Clara Orsini - Romano

This first full-length study in English beautifully conveys the life, ambiance and achievements of Elena Lucrezia Cornaro Piscopia.

Benjamin G. Kohl, *Vassar College*
ANDREW W. MELLON PROFESSOR OF THE HUMANITIES

Elena Cornaro's prodigious intelligence and fervent faith are luminous constants in this warmly human story of her brief, conflicted life.

E. Maxine Bruhns
National Chairman
U.S. CORNARO TERCENTENARY COMMITTEE
Director, NATIONALITY ROOMS AND INTERCULTURAL EXCHANGE PROGRAMS, University of Pittsburgh

"Think not this is a portrait of Minerva."

The Lady Cornaro

PRIDE AND PRODIGY OF VENICE

JANE HOWARD GUERNSEY

Jane Howard Guernsey
May 1999

COLLEGE AVENUE PRESS
Clinton Corners, New York

THE LADY CORNARO: Pride and Prodigy of Venice

ILLUSTRATION ON FACING PAGE AND PAGE 233: *La Conchiglia Celeste,* Giovanni Fabri. Venice, 1690. Spencer Collection. The New York Public Library. Astor, Lenox and Tilden Foundations.

COLLEGE AVENUE PRESS
is an imprint of
The Attic Studio Press
P.O. Box 75 • Clinton Corners, NY 12514
Phone: 914-266-8100 • Fax: 914-266-5515

PRINTED IN THE UNITED STATES OF AMERICA

10 9 8 7 6 5 4 3 2 1 FIRST EDITION

Library of Congress Cataloging-in-Publication Data

Guernsey, Jane Howard, 1927–
The lady Cornaro : pride and prodigy of Venice / Jane Howard Guernsey
p. cm.
Includes bibliographical references and index.
ISBN 1-883551-44-7 (alk. paper)
1. Cornaro Piscopia, Elena Lucrezia, 1646–1684. 2. Scholars—Italy—Biography. 3. Authors, Italian—17th century—Biography. 4. Philosophers—Italy—Biography. I. Title
PQ4621.C8Z68 1999
378.45'32—dc21
[b] 99–14133

For

Geraldine Wyman Treadway

1930–1988

Mother, Educator, Nuclear Physicist
Widow of William E. Dampier and
Wife of the late L. Donald Miller
Vassar College, Class of 1951

*Gerry enriched our lives with
her beauty, her genius and her love,
embodying the spirit of Lady Elena
in the twentieth century.*

For

My Class of 1948–'49 at Vassar College

VENICE, "MISTRESS OF THE SEAS," SHOWN IN EARLY SEVENTEENTH-CENTURY MAP *(detail)*

(La Città Di Venetia. Venice, 1614. The John M. Wing Foundation, The Newberry Library, Chicago)

CONTENTS

ILLUSTRATIONS

CHRONOLOGY

Elena Lucrezia Cornaro Piscopia (1646-1684)

1646 Elena is born on June 5 in a Grand Canal palace, Venice.

1651 Even as a young girl, Elena is seen as an unusually graceful, generous and studious child.

1653 Recognizing the girl as a child prodigy, parish priest and Aristotelian scholar Msgr. Fabris offers to tutor seven-year-old Elena, urging her father to provide a classical education.

1654 Elena's father, Gianbattista Cornaro, marries her mother, Zanetta Boni, who had been his mistress for many years.

1654 As her prodigious mind emerges, the eight-year-old Venetian becomes fluent in both French and Spanish.

1657 Elena makes a secret vow of chastity at the age of eleven, having earlier expressed a desire to become a nun.

1658 With leading scholars among her private tutors, the young Cornaro's academic subjects expand to include Greek, Hebrew, Latin, Scripture, history, literature, and the arts.

1663 Carlo Rinaldini, a noted philosophy professor, and Rabbi Shalma Abbroff, her beloved Hebrew teacher, are major influences. By the age of seventeen, Elena is proficient in mathematics, dialectics, physics and astronomy.

1664 Elena's father, Gianbattista, is chosen for the coveted position of Procurator of St. Mark in Venice.

1665 The Lady Cornaro is a prominent celebrity in the annual "Marriage of the Sea" celebration, but she rebuffs her father's elaborate betrothal arrangement during the festivities.

1665 With the blessing of her confessor, Abbot Codanini, Elena becomes a Benedictine oblate and begins to wear a monk's habit underneath her ornate gowns.

1670 Drawn to severe ascetic practices and spiritual exercises in the midst of opulent surroundings and daunting social appearances, Elena shows symptoms of "holy anorexia."

1671 Frequently ill and suffering numerous fevers, Elena is sent to recuperate at the family's summer palace in Padua.

1672 Professor Rinaldini recommends that Elena concentrate on the requirements necessary for a degree at the University of Padua. With her father's encouragement, this pursuit becomes her academic focus.

1675 As her scholarly reputation grows, Elena is much in demand as a public speaker, and prominent Italian academies seek her membership.

1677 Cardinal Barbarigo of Padua, after first rejecting the idea, accepts Gianbattista's proposal to allow Elena to be an official candidate for a university degree.

1678 In a special convocation in a Paduan cathedral, Elena Cornaro receives a doctorate in philosophy from the University of Padua on June 25. She becomes the first woman in history to receive a university degree.

1679 Though the fame accompanying her history-making degree brings additional demands, Elena, plagued by ill health, moves to the family palace in Padua. She is attended by her mother Zanetta and cherished companion Maddalena.

1683 Seriously ill, Elena selflessly continues to express her concerns about family, social issues and the poor.

1684 On July 26, Elena Cornaro dies in Padua at the age of thirty-eight. Memorials are held for her throughout Italy, and posthumous tributes to *"La Prima Donna Laureata nel Mondo"* in Europe and America continue to the present.

I say give me the portraits of an Isabella of Arragon or Castile, and her foure daughters; Lucretia d'Este (to whom our Queene is related), Victoria Colonna, Hippolita Strozzi, Petrarch's Laura, Anna Maria Schurman, ***and above all Hellen Cornaro, daughter of a procurator of St. Marco (one of the most illustrious families of Venice) who received the degree of Doctoresse at Padua for her universal knowledge and erudition, upon the importunity of that famous University prevailing on her modesty.***

– Letter to Dr. Samuel Pepys
in the *Diary of John Evelyn.*
Says-Court, Kent, England
AUGUST 12, 1689

PREFACE

"WOMAN is made for motherhood, not for learning," thundered the university chancellor at the aristocratic father of Elena Lucrezia Cornaro Piscopia. In the seventeenth century, life decisions for young women concerning their education, marriage, or monastic calling were made through families, churches or governing circles by men who dominated European mores of that time.

Into this rigidly confined environment was born the beautiful and brilliant Lady Elena Cornaro. Raised in a palace on the Grand Canal of Venice and driven by an ambitious and exploitive father, Elena experienced the privileges and strictures of being part of one of the largest, wealthiest and most powerful dynasties in Italian history. By the age of fifteen, she was already recognized as a classics scholar. In early adulthood she was considered the perfect candidate for an international marital alliance and, even more notably, for more than one university degree. The gentle patrician also became a pawn in power politics between her father, a reigning cardinal, and the Vatican.

What noble legacy sparked an unprecedented quest that would affect all subsequent generations? How did Elena emerge? Who was responsible for her astonishing achievement? What were the difficulties and hostilities that threatened? Was there genuine heroism displayed? And why was the most learned and vastly admired woman of her century so soon forgotten?

Pursuing these questions for nearly thirty years, my study has unearthed significant defining details which are woven into every chapter of *The Lady Cornaro.* This book, bearing the fruit of extensive collaboration with leading Italian and American scholars, reveals illuminating features which provide significant insight into the brief life of the Baroque maiden who greatly impacted the course of modern history. Although little was published about women during Elena's life, ample scholarship exists about this Venetian noblewoman; regrettably, it is not readily accessible. Extant accounts are old, rare, and written primarily in Latin and Italian. Elena Cornaro's own reflections are unavailable. Unfortunately for us, she insisted that all her writings be destroyed.

The Lady Cornaro combines available, scholarly evidence which we have unearthed over the past three decades with a journalistic approach, designed for both the general reader and the academician. For the benefit of all readers, it should be noted that a biographical work of this nature necessarily requires reliance on various sources that sometimes do not fully agree; for instance, the spelling of proper names, dates of events, and even the specifics of events may vary. In all cases, we have sought to use the most reliable sources to accurately record our intriguing tale—while recognizing that some facts, figures, and events are still the subject of debate and speculation among scholars.

The contemporary emergence of Elena's biography is a fascinating story which spans both sides of the Atlantic. As *THE LADY CORNARO* celebrates the remarkable life of a Venetian woman of the seventeenth century, it also chronicles the leading role of twentieth century Americans and Italians in a triumphant transatlantic endeavor to honor the world's first woman university graduate.

Jane Howard Guernsey
WILMINGTON, DELAWARE
April 1999

The first place in the New World to recognize the legacy of Elena Cornaro was Vassar College in this 22-foot-high stained-glass window. Installed in 1906 in the college's Thompson Memorial Library, the "Great Window" (also called the "Cornaro Window") shows the first woman laureate defending her thesis on Aristotelian dialectics before an international audience at the University of Padua in 1678.

(Photograph by Charles Porter)

PROLOGUE:
Who Is She?

Try and make all the faces intelligent, and where possible, use likenesses. . . . Be careful that your details are historically correct.

– LETTER FROM CHURCH GLASS & DECORATING COMPANY, NEW YORK, NEW YORK, TO JOHN HARDMAN & COMPANY, BIRMINGHAM, ENGLAND, WINDOW DESIGNERS. FEBRUARY 9, 1905

SUNLIGHT STRUCK THE FACES of five winged cherubs, shown gently unfolding a parchment scroll that swept across the lower panels of the vast stained-glass window. An inscription on the banderole they held proclaimed, *"In Laud[e] Helenae Lucretiae Corneliae Piscopiae Laurea . . . Unico exemplo Donatae"* ("In praise of Elena Lucrezia Cornaro Piscopia . . . Doctored, without Precedent").

The middle cherub with silver wings proudly displayed an ancient coat of arms. Nearby, robed men were gathered in a circular tribune, all eyes fixed upon the window's central figure, a majestic young woman standing before them. The queenly maiden, framed by pink marble columns, was elevated on a stepped podium. Dressed in pleated silk brocade and adorned with a jeweled cross hanging from pearls at her neck, she was clutching a document in her right hand.

In 1908, another young woman, Ruth Crawford of St. Louis, sat beneath this great window in the central wing of the Frederick Ferris Thompson Memorial Library at Vassar College. In her long, white Edwardian dress, Ruth contemplated the magnificent stained glass rising above her, which had been installed only two years earlier. As the inquisitive history student studied the striking images, she pondered their meaning. *How did they come to be portrayed there? Who were they? Why was a beautiful maiden given primacy in the center of this splendid scene?*

Searching for a story in the window, the eighteen-year-old Vassar freshman noted hooded mace bearers, examiners with texts and a seated archivist recording. Clerics in pairs were there, and a scholar on either side of the enthroned feminine figure. The one to the maiden's right held an ermine cape, the other a laurel wreath.

Forming the window's background appeared what was described by the New York glass manufacturers as "a multitude of people of all sorts and conditions," gesturing and listening. In the upper lights was a canopy of allegorical personifications entitled Grammar, Dialectic, Music, Philosophy, Astronomy, Medicine, Geometry and Theology. The entire richly patterned setting was ornamented with braided swags on arches and greenery, grapes, and pomegranates in delicate tracery.

As afternoon glazed the colored patchwork, two individuals predominated in the lower foreground. On the viewer's right, an ascetic gentleman stood in scarlet; on the left, a bearded nobleman in gold, adorned with heavy chains over vest and velvet cape. Beneath a plumed hat, he peered at the woman with an enraptured gaze.

The lady of the window, Elena Lucrezia Cornaro Piscopia, was to be a central focus in the life of the student seated there in the autumn of 1908. The young historian would come to know well this lustrous and tragic figure. Ruth would find Elena to be a heroine lost, but one whose towering intellect had served in her lifetime to advance the role of all women in western civilization.

In this Venice scene of the "Marriage of the Sea," *(above, and detail below)* painter Girolamo Pilotti depicts the arrival of the "Serene Highness" for the festivities. The Marriage of the Sea has been a lavish annual celebration enjoyed by Venetians for centuries, including many generations of the Cornaro Family. But in 1665, the holiday brought anguish to young Elena Cornaro.

(Museo Correr, Venice. By permission of the Minister of Culture and the Environment)

1

AN ARRANGED MARRIAGE REBUFFED

...I would rather elect being treated as a slave and be kept for all my life, like a dog to a chain, than to squander the treasure of my virginity.

– ELENA TO HER CONFESSOR

AS CHAMBERMAID Angela withdrew, a carved ivory casket of jewels was flung across the room, landing on an ornate silver looking glass, cracking gems encrusted on the mirror's frame. Sobbing, Lady Elena yanked both of the pendant pearls on her gold filigreed earrings. She tore the embroidery fastening the lace bodice of her ball gown, revealing a crude, woolen monk's habit and a scapular hidden beneath.

Scattered across the Persian carpet in Elena's room were snarled hairpieces, overturned pots of rouge and powder, a ripped, striped petticoat, diamond pins for curls, brooches and crushed ribbons. "The whole arsenal of beauty [was] sacked and destroyed," an orator later recounted.

All that remained intact in her bedroom that evening were several exquisitely crafted Chinese writing implements from a Jesuit missionary and Elena's tiny, treasured Spanish cross. Its gleaming crystal rested comfortingly against the noblewoman's delicate young neck.

Elena Lucrezia Cornaro Piscopia was emerging as an international celebrity. Born to a leading Venetian aristocrat in an opulent seventeenth-century court, this exquisite Italian maiden would be the first woman in the world to earn a college degree. At the age of 32, Elena was granted a Ph.D. by the University of Padua in the year 1678. Earliest records, written by two Benedictine monks and a seventeenth century biographer from Messina, confirm that she mastered much of the ancient, medieval and contemporary learning available in her era.

Her countrymen affectionately referred to Lady Elena as "The Cornaro." European rulers were captivated by her brilliance and beauty. Pope Innocent XI and France's Sun King, Louis XIV, as well as the monarchs of Spain and Poland, would pay her homage. But it was fame that she shunned.

The scene of disarray in Elena's palace bedchamber followed a courtly evening ball at the *Palazzo Ducale* (Ducal Palace) on St. Mark's Square. It was a day that had begun with the annual "Marriage of the Sea" celebration. In the evening, the eighteen-year-old Cornaro was to be honored at the palace with a surprise announcement of her engagement to a valorous war hero. But no one had told Elena!

It all had been decided by the lords of her native republic of Venice. At a secret session, the Great Council arranged to pay tribute to the young lady by decreeing their choice of a husband for her: young Captain Marco Contarini, the popular, victorious ship commander, nephew of the reigning sovereign.

Rarely were individuals ever honored by this august governing body and, more rarely, a woman.

Along flowered balconies of *Procuratie Vecchie,* a delegation of elegantly attired "gentledonnas" (referring to daughters and wives of nobility), had assembled to witness the morning procession to the sea. The Procuratie Vecchie were law courts next to the Romanesque clock tower where Cornaro's father, Gianbattista, enjoyed a first floor apartment overlooking St. Mark's Square.

In the lead of the procession was Lady Elena, totally unaware of her pending betrothal. Its disclosure had been planned to be a special added attraction at this favorite annual holiday—an event which continues to be a highlight of the Venetian calendar year.

Gentry and townsfolk were coming together to reenact the historic Marriage of the Sea. At the consummation of the festival, Domenico Contarini, the highly regarded doge (chief magistrate) of Venice, cast his jeweled signet ring of onyx, malachite and lapis lazuli into the ocean. It was an expression of gratitude to the Adriatic for its many gifts to Venice, a humble repayment of the Republic's debt to the sea.

According to historians, this nautical custom took place in its earliest form on Ascension Day in the year 1000 to celebrate the Venetian conquest of Dalmatia along the western border of Yugoslavia (now Croatia). One legend arose that a fisherman presented the first ring to the reigning doge, establishing a time-honored tradition. By the Renaissance era, six centuries later, the nuptial fete, long since authorized by the pope, had come to symbolize Venice's maritime dominance.

The lavish Baroque setting on this May day in 1665 was unparalleled in pomp and pageantry. The royal entourage of the procession had begun at the basilica's piazza with heralds who held aloft tall shafts woven with ribbons and crowned by official standards.

Next came the trumpeters, their heavy, long silver horns requiring the support of young pages, followed by ambassadors and European court envoys in embroidered cloaks and plumed hats. Then appeared "The Great Admiral" in crimson satin, wearing a vest down to his knees and a violet cap banded in braid. The Admiral served as Director General of The Arsenal, where shipbuilders' skills had helped make Venice one of the leading naval and mercantile centers in the world.

Esquires and secretaries marched ahead of the patriarch, joined by the canons of St. Mark's, Byzantine-seeming figures in clerical robes accompanied by choristers. The chaplain and the pope's emissary walked in front of Doge Contarini's suite, which carried all the accessories of office: the ducal coronet, enriched with large precious stones and squired on an enameled tray; a chased silver candelabrum; the doge's pleated leather chair, covered in golden cloth; and his kneeling cushion, embroidered with arms of the Republic.

The grand chancellor preceded the doge, called "Serenita" in Venetian dialect, who was splendidly dressed in ermine robes of state, well-shaded by a white silk canopy. The doge's nephew—the Cornaro's designated fiancé—marched proudly in an armorial Brescian breastplate, holding his sword with a silver crescent on its hilt, symbolizing victory over the Turks. Elena barely noticed him.

Church bells, trumpets and cannons resounded across the Piazza in front of St. Mark's Basilica. As the triumphal procession advanced through the square, it passed to the edge of the Grand Canal between granite columns. Glancing at the two columns, Elena could see a statue of St. Theodore, the third-century commander and patron saint of Venice, standing boldly on a crocodile. Atop the other column was an ancient bronze winged lion, symbol of St. Mark.

Waters across the lagoon were obscured by the voluminous flotilla of barques, large boats, and holiday gondolas gathered from all over the island city and from villages near the sea. Crammed with joyous celebrants, lively bands, and foreign visitors, vessels with bright banners and flowing streamers crowded in festive clusters near the parade route. With utmost dignity, nobles of the realm escorted their doge to his great gilded galley, the *Bucentoro* (Bucentaur). "Its fittings, gorgeous in the extreme," wrote a nineteenth-century historian, "were brilliant with scarlet and gold; its long banks of oars brightly burnished; and its decks and seats inlaid with costly woods."

On board the Bucentaur, with six standards floating at its bow, was an elevated throne for Doge Contarini. It had been constructed over a carpet of flowered damask fringed with gold that ran the full length of the boat. At the doge's left stood an ascetic figure in scarlet and a select group of young boys. In designated seats to the doge's right were a girls' chorus and fair Lady Elena Cornaro, selected to sit next to the beloved Contarini.

The celebrators then sailed over to Lido Island, two miles to the southeast, on the outer edge of the lagoon, where prescribed prayers and formularies were read on board the Bucentaur. Doge Contarini tossed his marriage ring into the water while reciting a Latin phrase heard to this day at the annual festival ceremony:

> *Desponsumus te, mare, in signum veri perpetuique dominii.*

> *(Sea, we espouse thee, in the sign of true and everlasting dominance which we have over thee.)*

Filled with the majesty of the moment, the jubilant crowds threw nosegays of flowers and herbs overboard while they roared and cheered, "Long live the Adriatic!" "Long live the Doge!" "Glory and prosperity to Venice, the queen of the seas!" The merry voyagers then sailed back to the mainland for evening parties and the great ducal ball, where Elena Cornaro was to be feted.

It was time once again to display the region's splendor. Exhausted by the Thirty Years' War (1618-1648), Europeans had been flocking to Venice for needed respite. They were welcomed by local citizens, who themselves had been diminished in number and in spirit from epidemics of the bitter plague that had killed over one-third of their people.

The holiday brought general rejoicing. At sundown there was dancing in the streets by torchlight. Gold coins were tossed from palace windows along the Grand Canal. Over at The Arsenal, shipwrights were given their own banquet.

While free bread and wine were being distributed to the poor, a starkly contrasting scene was emerging as the *beau monde* of Venice, for which it was so famous, descended from crested coaches at the portal of the Ducal Palace. Its pink and white marble façade reflected the beam of hundreds of slender wax tapers that night.

Courtly cavaliers were dressed in handsomely embroidered capes, clasped by diamond and amber buttons. They escorted smiling, gloved noblewomen in low cut gowns of silver and gold tissue silk over point lace, with clusters of rubies and ribbons at their shoulders and fresh flowers in

Ceremonial processions: inauguration of the Admiral of the Fleet receiving official scepter *(above)* and the "Marriage of the Sea" were full-dress parades through St. Mark's Piazzetta. The Marriage of the Sea still commemorates Venice's gifts from the Adriatic. As Republic leaders, the Cornaros participated in these splendid rites.

(La Città Di Venetia. Venice, 1614. The John M. Wing Foundation, The Newberry Library, Chicago)

their hair. The finest pearls from the Orient adorned their necks and wrists, and others were sewn into beaded bouquets and foliage over skirts and sweeping trains. It was whispered, wrote the visiting French embassy attaché, Limojon de Saint Didier, that some ladies on these evenings had to pay excessive rental fees to happy jewelers for the privilege of displaying their heavy, glittering gems!

On the arm of her father, a radiant Lady Elena arrived at the Ducal Palace. Amid a distinguished gathering, they were two exceptionally striking figures: Gianbattista, the bearded nobleman in gold, proud, erect, imperious; beside him his petite, teen-age daughter, her gown silver-damascened over turquoise silk, sweeping back in graceful curtsy. Both were warmly welcomed to the party by the doge's family and caused no little stir before dinner was announced.

And such an Italian feast of "plentious food" it was! For banqueting in the Great Council Hall, liveried servants were carrying engraved silver decanters and crystal platters laden with seaport specialties among the seated guests. Typical of this annual feast, there were mussels marinated in wine, fried oysters, limed bass and chilled rings of sole under piquant anchovy sauce. Enameled red glass baskets were passed, brimming with gorgonzola biscuits, herbed breads and fried mozzarella cheese. One entrée offered was a selection of small roasted game birds, another chicken polenta, garnished with prawns, fried eggs and black olives. Molded salads consisted of risotto with roasted chestnuts, white beans and caviar.

Desserts included *macedonia* (fruit salad) with fresh strawberries and melon, candied figs from Greece, and, best of all, *Il Diplomatico.* A sumptuous rum layer confection baked with newly imported chocolate and coffee flavorings, *Il Diplomatico* was served on plates made of spun sugar, beside napkins of fine lawn edged with Flemish lace, monogrammed with each guest's coat of arms.

Groomed in good manners, a poised Elena appeared to be enjoying the festivities. The gala evening included dancing and music, madrigal singers and comic skits, and mimes performing in the courtyard. From the upper balconies festooned with pennants, guests watched as fireworks covered the sky and lighted arrows were shot continually from church towers all over the city.

As Elena was greeting friends from a neighboring palace, her father beckoned a servant. Gianbattista ordered him to escort Elena behind heavy drapery at one end of the ballroom to witness the arrival of the much-admired nephew.

"Whatever for?" she pondered. Why had she been made the center of attention this day, courted earlier by the ducal party on board the Bucentaur, and now singled out again in the ballroom?

Unknown to Lady Elena, rumor and excitement had been building over a new alliance of two powerful Venetian dynasties, the Cornaros and Contarinis. It had all the aura of a fairytale romance.

Both families were immensely rich and of titled lineage. Elena's Cornaro Piscopia line boasted three popes, nine cardinals, four doges, many great statesmen, and a celebrated Queen of Cyprus. Her chosen suitor was descended from a succession of doges, prelates, merchant princes, and loyal defenders of the Republic. And both could claim in their histories distinguished Italian men of letters and patrons of the arts.

Elena's designated groom, Captain Contarini, aboard the *Santa Maddalena* galley, had helped lead the naval fleet against the menace of the Turks in a series of victorious campaigns

THE BUCENTAUR WAS THE GILDED ROYAL BARGE OF THE DOGES. MANNED BY 168 ROWERS, THE VESSEL ESCORTED THE DOGARESSA AND DISTINGUISHED VISITORS TO THE DUCAL PALACE AND LED FESTIVE CELEBRATIONS.

(La Città Di Venetia. Venice, 1614. The John M. Wing Foundation, The Newberry Library, Chicago)

under the courageous commander-in-chief, Admiral Francesco Morosini. Her father, Gianbattista, had been elected the previous year as *Procuratore di San Marco de supra,* the Treasurer of St. Mark. Next to the doge, he was now the highest ranking officer in the Republic.

In fatherly fashion that evening, these two powerful men—doge and senior procurator—took the earnest young girl aside. They had chosen this moment to finally reveal, before announcing it publicly, their cherished secret: her forthcoming marriage to Captain Contarini.

Elena, however, had kept her own secret: a personal pledge of chastity made when she was eleven years old. Although this pledge was not an uncommon practice in her day, Elena had never spoken of it at home. She thought that none of her family knew.

Taking her hand, the doge spoke gently, "My daughter, do not any longer refuse to crown with joy the whole Republic by accepting as your husband the suitor she has chosen for you; both your father and I join our entreaties with those of all the people." Before she could voice her objection, her determined father produced a document carrying the official seal of Rome and exclaimed, "Obey, Elena, obey! It is not only your privilege, but your duty, for you are free!"

Seizing the parchment, she discovered that it contained a papal dispensation from chastity vows. Without her knowledge, her father had appealed to Pope Alexander VII to negate her sacred promise. Because she had taken her vow at such a young age and without his consent, Gianbattista insisted that it was void.

Elena was stunned. Her heart raced and her mind was filled with thoughts of horror and foreboding at the mere suggestion of any marital prospect. Much to the astonishment of the two power brokers confronting her that evening, a shaken Elena moaned aloud and then fainted. She was immediately removed from the party and taken home in her carriage. The Cornaro Piscopia Palace was ablaze all night.

Gianbattista was furious. His adored and usually cooperative daughter, whose spectacular intellectual achievements were already bringing glory to his city and state, had precipitously let him down. Even his prized Elena, so vital to Gianbattista's desire to cleanse the Cornaro name, had unexpectedly scorched it.

There had been several recent family stains tarnishing its luster, and Elena's politically ambitious father was resolved to erase them. The children of Giovanni Cornaro, a previous doge of fine reputation and principle, had profited unfairly from their father's position. One son was appointed to a cardinalship illegally and two others were elected to the Senate in fraudulent balloting. The most notorious one, Giorgio, amassed a large fortune over two years importing cattle from Dalmatia while his father was in office. Involved in highly questionable dealings, Giorgio sought at one point to silence the voices rising against him. He arranged for a group of masked assassins to kill one leading accuser, but the accuser outmaneuvered the murderers and lived to tell the tale. Giorgio then fled from Venice and was later found in Ferraro, hiding with his gondoliers. He was exiled, deprived of his wealth and rank, and subsequently killed. The scandal rocked the Republic and every Cornaro.

After three unsuccessful petitions, Gianbattista was finally chosen in 1664 as Procurator of St. Mark, the head Senator charged with overseeing the basilica's treasury and directing its library and archives. Over the years, doges were often selected from Gianbattista's newly acquired office, *Procuratore de supra.**

Wealthy Venetians greatly valued their Procuratia, the ranking office that developed into an institution which administered vast amounts of public and private funds and served in a custodial capacity for the Republic. The office was believed to have originated after A.D. 829 when two Venetian merchants supposedly transported the body of St. Mark from Alexandria to Venice and the new repository required supervision. In A.D. 977 Doge Peter Orfeole assigned a procurator to rebuild the severely burned "Ducal Chappel."

Seventeenth-century records of historian Amelot de la Houssaye (secretary to the French ambassador at Venice) list the first documented procurator under Prince Dominick Contarini, an ancestor of the reigning doge. He appeared in the archives as a single officeholder until 1231. Eventually, the procurator was to handle revenue from lands left to St. Mark's and distribute it to the poor. This was to become Gianbattista's role.

As St. Mark's grew and its great riches vastly increased, the Procuratia became the Republic's controlling financial power. By the thirteenth and fourteenth centuries, these custodians were elected by the Great Council and supervised trusts, loans and investments, both domestic and foreign.

The positions were coveted ones. Grand Canal palaces were built for officeholders, and by the fifteenth century the duties of nine procurators were divided into the three chambers. Gianbattista, highest of the three ranking procurators,

---

* The other *Ridotti* (chambers) were *de citra* (this side) and *ultra* (beyond), delineating the areas on the right or left sides of the Grand Canal the procurators governed.

was designated to administer the basilica and the piazza. Incessant wars with the Turks and the Republic's great need for money elsewhere led to the bending of the rules; as a result, a man of substantial means, even without the prescribed lineage, might attain one of the offices.

Procurators' inaugural ceremonies, deemed as eminently important, were accorded grand Venetian pageantry, in all its splendor. When a procurator died, *La Trottiere*—the special bell designed only to assemble the Great Council—was rung. It signaled the Council to elect a successor.

Upon his appointment as the new top procurator in 1664, Gianbattista was to choose a special day for his induction ceremony, following ancient custom. Cornaro friends and relatives escorted him from his palace to participate in Mass at St. Mark's. He was welcomed there with the right hand of the doge, who was flanked by senators and other officials in scarlet robes marching in double file to pay homage.

Swearing allegiance to the Republic and to his duties, Gianbattista took his seat in the Great Council hall where he received his symbolic keys, presented in a crimson velvet purse from the "Farmers of the Company." He then swore another oath of office upon an ancient document held by the grand chancellor. At that point, he could wear the procurator's velvet stole and prestigious gold chains.

Part of Gianbattista's role as treasurer included the humanitarian duties not only of allocating money for the needy but also of assigning housing allocations. "[P]roperly these Procurators are the common Fathers of all People in distress," de la Houssaye wrote in 1675. Elena was especially proud of this dimension of her esteemed father's post.

In his youth, Gianbattista had been a charming and spoiled playboy, rather typical of many frivolous and perfumed noblemen of the era. But he outgrew the fast, sporting life when he met a very beautiful Brescian, Zanetta Giovanna Boni.

The vivacious Zanetta was from an extremely poor peasant family, born in the Piedmont town of Val di Sabia near the city of Novara. In Cinderella fashion, Zanetta had fled to Venice—most likely to escape starvation at home—and sought work as a servant girl in one of the grand palaces. Gianbattista saw her there and fell in love.

A strong, clever, and vibrant woman, Zanetta Boni became Gianbattista's mistress, as well as the mother of his five children. Three of them, including Elena, were born out of wedlock. "The Laws of the State," declared the rules of the Senate, "do not esteem such issue to be Noble."

Further hindering the Cornaro reputation, Zanetta was a commoner. The loss of certain noble rights and the exclusion of his male children from the lists of Venetian nobility galled young Gianbattista and continued to irritate and frustrate him for the remainder of his life. It also caused him to be an excessive striver. The senior procurator's sons could merely be considered "Gentlemen of the Republick"—until he purchased better titles for them.

Through years of strategic maneuvers and high fees, Gianbattista continually strove to have his two boys listed in the register of Venice's nobility, *Libro d'oro.* This was the exalted Golden Book that, beginning in 1315, recorded the births, marriages and deaths of the Republic's leading families. Inclusion in this "Who's Who" of Venice would make Gianbattista's sons eligible to serve on the governing Great Council. But because of their mother's lowly birth, his daughters could never be included, and, as women, they would have no voice in administering the Republic.

Gianbattista was an intelligent and pragmatic man, as well as a sensitive one, and he married Zanetta in 1654, when Elena was eight. During his lifetime, he was to pay a very high price socially and politically for this union.

The marriage could never be registered in *Libro d'oro,* and it was reported to have been censured by the Senate's Council of Ten "as ill assorted in point of rank." Nor was Zanetta ever elevated to ranking circles of society. Haughty local gossips had a busy time chewing over her prominent husband's alleged affairs. Referring to his wife by the derogatory nickname "La Valsabbia," derived from the name of her hometown, they fabricated the rumor that she was the daughter of a gondolier.

Early in his marriage, Gianbattista's rightful knighthood title, "The Order of the Sword"—to be inherited from the Piscopias—was being denied him. Now his prized Elena had thwarted an important marital scheme. As the evening of her planned betrothal waned, Gianbattista left the Ducal Palace fuming.

Soon after her maid Angela retired from the palace bedroom where Elena had fled, the young Cornaro seized her ill-fated ornaments in feverish rebellion. Tomorrow morning, she determined, she would seek solace somewhere. Elena thrust shut the heavy, iron bolt on her inner door and struggled to sleep. Soon Gianbattista's boots clattered up the rear marble staircase, and he slammed the lion's head knocker on her door.

An explosive scene followed: Elena, dragged out of bed, hysterical and pleading; Gianbattista in fitful rage, harshly accusing her of intolerable behavior and disgraceful wrongdoing. Elena's mother, Zanetta, stood shrieking coarsely in the background. The encounter continued for some time, both father and daughter unyielding.

There were two choices for young noblewomen like Elena: marriage or the convent. Matrimony offered escape from the constricted environment of these "hothouse plants." The conventional nuptial route allowed wealthy girls to break out of their cloistered existence in high-walled gardens and shelve the required long white veil. A new bride would be given her own staff of servants and liveries, receive individual invitations to grand balls and assemblies, and be asked to help entertain at receptions for ambassadors and visiting monarchs.

Most of the bridled female gentry deemed marriage a welcome release. But the stuff of this society, with its salons of polite conversation and gentle banter, its undemanding daily routine refining manners and practicing stitchery, was not for Elena Lucrezia.

Church dignitaries welcoming a visiting prince, escorted by the City Council, to Christmas vespers at San Giorgio Maggiore Basilica. Andrea Palladio designed this architectural masterpiece across from Venice in 1566. It is the site where Elena secretly became a Benedictine oblate. The basilica's Abbot Codanini was of great spiritual and academic guidance throughout the Lady Cornaro's life.

(La Città Di Venetia. Venice, 1614. The John M. Wing Foundation, The Newberry Library, Chicago)

2

BIRTH IN A GRAND CANAL PALACE

Father, Sir, although I were asked by the greatest sovereign on earth, I will never consent to it.

ELENA TO GIANBATTISTA
ABOUT HIS MARRIAGE PLAN

AFTER COLLAPSING at the ducal ball and enduring a troubled, sleepless night, a frantic Elena had her personal maid rush a note to Abbot Cornelius Codanini at the San Giorgio Maggiore monastery. It was just past dawn, before the rest of the palace had awakened, when Angela journeyed in her mistress's gondola over the water to the stately Palladian monastery church on an island across from Venice.

"Hasten, my father," Elena had written to her confessor. "Come and save one of your children. Hasten, for the danger is imminent."

In response to her urgent message, Abbot Codanini soon arrived by way of a little-used service entrance of the Cornaro mansion. Elena sank to her knees in front of the prelate and cried imploringly, "Save me, father. Save me from a freedom that I have never demanded and that I do not wish to accept."

Fr. Codanini, well aware that both parents desired a brilliant match for their daughter, strove to change Elena's mind about the betrothal. Traditionally, church ties with the Cornaros were close. In addition to serving as high ranking ecclesiastics down through the years, Cornaro family members had built entire churches in the region.

Quite naturally, Codanini used every method of persuasion in his training with Elena on that late spring morning. And Elena deeply admired the learned and articulate Benedictine cleric of San Giorgio Maggiore, whom she had asked her father to choose as her confessor. He urged the anxious girl to consider the great benefit of a splendid marital alliance for Venice and for the two families. Each had always been considered among the top twelve governing élite who were founding fathers of the Republic, he reminded her. But his conscientious efforts were in vain.

Finally, assured of the young girl's unwavering determination, he agreed to make official Elena's desire for chastity. She had consistently expressed this wish, keeping a private childhood vow.

To those who urged marriage as a licit and holy state, including her parents, she would answer, "I don't deny that, but virginity is more pleasing to God; and at the moment of death, the devil doesn't have the power over virgins that he has over everybody else."

That early morning, in furthering her steadfast desire to become a nun, Elena prevailed on her confessor to administer vows making her a Benedictine Oblate of the Third Order. After a private ceremony at San Giorgio Maggiore, she asked permission to always wear a monk's habit hidden underneath the socially approved fancy gowns imposed by her mother.

As an oblate—one dedicated to the religious life but not bound by monastic vows—Elena would always be close to convents while still living at the palace, "in secolaro" (as a layperson, in the secular world). She presciently chose the name "Scolastica," in honor of a nun who was the twin sister of St. Benedict and foundress of the Benedictine order of nuns.

Elena begged Abbot Codanini to keep all of these commitments quite secret from her father. With the priest's support, she approached Gianbattista and tried to convince him that a celibate life was what she desired. "In other things I will always live a slave to your commands," she promised her father, "and will die if necessary a holocaust to my reverence for you."

Gianbattista, as described in several old records, was an authoritative gentleman, at times impatient and headstrong. But he was also wise, knowing when to compromise. With his daughter Elena, he eventually relented from pressing further this advantageous Contarini marriage, but he remained adamant in refusing to allow her to enter a convent to become a nun.

There were over thirty convents in Venice during Elena's childhood; most of their inhabitants were from the nobility. Unlike Elena's parents, many would enroll their sometimes unwilling girls as novices to spend the rest of their lives in seclusion. Why? A matter of dowry! Monastic tuition was far lower than most nuptial donations. Few families could afford the expenses of having one daughter, or more than one son, marry. The Cornaros easily could.

Elena was greatly relieved when her father allowed her to refuse the Contarini proposal. But her mother was not won over as quickly. A fast-tempered, dramatic woman, Zanetta screamed in protest vulgarly when told of Elena's balking. She yearned for an important marriage for this unusual daughter.

Vehemently opposed to both Elena's religious interest and her academic pursuits, Zanetta continued to nag her husband about arranging for appropriate and glamorous suitors to meet the unwilling maiden. Ignoring his wife, Gianbattista acquiesced this time to Elena's request; he was beginning to have a very different future in mind for her. Preparation for this path had begun long before.

She was born in the Cornaro Piscopia Palace, a magnificent and princely setting, at 6 o'clock in the evening on June 5, 1646. It had been a simmering, hot day in Venice, and there was much rejoicing when the tiny girl, a third child—named for a sixteenth-century family member, Elena (born in 1549)—arrived as the sun set and the evening softened and cooled. While Elena was cradled in her nurse's arms, household servants scurried toward balconies and called to a gathering of gondoliers. These scrappy, wily purveyors of news and gossip had been waiting below on the front steps, by the water's edge. Their happy cry, a prelude to the acclaim that would accompany Elena later in life, spread quickly over the lagoon.

Torches gleamed across the Cornaros' russet and green Greek marble edifice that night. In celebration, the new baby's delighted mother instructed one of her gardeners to plant a cypress tree at the summer palace in Padua. The gesture would prove to be prophetic.

In 1641 Gianbattista became sole owner of the Cornaro Piscopia Palace on *Piazza di San Luca* (St. Luke's Square). A large and imposing winter mansion near the new Rialto Bridge, it had come down through the family from Federico Cornaro in the early 1300s. The palace was thought to have

The birthplace of Elena Cornaro, the Cornaro Piscopia palace was described by John Ruskin as "the most beautiful palace in the whole extent of the Grand Canal." Later named the "Loredan Palace," it is connected to the Farsetti Palace which now serves as the *Municipio* (City Hall) of Venice.

(Courtesy of Father Francesco Ludovico Maschietto, Basilica of San Giustina, and Editrice Antenore. Padua, 1978)

been designed by the Lombardian Nicolo Barattieri around 1200. It was rebuilt several times but adhered to "its old form," the twelfth-century Venetian-Byzantine style, as John Ruskin observed when he journeyed to Venice in 1849. In *The Stones of Venice,* the famed English critic proclaimed it to be "the most beautiful palace in the whole extent of the Grand Canal."

Raised in this sumptuous setting, Elena rarely showed any interest in the grandeur of her surroundings. Instead, she exhibited an inner grace and a seriousness even as a small child, which would predominate her persona. Her clearly evident love of church was a characteristic which greatly amazed her parents in one so young. Contemporaries wrote that when she was barely able to walk down the great marble steps of the palace by herself, Elena begged to accompany her nurse to church at St. Luke's around the corner. In white veil and clutching a rosary and prayer book, Elena regularly toddled over for daily Mass. When still too young to articulate, she would imitate others by mumbling responses at the morning worship service. It was there she came to believe she could always be free from the seductions of her environment.

Among those who idolized her, the Capuchin monk Antonio of Breganze attested in his homilies about witnessing Elena's generous spirit. He spoke of seeing her as a five-year-old, staring at stuccoists gilding fretted ceilings of the palace and embellishing its façade with elaborate sculpture. When Elena asked her father about the cost, recalled the astonished priest, she was deeply grieved by his reply. Taking Gianbattista's hand, his daughter said to him, "Father, Sir, wouldn't it be better to give this money to the poor and with the alms build ourselves a palace in heaven?" Although the story may be somewhat apocryphal, this generosity of spirit was a trait Elena would often exhibit throughout her days.

Early in her life, Elena's family viewed her intense curiosity as simply natural and childlike. But Gianbattista gradually began to recognize that, in addition to her uncommon compassion and comely looks, his daughter was blessed with a truly extraordinary mind.

St. Luke's parish priest, Monsignor Giovanni Battista Fabris, was the first to recognize Elena as a child prodigy. He noted that by the age of seven she was showing remarkable reasoning powers and a prodigious memory.

A well-known Aristotelian scholar, Fr. Fabris spent several mornings at the palace testing young Elena by having her read and memorize difficult philosophical passages in translation. As he worked with Gianbattista's exceptional daughter, the priest discovered her superior facility in learning Greek. As a result, he urged her father to provide for Elena what he would for a promising son: a classical education in the humanities, fine arts, and science.

Gianbattista fairly leapt at the idea. Princes honored men of letters, and scholars were greatly respected throughout Italy and the rest of Europe. All those publicly recognized were men.

Now, through this unique, female child, an outstanding opportunity was unfolding for him. It was a path pointing toward a notoriety that this driven nobleman was seeking in order to magnify his illustrious Cornaro name. It could be "a glory for the family yet unknown." Gianbattista would make certain that his daughter was the most learned woman of her century. But there were many obstacles along the way.

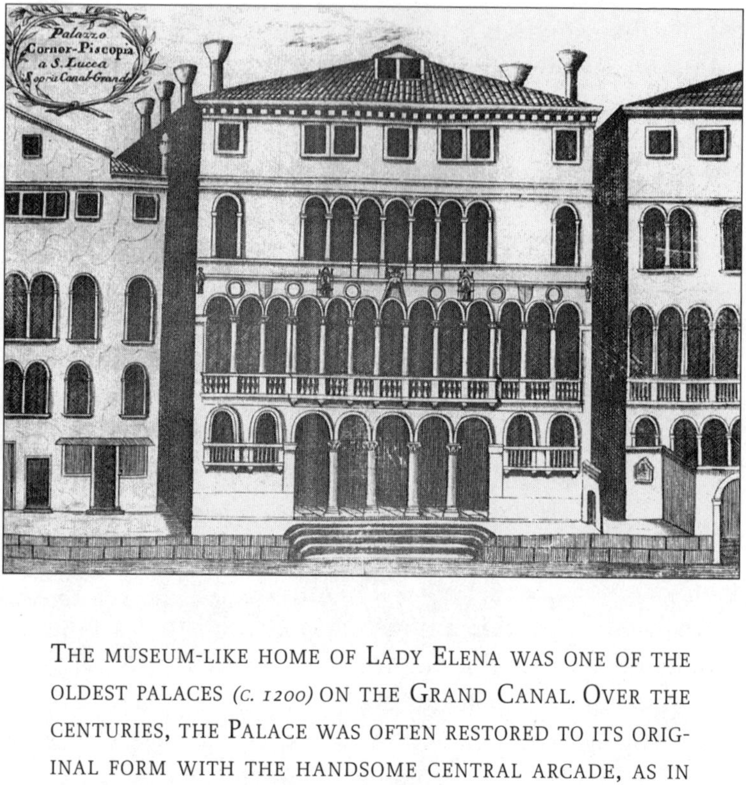

THE MUSEUM-LIKE HOME OF LADY ELENA WAS ONE OF THE OLDEST PALACES *(c. 1200)* ON THE GRAND CANAL. OVER THE CENTURIES, THE PALACE WAS OFTEN RESTORED TO ITS ORIGINAL FORM WITH THE HANDSOME CENTRAL ARCADE, AS IN THIS 1709 ENGRAVING.

(Elena Lucrezia Cornaro Piscopia, Maria Tonzig. University of Padua, Abbey of San Giustina. Vicenza, 1980)

3

THE YOUNG YEARS OF A PRODIGY

Amongst the families thus pledged to justify a fabulous origin by deeds of adequate splendor, the Cornari were foremost.

French diarist Alexis François Rio
1856

A quest for glory was certainly not what drove Elena to overcome every academic barrier placed before her. But for Gianbattista it was clearly a different story.

To inspire his young daughter, Gianbattista would spend special time with Elena, walking through their vast palace, reviewing family history and noting the ancestral trophies and treasures of their museum-like home. There were many of these mornings, for Gianbattista was resolved to have Elena well familiar and appreciative of her heritage. Determination consumed him.

As part of his home schooling efforts, Gianbattista would lift up the small girl, giving her a better vantage point to see the palace's roundels and sculptured plaques of knightly insignia ornamenting its arched and pillared facade. He would point excitedly to heraldic coats of arms above carved balustrades of both the Cornaros and the Piscopias. No child, he lectured, could ask for a prouder lineage.

The Cornaros claimed to have been descended from the famous Cornelii* Scipiones of ancient Rome who had commanded armies and served as consuls. One of them, Cornelia, was mother of the two Gracchi (whom she called "her jewels"), and whose outstanding traits of beauty and intellect would be seen generations later in her Venetian descendant.

Cornelia's sons, in the latter part of the second century B.C., championed impoverished farmers, ordered kind treatment for prisoners, and freed volunteer slaves who fought for them. Their humane compassion, so valued by Elena, would be reflected centuries later in the little girl who was listening to their tales.

Over the centuries, pride in family—strongly linked with loyalty to the state—was a tradition among most Italian noblemen; it often inspired glorious feats. The pride clearly ignited Gianbattista's fervor. Was it not a Cornaro ancestor, Gaius Cornelius, who, when Julius Caesar came through Padua in 50 B.C., predicted Caesar's victory over Pompey in the civil war? Having been rebuffed by Rome over his second consulship, Caesar met with Cornelius before returning there to take over as dictator. From another branch of the family, it was Caterina Cornaro who became the legendary Queen of Cyprus when she married the King in 1472. This marriage

* The name Cornelii became Cornelli, then Coronelli, Coronetti, Coronarii, and finally, Cornaro (Venetian) or Corner (abridged Italian form).

The Cornaro coat of arms—with two Greek crosses and two red lions rampant with gold crowns—is displayed with the Center cherub in the Vassar College library window featuring Lady Elena. In The Cornaro Piscopia coat of arms, the Order of the Sword insignia appears in the center.

(Photograph by J. J. Sinnott)

ultimately led to the securing of valuable properties for the Cornaro family and strategic land for the Republic.

Listening intently and courteously to all of Gianbattista's dazzling tales of war heroes and skilled statesmen in their ancestry, Elena was actually far more interested in the story of ancestor Francesco Cornaro. He was the Bishop of Paphos in southwestern Cyprus and, in 1519, he made a pilgrimage to the Holy Land. An eloquent Renaissance intellectual, Francesco astounded and enlightened the reformist Council of Trent with the extent of his knowledge. The Council had been called to reformulate the canons of the Catholic Church and commission a churchwide catechism in 1545. Elena admired this pilgrim forebear, as much for his piety as his scholarship.

In his desire to fully apprise his daughter of her illustrious family, Gianbattista persevered, "parading the great models constantly before (her) eyes. . . ." Exulting in his birthright, Elena's father also lived its legacy.

A polished aristocrat who inherited and amassed great fortunes, Gianbattista was born in Venice on April 1, 1613. His parents, Girolamo Cornaro Piscopia of Venice (1574-1625) and Caterina Thilmans of Holland, had been married in Padua three years earlier.

When his mother died in 1629, sixteen-year-old Gianbattista and his younger siblings were placed into the custody of a Flemish cousin, Matte Van Losen. As the eldest child, Gianbattista was put in charge of the large family. There were four surviving brothers and four sisters. All the girls eventually became nuns.

By the time Gianbattista was twenty-three, he had met Elena's mother, Zanetta Boni*, and taken her as his mistress. They had produced a son, Francesco, born in 1635, and a daughter, Caterina, a year later. Caterina died when she was seventeen.

Along with his offspring was born the great obsession of Gianbattista—having his sons listed in the aforementioned *Libro d'oro.* Vellum-bound and emblazoned with a gold seal on the cover, the book was quite petite; but the small size of the Republic's premier social listing belied its vast and vital political importance.

In 1637 Gianbattista was appointed *Provveditóre* (supervisor) of Peschiera, a frontier military fortress on Lake Garda, eighty miles west of Venice, where he had complete authority over the entire area. During his two years there, he directed all administrative and judicial systems and oversaw marketplaces, buildings and the surveying of public streets. He and his brother Baldassare, for whom Gianbattista would name his second son, inherited the Cornaro Piscopia Palace on the Grand Canal in 1640.

When his brother died a year later, Gianbattista became sole owner of the palace and heir to its collections. That same year he was named Captain of Bergamo, succeeding Giovanni Grimani. Bergamo, in the Lombardy region of present day Italy, was a beautiful and important hillside town, where Gianbattista was to command military fortifications, maintain public order and have a voice in Venetian affairs, upholding the policy of the Republic in its territories. He was notably successful at both Peschiera and Bergamo. And each assignment represented an advantageous political stepping-stone to his future procuratorship in Venice.

---

* Variations of Zanetta's surname in historical records include Boni, De Boni, and Del Buono.

Both positions paid only nominal fees, and Gianbattista used his own money in administering them. But his influence as a good Venetian was continuing to grow, and it was honor he coveted. In 1649 he first petitioned for the top procuratorship of St. Mark, *de supra,* the second most sought-after office in the state. "Procurators becom the principall pillars of the Republic ever after," the seventeenth-century historian James Howell tells us.

Gianbattista also was proving to be a shrewd businessman. His real estate holdings included palaces and houses he rented in the city and country; as time went on, he would own mills, riverboats, ferries and bridges throughout the region.

Elena was three when her father first applied for the office of Procurator of St. Mark. His application was made to the Great Council, which consisted of all male nobles over twenty-five and totalled about 2000 members. As noted earlier, Gianbattista did not receive the post at that juncture, but he was well positioned financially to nurture young Elena's genius.

Her ensuing childhood years were comfortable and generally carefree as the precocious little girl grew up in lively Venice. There were abundant and wondrous sights for her to see, engaging a vibrant and fertile mind.

Elena's nurse Lorenza—whom she affectionately called *"Nonnina"* ("Grannie")—would firmly clutch her tiny charge by the hand as the two scurried past the endless shops of Venice. They would walk along the busy Merceria lanes and onto the Piazza, St. Mark's Square. It was a surging scene of compressed splendor, complementing the ordered majesty of the basilica.

Once the small private chapel of the doges, the basilica had become the state church. Its golden domes and early mosaic treasures, created by the best artisans over many centuries, were merged in triumphal offering. The cathedral's arched portal reflected the Republic's benevolent acceptance of people from every land.

"Of the throng in the Piazza," wrote the visiting diarist Thomas Coryat, "Here you may both see all manner of fashions of attyre, and heare all the languages of Christendome." Elena and her nurse saw jugglers and fortune-tellers, goldsmiths, money-changers, English knights and Greek sailors. They witnessed fruit sellers, hatters and beaders and wool combers, veiled nuns and flower girls flocking to and gathering in St. Mark's Square.

Also in the Square were goatherds and mountebanks peddling medicine, watermen, coach and cheesemakers, Turks, Spaniards and toothdrawers (those self-professed dentists of the day!). Along the quays, fisherfolk from nearby Chioggia were mending nets while poor elderly wives in brown shawls huddled at bonfires. These women were seen in sharp contrast to clusters of splendidly attired ladies wearing veils of fine cloth, lined with taffeta in summer and fur in winter. The matrons chatted under blue and white striped silk parasols held by attending women. And scattered amidst the crowds were black-cowled monks asking for alms.

Elena absorbed all of this teeming life, with her curled hair bouncing as she strode, and her large dark eyes, serious and perceptive beyond their years, staring intently. She would often tug at Lorenza's sleeve, sometimes pointing to other children freely playing near wooden bridges along the canals, and other times asking her for silver ducats to give to the beggars they encountered.

The Piazza, which still attracts countless world visitors, was the site for morning gatherings of businessmen like Gianbattista. After greeting each other in a manner reflecting the formal courtesy of the day, they would discuss affairs of the Republic in the shaded square. In the mid-seventeenth century, the Republic totalled well over 170,000 people in its principal centers: Venice 140,000 and Padua 30,000. On hot and sunny afternoons the Piazza became a public place, with Elena and Lorenza sometimes being part of the spectacle.

On one afternoon, the two would wander over to the Piazza to watch glass-blowers exhibiting delicate wares. Another time they would visit the cook's shop for venison pastry wrapped in a napkin, or return to the palace with a brace of partridge or rabbit, and apple fritters for dessert. And often Elena would journey by gondola with her nurse Lorenza along the Grand Canal, that "Great Vein" of Venice, crossing it to San Giorgio Maggiore for morning Mass. This was the youngster's favorite time.

For a "hapless victim," asserted one nineteenth century Frenchman, there was little childhood. Elena avoided the usual games other children played, rarely even engaging in conversation with other youngsters. A brother and sister, Francesco and Caterina, were years older, Francesco often away on business. The "studious and genial" Caterina, who was very close to her little sister, died when Elena was seven. Another brother, Baldassare, had died while traveling on a boat just prior to his second birthday and a year before Elena was born. Her other brother Girolamo and another sister named Caterina Isabetta were much younger and tended to be overshadowed by the prodigious Elena. None of the siblings received advanced education.

The middle child of three surviving siblings, Elena was brought up largely as an only child, both in position and interest. Her early, innate seriousness was greatly encouraged by her father; he had embraced, in all contradiction to the convention of the day, the scholarly development of this promising daughter.

Monsignor Fabris, the Cornaros' parish priest and family friend, was her beloved first tutor. Unlike his new protégé, Fr. Fabris was self-made. He had grown up a poor boy, reportedly doing very menial work, assisting with monastery chores while attending a Jesuit school, *Collegio della Compagnia di Gesù* (College of the Society of Jesus). His abilities soon were recognized by the Jesuits, and they undertook to educate the promising youth. He was ordained to the priesthood as a Third Order Franciscan and rose to be an eminent figure in scholarly circles as a Latinist and theologian. He was celebrated for his Aristotelian commentaries and a treatise on the life of St. Luke.

After earning a doctorate in theology, Fr. Fabris became the much-admired pastoral priest of St. Luke's Church. Located in an eleventh-century building founded by Otho Dandolo, the church was rebuilt in 1581. The Cornaros worshiped there, only a short walk from their palace. The Franciscan Fabris's love of philosophy and theology and his expertise in all the works of Aristotle were to shape Elena's academic future at Padua.

Originally, Gianbattista had been uncertain about just how to begin educating his seven-year-old daughter. Although involved in many other activities in a busy parish, Fr. Fabris offered to give Elena her first private lessons. He began her studies with Latin grammar. Within a few months, he initiated Greek.

Elena grew close to the kindly and experienced priest, a man who was seventy-one and remarkably vigorous when he began teaching her. It was Fr. Fabris who encouraged Elena to read both secular and religious works. Thriving on this early intellectual stimulus and support, Elena quickly realized that she loved to study, even tedious works! Fabris was "ecstatic" over the gifted girl's progress; Gianbattista thoroughly reveled in it.

There was another pivotal figure in Elena's intellectual rise to prominence: Gregorio Barbarigo. The nobleman Barbarigo had come to Fr. Fabris as a twenty-three-year-old cleric, seeking counsel. He had just returned from the conclusion of the Peace of Westphalia (1648) in Münster, Germany, that ended the bitter Thirty Years' War. Young Barbarigo sought Fabris's advice on monastic orders. The priest advised him to go to Rome, confirming an opinion the nobleman had received from a priest in Milan.

Years later Barbarigo would don a robe of scarlet, just as Fabris had predicted, becoming Bishop of Padua and Chancellor of the Theological Faculty at its university. He was to be one of Elena's greatest obstacles, but ultimately her champion in life and in death.

4

FIRST CONVENT CONSIDERED

It must be reckoned a miracle if a woman who, desirous of rising superior to her own sex, has dedicated herself to study, escapes with her mind and spirit unsullied by vices and abominations.

FRANCESCO PONA, A VERONESE PHYSICIAN
1628

HAVING SUCCESSFULLY BEGUN her exceptional education with Fr. Fabris, Elena urged her parents to consider a teaching convent for her. After the family conferred with Abbot Codanini, eleven-year-old Elena began her postulancy in a Venetian order in 1657. It was late summer, the start of the church educational year. The convent's name and Elena's specific date of entry are unrecorded because she never officially joined the order.

The Cornaros were told that the convent had an exemplary reputation. Gianbattista, always having the last word, had narrowed the final choice to four. According to the Benedictine biographer Bacchini, who knew both parents, they arrived at their final decision by drawing lots from an urn!

Regardless of how the convent had been selected, Elena was overjoyed at the opportunity to follow her deep interest in the contemplative life. She undoubtedly expected that her first months there would be divinely blissful, as she outwardly wore the customary secular clothes, but inwardly became engrossed in the spiritual ambience of the convent's cloistered confines.

As it turned out, her time there was hardly quiet solitude.

Young Elena had already matured into a reflective and rather taciturn girl, with a propensity for scholarly introspection. She was thoroughly frightened by the irreverent, even raucous, atmosphere of this particular convent, and she grew increasingly uneasy amidst the turmoil.

"A house of discord and a centre of unworthy intrigue," as described by one French account, was scarcely the environment a devoted father and protective mother would select for their daughter. But the convent they had unwittingly chosen turned out to be just that.

The great majority of Venetian convents of the mid-1600s were engaged in education, as well as in charitable work. The nuns who ran them were typically intelligent and well-informed women, some of whom became politically influential for the public good. Lady abbesses were known to have been allowed to appear before legislators to plead, discreetly, for social reforms, including better education for women. Girls who lived at these convents were usually taught the rudiments of reading and writing, as well as singing and domestic skills such as sewing and weaving.

A few convents had become notorious rendezvous sites, encouraging secret liaisons and scandalous escapades, holding "assemblies, balls, theatricals and puppet-shows." Some "parlours were a field which offered fruit all the more tempting because it was forbidden," wrote an Italian historian. While these convents were rare, the one selected for Elena happened to be in uproar, apparently catering to the social and affluent, diverted from its serious religious purpose.

The Cornaros had clearly mischosen for their now unhappy daughter. She returned to the winter palace by fall, gravely disappointed but fervently hoping to be allowed to enter another religious house very soon.

Welcoming back his challenging pupil, Monsignor Fabris undertook to structure a private curriculum for Elena modeled on the public form—a form far less standardized than in modern times.

If qualified intellectually, both boys and girls of the wealthy seventeenth-century Italian upper class in their elementary years received the classical humanist training which was largely a contribution of the Jesuits. Although courses varied, the *patrizii* (patricians, noblemen) were usually taught classical languages and literature. Subjects included grammar, history, poetry, moral philosophy and rhetoric. This weekday focus was combined with religious study on Sundays and holidays at schools of Christian doctrine in churches and monastic houses.

In Venice, the majority of teachers were clergymen; there were also some lay masters. A number of the teachers were non-Venetians who were attracted to the city by better pay and by the flourishing printing houses where they could earn extra money. Considered public servants, teachers were respected as other professionals of the day, including lawyers and physicians.

Among the teachers were a small number of women—equipped with a convent education but no college training. Even though the numbers had increased since the Renaissance, females made up only a small portion of the students recorded from among all classes of that patriarchal society. Girls, even of the lower nobility, let alone of the poorer population, were generally semiliterate.

As Gianbattista had arranged for his daughter, rich children of grade school age were often taught by tutors who lived in their homes or came there for daily lessons. While young noblemen were being prepared for public service or professions in law, medicine and theology, such preparation was not possible for women, since they were not allowed to attend universities. But Elena Cornaro would be a leading pioneer in breaking that barrier.

Under Fr. Fabris' tutelage, her studies were first centered on the acquisition of languages and developing her command of them. Her natural gift was already apparent. The priest proposed to Gianbattista the idea of hiring a range of additional private tutors to instruct Elena further in Greek and Latin grammar and literature. And he volunteered to assist with arrangements. Predictably, the prodigy's father was highly receptive.

Fr. Fabris continued to teach Elena philosophy of the ancient Greeks, and for fifteen years he provided guidance for her spiritual life. Giovanni Valier, Canon at St. Mark's, was engaged to instruct her in Latin. Another canon, the well-known Dr. Bartolloti, served as substitute. Rapidly, Elena was moving forward in both languages.

At the youthful age of eleven, her academic fare already included extensive Scripture study, and she was likely reading such traditional classical Latin works as Caesar's commentaries on the Gallic wars, Cicero's speeches and philosophical works, Virgil's epic poem, *The Aeneid,* Livy's history of Rome, *Ab Urbe Condita,* and Horace's *Odes* and *Satires.* In comparable literature of ancient Greece, Elena would soon study Xenophon's *Anabasis,* Plato's *Apology of Socrates,* Herodotus' history and Homer's *Iliad.* An incredibly ambitious curriculum—even for this young girl!

French and Spanish had already been added to her studies at the age of eight, taught by educated natives of France and Spain who lived in Venice. Elena rapidly acquired fluency in both languages. In her early twenties, she had the facility to translate into Italian a small Spanish book by the Carthusian Giovanni Lanspergio, *Coloquios de Christo al alma (Colloquy of Christ to the Devoted Soul),* written in 1669.

To complement Elena's studies in language and history, the Jesuit Carlo Vota, head of the Venetian Academy of Geography, was enlisted to instruct her in scientific studies. Renowned as a man of "encyclopedic culture," Vota was an expert in mathematics, physics, astronomy, geography, as well as languages. The course of academic disciplines, originating with Fabris, was greatly expanded by Vota, who taught Elena for seventeen years.

Nor were the arts neglected. Gianbattista had constructed an art gallery to house his painting collection, which included works inspired by Titian and Veronese and of Jacopo Bassano (the "Portrait of a Doctor," considered one of his best paintings) and miniatures from the popular Bavarian, Carlo Loth, among others. A portrait of Gianbattista "His Excellency, a Lion-like Hero" also hung there. (It was listed in an inventory but has never been found.) Elena studied all the paintings and developed into something of an authority.

An organist, Maddalena Cappelli, came to live at the palace to provide a broad musical background for the girl, including instrumental and vocal instruction. She remained with Elena as teacher and close confidante for more than two decades.

This academic assemblage for a woman was quite unprecedented.

While the Venetian society of the 1600s was stretching the frontiers of scientific inquiry and maintaining deep pride in its cosmopolitanism, there also remained vestiges of the ignorance and superstition that marked medieval times. In order to equip them for earning a living in trade or government, Venice's noblemen, merchants and male professionals achieved a high level of literacy. Their wives and daughters, on the other hand, acquired only the basic skills needed to run a household.

In an unforgiving social structure, a learned woman was often considered evil and unchaste, and some thought likely to be a witch. Those with intellectual prowess were the most maligned, often perceived as temptresses. From the start, Gianbattista had to contend with such accusers, including his own wife, who were suspicious and disapproving of his revolutionary goal to educate Elena. Being a Cornaro shielded him; having a fortune clearly helped.

The very wealthy in Venice lived royally. The Cornaro Piscopias owned five large dwellings, surrounded by formal gardens and filled with oriental treasures, ancient Greek sculpture, and the finest Italian painting. And there were staffs of servants to maintain these properties for them. In addition to palaces on the Grand Canal and in Padua, the Cornaros enjoyed country homes with fields and farms overlooking mountains, and others by the sea. The family could visit their Italian villa at Codevigo or the one at Este. Male members journeyed south of Turkey to visit the Cornaro Piscopia plantation on the southern tip of Cyprus. Women, however, were "made only to stay at home, not to go abroad," Elena once wrote.

Gianbattista kept his own fleet of gondolas and gondoliers, one gondola assigned to each member of his family. A hidden, underground private passageway was constructed to get to the boats. (The mooring ring for tying them up was rediscovered at the Ponte Corvo bridge in the 1980s.)

The best governesses, music, dance, and fencing masters were provided for his privileged children. Gianbattista owned a private stable of horses, complete with grooms and fancy carriages. He built chapels in his mansions and commissioned works of art to adorn them. From his father Girolamo, he also inherited a large personal library, whose holdings he greatly expanded. This was yet another Cornaro tradition. The family's ancestor Federico of San Luca, grandson of Il Grande, had assembled a rich and recognized library from his travels in the east with his brother Fantino.

Considered one of the finest private collections in Venice, Gianbattista's library augmented the expert teaching team that he and Fr. Fabris had assembled for Elena. It contained sets of mathematical and astronomical instruments and was well stocked with valuable Greek and Latin manuscripts, rare early printed editions of history and writings of all the major philosophers: Plato, Seneca, Cicero and Plutarch. It also housed the family arms display, trophies and marble busts, navigational charts, globes and maps.

The Cornaros' collection included various commentaries and the complete works of Aristotle in Greek as well as vernacular translations. In his book *A Journey Through Italy* (1698), the learned Benedictine monk Bernard de Montfaucon stated that the Cornaro library had the most extensive collection of works on the Venetian Republic. Scholars and area people were invited to consult the library at the Cornaro Piscopia Palace, and Elena had the advantage of using it constantly. Her mastery of its resources for local history would be evident in future years when she was called upon to adjudicate civil disputes.

Quite by accident while Elena was studying there one day, a noted professor from the University of Pisa arrived unannounced to examine the rich library and to meet Gianbattista. Awestruck, Carlo Rinaldini wrote a letter in Latin describing the scene:

> I was leafing through works of [Greek mathematician] Archimedes which were on the table. I fell upon the theory of the application of a straight line drawn between the circumference and diameter of a circle. Suddenly there appeared a very young girl, quite beautiful, her head majestic, her features well proportioned, with delicate coloring and very dignified in manner. She began to explain the theorem. I was dumbfounded and lost my words. Taking courage I asked the name and origin of this illustrious girl.

A lifetime friendship began there, and Professor Rinaldini would play a leading role in Elena's future academic triumph.

She gloried in her studies quite naturally, encouraged and sustained by the invigorating Monsignor Fabris, a lover of philosophy who served as both her first Father Confessor and the discoverer of her potential.

Early one morning during Mass in 1668, the eighty-six-year-old Fabris died of a stroke. As the priest had wished, his death was sudden and unannounced. When Elena learned of her mentor's death, she fled in tears to the summer palace in

Padua, which offered the grieving girl quiet refuge in its great gardens.

As Fr. Fabris had taught her, Elena would sit and pray for long periods near her birthday cypress tree. And it was there during an afternoon of the following spring that she found inexplicable comfort—upon discovering that nightingales were nesting in its lower branches.

"IN HER," WROTE MASSIMILIANO DEZA, "GRACE BEGAN SO EARLY THAT IT SEEMED NATURAL." A BENEDICTINE MONK, DEZA KNEW AND ADMIRED THE CORNARO FAMILY. HE WAS ELENA'S FIRST BIOGRAPHER.

(Vita di Helena Lucretia Cornara Piscopia. Venice, 1686. Biblioteca Civica, Padua)

5

EARLY FAME

I have ever had two altars erected in my heart—
one to God, the other to my country.

GIANBATTISTA PETITIONING THE GREAT COUNCIL

ELENA WAS READY to move forward intellectually in any direction. An Englishman, Professor Alexander Anderson, succeeded Monsignor Fabris as her advisor.

Living in Venice at the time, Professor Anderson became Elena's Latin teacher, building on the solid foundation she had already received. The Briton also added a new language to her course of instruction: English. This addition was most unusual in the 1600s, as noted by philosopher-historian Paul Oskar Kristeller. In *Beyond Their Sex*, a collection of scholars' essays, Kristeller observed that very few students on the continent learned any English until the eighteenth century.

It was through Professor Anderson that the nobleman Abbot Luigi (Alvise) Gradenigo was engaged to continue Elena's studies in Greek, his native language. The Orthodox priest, future Head Librarian of St. Mark's, was a member of the large Greek colony in Venice. It was a colony that had been established at the end of the fourteenth century, as a result of the Great Schism of Latin and Greek churches which had begun over disputes regarding authority and discipline. Separation drove some of the schismatics to Venice, where they were more welcome than anywhere else in Italy.

By Elena's time, Hellenic studies flourished and had become increasingly influential because of the Republic's exposure from trade with the Levant—the coastland countries bordering the eastern Mediterranean Sea from Greece to Egypt—and because of international voyages of the wealthy. Firmly established as a center of Greek studies, Venice boasted of several great printing houses, particularly that of Aldus Manutius, whose press had Greek type. "This was the moment in history when the Aldine Press was transforming man's horizons,"noted a British art historian.

From 1495 to 1515, the writings of Plato, Aristotle, Plutarch, Herodotus, Thucydides, Xenophon, Sophocles, Aristophanes, Demosthenes and other Greek authors were published in Venice for the first time by the Aldine Press. Each Aldine edition featured their famed device, a dolphin entwined around an anchor. These elegant Aldine books became part of the Cornaros' distinguished library, available for their gifted daughter to read.

Gradenigo was from an overseas Venetian family long settled in Candia (now Crete), and Anderson personally recommended him to Gianbattista. Expanding Elena's knowledge of the ancient Greek she had first learned under Fabris' tutelage, the priest also undertook to teach her the modern tongue.

For a decade Elena studied with Gradenigo, interrupted briefly by her time in the convent. His pupil quickly mastered both forms of the language so well that when Gradenigo was being considered for the abbacy of the Cardauchi on the Greek island of Corcyra (now Corfu), a treatise composed by Elena served to convince church authorities of his scholarship.

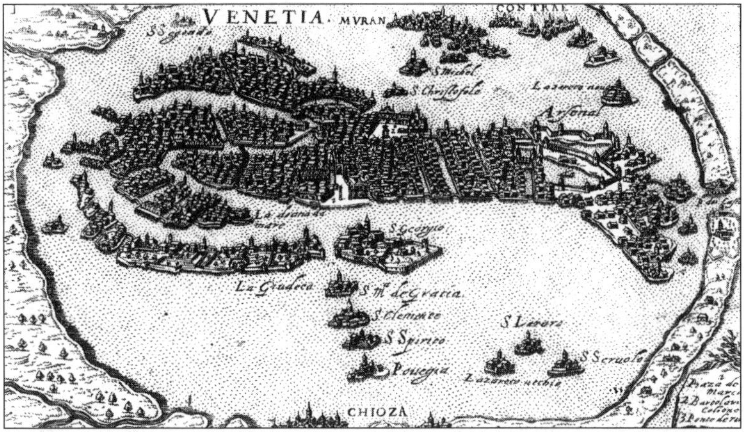

A seventeenth-century map of Venice *(detail above)*, written in Venetian dialect, includes San Giorgio Maggiore Island with the Basilica where Elena worshiped, and the lagoon island of Santa Maria della Grazie, site of her Capuchine retreats. Facing San Giorgio Maggiore is *La Giudeca,* the Jewish section of Venice and home of Elena's beloved Hebrew teacher, Rabbi Shalma Abbroff. *Lazaretto Vecchie* in the foreground is the city's old hospital; on the other side of the city is the famous glassmaking center, Murano, and *Lazaretto Nuovo,* the new hospital. *(A larger version of this map is found on page vi.)*

(La Città Di Venetia. Venice, 1614. The John M. Wing Foundation, The Newberry Library, Chicago)

The famed Aldine device *(right)* was the press symbol used by Aldus Manutius (1450-1515), first publisher of Greek and Latin classics in Venice. Similar devices are used today.

(Il libro del Cortegiano [Book of the Courtier]. Baldesar Castiglione. Venice: Aldus, 1541. Annenberg Rare Book and Manuscript Library, University of Pennsylvania)

Submitting her work, the priest countered opposition and secured his appointment.

Elena was emerging as an outstanding linguist. By the age of fifteen she was considered an accomplished scholar in both Greek and Latin. She spoke, wrote and debated skillfully in both languages.

During these years, Carlo Rinaldini, who had originally met Elena during their memorable and unexpected encounter in Gianbattista's library, was frequently coming to consult the Cornaro collection and to visit the young girl. He often stayed several days at the palace and was charmed by Elena's grace and unusual facility in erudite conversations. "She is beautiful as an angel," he wrote in a letter, "and speaks Greek, Latin, French, English and Spanish with perfect ease."

A man of prominence and great learning, Rinaldini was born in 1615 in Ancona, a seaport town in the Marches Region. He studied philosophy and mathematics at the University of Bologna, Europe's oldest university, and began his career as mathematician for the Duke of Tuscany.

When Elena first knew Rinaldini, he was professor of philosophy at the University of Pisa, having begun his tenure there in 1649. After eighteen years at Pisa, he went to the renowned University of Padua, which was under Venetian rule. Rinaldini became head of the Padua philosophy faculty, and he began to tutor Elena privately during his tenure there.

To further Elena's scholarly pursuits, another highly innovative arrangement developed in her life. A distinguished rabbi from a Venetian synagogue (no synagogue's name recorded) came to teach her Hebrew and Aramaic. This provided Elena the unique opportunity to study Old Testament sources in the original tongues and to discourse with Jewish masters.

In what was becoming his typical move, Gianbattista had selected the best person in the field, Rabbi Shalma Abbroff (also known as Shemuel Aboaf). He was an esteemed leader of the small but prosperous Jewish community whose ancestors had been expelled from Spain in the 15th century. Originally fleeing to Germany, Poland and the Aegean Islands, some of these Sephardic Jews eventually migrated to Venice, where they found general acceptance. By the 1600s, the Jewish community in the Republic numbered nearly 6,000, with seven synagogues.

Rabbi Abbroff was born in Hamburg in 1610 to a Sephardic family of scholars. He later moved to Venice, where he was called to head the Jewish community in 1650. Spanish by birth, the Abbroffs became Italian in culture. They sent their thirteen-year-old son to be educated in Verona where his grandfather lived. Soon, the young Shalma Abbroff achieved fluency in Italian, Spanish, Latin and German. He founded an academy, and his expertise as a rabbinical authority was sought throughout Europe.

A very strict Orthodox intellectual, Rabbi Abbroff made an exception in teaching Elena Hebrew, assenting to the procurator's unusual request. He soon became a valued friend of the Cornaros, who consulted him often. Despite the rabbi's general disapproval of public ceremony (and wasting time smoking and snuffing!), he received invitations to their social gatherings. His teaching inspired Elena, and his personal piety and compassion deepened her admiration.

Elena rapidly learned Hebrew and also Aramaic—the Semitic language spoken by Jesus—enhancing Elena's understanding of the Holy Scriptures. She further expanded her knowledge of languages with the study of Arabic. Scholars from France and Spain, countries whose languages she had learned so early, often commented that she spoke like a native.

When Elena began the study of theology, this proved to be her favorite subject—and it would determine her future academic course.

Lessons in philosophy, begun early by Fr. Fabris, were continued by the Conventual Fr. Felice Rotondi, a confidant of Gianbattista and a teaching theologian from the University of Padua. Elena was then sixteen, the Franciscan friar thirty-two. Rotondi was born in Monte Leone Sabino, a small hill town northeast of Rome. Having earlier earned a doctorate, he became Provost of Academic Affairs in the Franciscan order of Venice in 1662. Three years later he went to Padua and eventually was associated with the Venetian Academy of the Ricovrati (or Ricoverati), where his university friend Carlo Rinaldini also held membership.

Much to her delight and fascination, Elena's studies now covered the works of all the church fathers. In both Latin and Greek, she read the writings of St. Augustine, St. Thomas Aquinas and many other doctors of the church. The *Apologeticus* of Tertullian (who initiated Christian Latin literature in the second century), and the writings and sufferings of the ancient martyrs St. Basil and St. John Chrysostom were of particular interest to her.

According to Professor Rinaldini, Elena was well versed not only in philosophy but in mathematics, dialectics and astronomy by the age of seventeen. The widely known seventeenth-century Messinian writer, Antonio Lupis, observed that she knew the problems of history, both ancient and modern: changes in states, origins of empire, laws of the people, and the extent of war.

At this age, Elena was also recognized as a skilled musician, singing and accompanying herself on the harpsichord, harp, and lute. In addition, she was composing music and writing serious poetry. Her fame as an astonishingly accomplished young woman was spreading, and her father promoted it—concurrently promoting his own advancement.

When Gianbattista had begun petitioning for the leading procuratorship of St. Mark's in 1649, paying 25,000 ducats to the public treasury, he failed in this first attempt. Ten years later he tried again with 40,000 ducats and was again refused. He finally succeeded in 1664.

On March 1, Gianbattista Cornaro was named Treasurer for life. This position included the privileges of having an office in the Ducal Palace, an entrée to the procurators' council chamber, and an apartment in the new Procuratie overlooking St. Mark's Square. The post cost him 105,000 ducats, an enormous sum!

Also at this time—after being refused twice in 1659 and once earlier in 1664—Gianbattista again sought to have his surviving sons, Francesco and Girolamo, included in the *Libro d'oro.* For this honor, Gianbattista had to plead before the Senate, the upper house of 200 men, and the Great Council. He was determined to overcome the recent political scandals that had eroded the family's good name—scandals which were well known to these rulers, the "great Sages" of Venice.

With considerable eloquence, Gianbattista forcefully recounted proud, personal chapters in his family's history. He spoke of the "Golden Age" of the Cornaros, when valiant Federico Cornaro *(Il Grande)* impoverished himself by donating his entire fortune to Venice to win the War of Chioggia in 1381. Gianbattista noted that Federico di San Luca had been listed as the Republic's wealthiest citizen in a 1379 census.

Moreover, his grandsons, Federico and Fantino, compiled yet another fortune from business ventures in the eastern Mediterranean and from the family's fief in Crete, Venice's most valuable colony (which it was to lose during Elena's lifetime). The Cornaro Piscopia branch of the family was directly descended from Federico, *Il Grande,* through Fantino.

Focusing next on his fifteenth and sixteenth century ancestors, Gianbattista told of Marco Cornaro who was honored by being elected doge—despite being poor and elderly and with a commoner wife. In 1515 Abbot Giovanni Cornaro enlarged Benedictine libraries in Venice and Padua from his own collections, a contribution for which he was venerated by young biblical scholars.

Gianbattista reminded his listeners of Cornaro heroism at the decisive Battle of Lepanto which occurred later in the sixteenth century—a battle in which many of the family had served, helping Venice win a huge victory at sea against the Turkish Ottoman Empire. Of the four Cornaros who commanded ships, one captain died, another lost a son, and a third was killed during combat along with his three sons.

It was said that the doge, so deeply touched upon hearing the candidate's tales, was moved to tears. Gianbattista's strong appeal for his sons was finally granted.

Now he could devotedly turn his attention to the pursuit of his larger quest: the historic renown of his seventeen-year-old daughter.

Elena was well aware of her father's contribution to the Republic in his role as an important public official. She also knew that he was one who exercised his duties with exceptional discipline. Some of the richest noblemen merely gloried in their titles and neglected their duties, a practice with serious consequences for Venice. Not so for Gianbattista Cornaro.

As Procurator of St. Mark (there would be twenty-two Cornaro procurators), he was a commanding figure in Venetian affairs. "All degrees of peeple do shew them special reverence," wrote English historian James Howell in 1651. "And they have priority of place... given them." Gianbattista sat in on the Great Council that made all the rules of the Republic. He administered its treasury with efficiency, pride and aplomb, no small task for a Republic under economic and political stress.

Spectacularly situated, Venice was one of the wealthiest and strongest cities in Europe during the Renaissance, when it controlled the Adriatic and very lucrative trade between east and west. In the early fifteenth century it captured Padua, Verona, Vicenza, Brescia, Bergamo, Treviso and Bassano, among other mainland areas. Its eastern possessions included Crete, Cyprus and the Morea (the medieval name for the Peloponnesus).

In the post-Renaissance seventeenth century, Venice's role was diminishing from an international to a regional port city. It had long lost its monopoly in the valuable spice trade with Diaz's discovery in 1486 of a new route around the Cape of Good Hope to India and the East Indies. By the year 1600, its position as an important textile center making wool cloth had vanished.

Portugal, England, France, and Holland had become commercial competitors, but during Elena's lifetime Venice still maintained the largest markets between Germany and the eastern Mediterranean for Persian silks, Turkish cotton, and a variety of other wares.

Venetian craftsmanship in glass, leather, and mosaics and the new, flourishing industries of printing and sugar refining strengthened its economy. And the government protected its glass, wool, and silk businesses. But the Venice of Elena's childhood was slow in recovering, having lost the Morea, Cyprus and then Crete, along with much of its labor force in the devastating plagues.

Wealthy men like Gianbattista, however, retained their power and vast fortunes with commerce and industry dealings, real estate ventures and shipping. Born in a "defined, hereditary aristocracy," they completely controlled the Republic.

Politically, Venice maintained its guard against Spanish domination and the Inquisition, its neutrality in European wars, and its independence from the Vatican. Repeatedly, it had to defend itself against invasion by the dreaded Turks. The fifth war, started in 1645, lasted for twenty-three years. The Venetian upper class was called upon continually to contribute to drained coffers. Gianbattista's position as treasurer of a Republic in decline was no small challenge.

During his time as procurator, Gianbattista moved easily among the erudite. He came to know many scholars of the day, both those who lived in the area and others who traveled to Venice to consult the Library of St. Mark's (now *Biblioteca Nazionale Marciana*), which was under his jurisdiction. This great library was said to have begun with a donation from the poet Francesco Petrarca (Petrarch), who so significantly stimulated the revival of learning in late medieval Europe. Having fled to Venice to escape the plague at Padua in 1362, Petrarch served as court historian for the doge. In exchange for a grand house in Arquà, a small village near Padua, he bequeathed his books, including classical manuscripts, to the Republic. The house had been given to him by Francesco de Carrara.

A century later, the scholar-patriarch of Constantinople, Johannes Bessarione (1395-1472), also contributed to the revival of letters and donated his extensive library to Venice.

Forming the nucleus of the Library of St. Mark's, the Greek cardinal's gift (he had paid 30,000 gold florios for 500 texts) comprised 482 Greek and 264 Latin manuscripts. Homer codices, a rare edition of Dante and precious examples of Byzantine bookbinding were among its treasures.

Over the years, clergymen, procurators, and benefactors, including Gianbattista and his father, enriched St. Mark's valuable collections from their private holdings. Pietro Bembo, credited with making Venice and Padua active centers of classical culture, was among its illustrious head librarians. The Florentine sculptor Jacopo Sansovino designed the old library building (*Libreria Vecchia*) in 1537. Since 1905 the Library of St. Mark's has been housed in an addition, the *zécca* (mint) building.

San Giorgio Maggiore also possessed an outstanding monastery library which Fr. Codanini made available to the Cornaros. Through Elena's tutors, Prefect Luigi Gradenigo and Canon Giovanni Valier, both with great family book collections, and through her father, who oversaw the basilica, Elena had access to extraordinary resources.

Following in his family's footsteps—marked for generations by close association with some of the most famous and learned men of their times—Gianbattista gathered the very best scholars of his day. He knew that Lorenzo de Medici ("The Magnificent"), who created the brilliant coterie of accomplished artists and writers at Florence, was often a guest of the Cornaros in the late 1400s. A leading figure in European scholasticism and son of the ambassador to Florence, Pietro Bembo presided over the palace circle of Cyprus Queen Caterina Cornaro at Asolo.

In the sixteenth century the architect Andrea Palladio was a young member of Luigi Cornaro's set, his work influenced by the elderly Luigi's architectural interest. The skilled reformer Carlo Cardinal Borromeo was a friend of Elena's great-grandfather, Giacomo Alvise Cornaro, a hydraulic engineer who helped conserve the Venetian lagoons.

Galileo Galilei, the great Tuscan astronomer at the University of Padua from 1592 to 1610, was an intimate of Marco Cornaro. Another family visitor was the noted scientist and historian Paolo Sarpi. Credited with discovering eye dilatation, Sarpi was also known for his wise counsel when the Jesuits were banished from Venice in 1605, an event that was to personally impact Gianbattista.

Yet another participant at Cornaro palace affairs was Torquato Tasso, a poet widely read in Europe by 1650. Many more honored men were to be welcomed during the lifetime of Gianbattista's celebrated daughter.

There was an additional and pervasive influence in this Cornaro house of culture: the fabled *Il libro del Cortegiano* (The Book of the Courtier) by Count Baldesar Castiglione. Son of a wealthy nobleman whose mother was from the royal house of Gonzaga, Castiglione served as the representative for several Venetian doges in England and Spain. His book of manners was first printed by Aldine Press in Venice in the spring of 1528 and subsequently published in 140 editions in four languages! A later English edition contained an introduction by Sir Walter Raleigh. The Count ultimately bequeathed his entire library to the Vatican.

Castiglione's popular tome, ten years in the making, laid down rules of etiquette and social standards required of Italian aristocracy. It became the model for all of Europe.

In the charming language of the time, Castiglione spoke of "To my thynkyng, the trade and maner of Courtyers... whyche is most fyttynge for a Gentilman that lyveth in the

Court of Princes. . . ." The "trade and maner" were carefully spelled out, including skill with arms and athletics; playing a lute and flinging a dart; and the manner in which a man should disclose his love to a woman. In particular, "noblenes of birthe" was rehearsed for the "stout herted."

The code set in the *Book of the Courtier* was followed for centuries. And Gianbattista hit every mark. "To be well borne and of a good stocke" he was indeed. The Cornaro legacy fired his tireless ambition over a lifetime.

Nevertheless, a carefully molded society never accepted his commoner wife. "A Waytyng Gentylwoman" had "to be well born and of a good house," preached Count Castiglione, "to daunse, drawe, peinet and to be learned." Zanetta could barely read.

Their daughter, however, would push the definition of "to be learned" far beyond the boundaries which Castiglione envisioned—to the point of being honored throughout Europe for her unparalleled scholarship. In the process, Elena would end up pressing the limits of physical endurance too far. In absolute obedience to Gianbattista, she completely immersed herself in her studies. And, while fueling her academic pursuits, Elena's desire to please her ambitious father would lead to dire consequences.

A TWENTY-TWO-YEAR-OLD ELENA IS SHOWN HERE IN A COWL. THIS 1668 ILLUSTRATION, SIGNED BY ABBOT GRADENIGO, HER GREEK TUTOR, AND AUGUSTINIAN CLERIC FRANCISCUS MACEDO, FEATURES BOTH LATIN AND GREEK COUPLETS WHICH PRAISE THE YOUNG PRODIGY.

(Biblioteca Civica, Padua)

6

EXTREME PENANCE

What loving slaughter on the eyes of God! What a noble spectacle to the Angels' sight!

ANTONIO LUPIS DESCRIBING ELENA'S TORTUROUS DISCIPLINES, 1689

SHARP NAILS PIERCED HER SKIN through a rough hair shirt as she drew the chains more tightly around her hips. Desperately trying not to submit to pain, the girl moaned in agony. Shoving up the sleeves of her nightdress, she further twisted the harsh roping, which consisted of knotted whip-cords soaked in pot vinegar. The roping cut into her wrists, still raw from a previous lashing.

All the servants had retired when Elena began her penance. It was close to midnight and, continually depriving herself of sleep, she had quietly retreated into the private chapel that adjoined her bedchamber. She tied both her arms to her sides and fell on her knees in meditation. An hour later, feeling faint, she collapsed across a wooden board on the floor to sleep.

It was a time just before a feast day of the church. Prior to religious festivals, Elena's voluntary disciplines and extraordinary penances became more frequent and often as lengthy as a full liturgy. Would that she could scourge her face and cut off all of her hair, she mused, knowing that only unseen self-punishment was possible.

As an adolescent entering her teen years, Elena began to starve herself more often. Not only was she known to urge the maids to eat her food, the young Cornaro also had them take some of her meals to hungry people outside the palace. It was her firm belief that physical suffering by self-maceration and other corporal abuse would lead to sanctification. Subjecting the body in order to attain spiritual perfection was her continuing goal.

Was holiness the primary motivation of this complex young girl? Was she reacting to excesses of a once brilliant society now in decline? Or was her extreme and brutal behavior actually a form of rebellion against strong and conflicting family pressures in a time when women had little voice?

Going well beyond ritual fasting, it seems that Elena was becoming, in modern parlance, anorexic. Anorexia nervosa is an eating disorder, primarily exhibited in young women, characterized by aversion to food and obsession with weight. Widely recognized in the medical profession today, the symptoms include severe and prolonged undernutrition caused by self-induced starvation.

For those suffering from anorexia, this aversion to food and eating may be an attempt to gain control over their lives. Their obsessive fear of weight gain results in weight loss, hyperactivity, and other nervous disorders.

Characteristics of anorexia in female patients were first medically recorded by Richard Morton in the seventeenth century. Morton distinguished these traits from the prevalent but vaguely diagnosed evidence of a disease then called consumption—which, two centuries later, was named tuberculosis.

A modern work by Rutgers University historian Rudolph Bell ascribes to early Italian female saints (some of whom were Elena's heroines) the clinical diagnosis of "holy anorexia." Unlike many cases today, their motivation was neither vanity nor a desire to be extremely thin; rather, it was a desire to attain mastery over and suppress such bodily functions as hunger in the belief that this would empower the spirit.

In *Holy Feast and Holy Fast,* Caroline Bynum, of Radcliffe College's Bunting Institute, traces the symbolic importance of food for women in a cultural context. She cites present day anorexic traits which were all clearly exhibited by Elena Cornaro: sleeplessness, euphoria, and hyperactivity. For Elena, this "holy anorexia" represented a way of doing penance, repressing the appetite to nourish the spirit. The numerous serious illnesses that were precipitated by this disorder—and endured the rest of her life—would finally cut short her achievements and end Gianbattista's further aspirations.

Historians have noted that these holy anorexics of the Renaissance were often quite happy children with healthy, loving parents. The girls tended to be obliging and highly intelligent, from prosperous, even titled families, who prayed earnestly and gratefully for their parents. But they often expressed feelings of worthlessness, showing clear signs of repression in a society ruled by notably autocratic and ambitious men. Anorexic behavior is now believed to be often precipitated by parental suppression and overcontrol, as seems clearly the case in Elena's life.

For many Renaissance saints, rejecting worldliness and embracing bodily abuse were their expressions of martyrdom. Elena deeply admired these saints; having avidly studied each of their stories, her own disturbed behavior appears to be a patterned reflection.

Some of the female saints were known to have adopted various shock techniques for penance and publicity. They practiced rigorous self-discipline and self-denial, often in an extreme manner. Biographers and historians have recorded instances of eating lice, drinking pus, and mixing dirt and ashes with food to make it unpalatable. Several consumed nothing for weeks on end except the bread of the Eucharist.

Considered by some observers today to be a classic holy anorexic, the revered St. Catherine of Siena was the most well-documented woman of the fourteenth century. One of twenty-five children of a dyer, Caterina Benincasa had qualities later to be evidenced in Elena.

Now a venerated and influential saint of the Roman Catholic Church, Caterina displayed great imagination and sensitivity at a very early age. Like Elena, she dedicated herself to a life of asceticism, pledging chastity in her youth. She struggled to persuade her parents for permission to join the Dominican order as a lay tertiary when she was sixteen.

Staying at home, she gradually became a recluse, eating almost nothing and remaining in constant meditation and prayer. When she returned more fully to the family routine, she began tending to the needy in her community, including the ill, the poor, and, eventually, the victims of the plague.

At twenty-one, Caterina was thrust onto a wider stage as a peacemaker. Traveling to Pisa at the invitation of its ruler, Piero Gambacorti, she enlisted participants for a crusade and was reported to have received there the stigmata—marks resembling the crucifixion wounds of Jesus Christ—on her hands, feet and heart.

The great political accomplishments that made Caterina famous were persuading Pope Gregory XI to abandon the sordid papal court at Avignon and return to Rome. Upon his arrival in the Eternal City, Gregory XI concluded a peace treaty between his successor, Urban VI, and rebellious Roman citizens.

This was certainly a unique role for a woman of the fourteenth century!

Never having learned to write, Catherine contributed to Italian literature by dictating 400 letters to various princes. Her eloquence has been compared to that of the renowned lyric poet and scholar Petrarch.

Elena would surely have admired this chaste, holy woman. The letters of St. Catherine offered great inspiration for Elena, who would also fully sympathize with her efforts to enter a convent and forsake marriage. The young Cornaro also sought to follow in the footsteps of her saintly predecessor whose courageous example of serving the needy has inspired many. The parallels between the two outstanding women are numerous and noteworthy, including their roles as peacemakers and important contributors to the literature of their time.

Extreme asceticism had been practiced by many of the early saints. Their biographies were Elena's favorite reading, even at a young age. Embracing their wisdom and dedication to humanity, she also was influenced by their selfless manner of living.

Elena's idol was the sixth century Umbrian monk, St. Benedict of Nursia, founder of the Order of Benedictines, whose great Rule she followed as an oblate. Written while he was sequestered in a cave for three years in Subiaco, *The Rule of St. Benedict* became widely regarded as a guide to monastic life and served as a noteworthy educational and civilizing influence in the western world. Elena thoroughly adopted the principles of discipline for mind, body, and spirit outlined in the Rule. She also sought to follow its requirement of manual labor and study as duties toward attaining perfection.

Accounts of Spanish saints were also popular literature in Elena's time. Ignatius Loyola, the eminent sixteenth-century Basque theologian, had a similar background to that of Lady Cornaro. The son of the noble houses of Onaz and Loyola, Iñigo López de Recalde (Ignatius) served as a page in the court of King Ferdinand and Queen Isabella. He attended the University of Paris *(la Sorbonne),* studying Hebrew in a class with two famous French students—Benedictine author and humorist François Rabelais, and Protestant reformer Jean Caulvin (John Calvin).

Loyola's father, Lord Beltran, directed the outset of his son's career by requiring him to join the military. The young aristocrat served as a soldier until he was twenty-six, when he was severely wounded defending a garrison against the French in the Navarre. Near death, he miraculously recovered but was left with a permanent limp. Realizing that his military career was over, he began reading religious works during convalescence. The writings transformed him profoundly.

Loyola renounced his inherited world of luxury and ease and became one of the "street people" of his day. Walking from Padua to Venice in 1523, he began begging bread and sleeping on the square in front of St. Mark's as a homeless derelict.

A wealthy Spanish visitor, touched by the scourged and emaciated figure of a fellow countryman, rescued him, furnished shelter, and obtained papal permission for him to board a pilgrim ship to Cyprus, where he would continue to Jerusalem. Later returning to Venice, Loyola was ordained there as a priest in 1537, at the age of forty-six.

A man of remarkable courage and powerful intellect, the new priest had within two years founded the Society of Jesus, with six associates. His Jesuit monasteries would subsequently train such men as Pascal, Descartes and Voltaire and impact many nations for centuries to come.

During his days as a courtier and a soldier, Loyola was hardly a saint. By his own admission, he had gambled and fought frequently, and had often engaged in illicit liaisons with women of the street. Later, he would champion the cause of these women—opening institutions in Rome to rescue them from the streets, providing orphanages for their children.

Repenting of his frivolous past, Ignatius chose to follow a path marked by great austerity and good works. A century later, his rejection of aristocratic living and his self-sacrificial lifestyle would captivate Elena Cornaro.

The Jesuit society created by the Spaniard clearly had a profound influence on the spiritual and intellectual life of the young Venetian woman. Fittingly, Elena's father would be instrumental in obtaining permission for the Jesuits' return to Venice in 1657. They had been expelled a half century earlier because they had sided with Rome during a time when the pope had placed the Republic under interdict—suspending religious services and the administration of the sacraments. Gianbattista was much admired for his efforts on behalf of the Jesuits, and his daughter would be a grateful beneficiary of their restoration.

A follower of Loyola to whom Elena especially was drawn was the Jesuit Aloysius, commonly known as Luís Gonzaga. In many ways, Luís's life paralleled her own. He was born in an ancestral castle of the distinguished Gonzaga family, the Renaissance rulers who brought artistic and literary genius to Mantua, including the Paduan court painter, Andrea Mantegna.

The young Gonzaga heir declared a vow of perpetual chastity when he was only nine years old! His father, the Marquis of Castiglione, was concerned about his eldest son's religious inclination and forced him to appear at courts in Mantua, Ferrara, Parma and Turin.

The boy was sent to the Medici in Florence in 1577, and while serving as page to the heir of the Spanish throne in Madrid, began silent periods of prayer and meditation. He abandoned royal life, and in 1585 joined the Jesuits. Six years later, while ministering to plague victims in Rome, he himself was infected and died. He was only twenty-three.

Extolled for his life of purity and service, Gonzaga became known as the "Patron of Youth," and was beatified in 1605. Several decades later, young Elena Cornaro, following his example, was inspired to take her childhood vow of chastity.

Another religious of noble birth and great stature was the sixteenth century Spanish Carmelite nun, Teresa of Avila. She, along with Ignatius of Loyola, was canonized in 1622 by Pope Gregory XV. Since Elena was fluent in Spanish, she read about Teresa in her native tongue, including the Spaniard's education in an Augustinian convent in Old Castile and her flight from home and a domineering father to join the Carmelite Convent of the Incarnation.

Inspired by personal visions of Christ, Teresa of Avila became concerned with the loss of discipline in some monastic orders of her land. At the age of forty-three, the Spanish mystic became determined to found a new convent that focused on the basics of a contemplative order: a simple life devoted to prayer. When her plans were discovered, she was denounced from the pulpit and urged to raise money for her present convent. Nonetheless, she persisted, and founded the reformed Descalced or Barefoots, in opposition to the parent body of Calzados. Their focus on prayer was coupled with an emphasis on work and service. And, while emphasizing an ascetic life, Teresa once observed, "There's a time for partridge and a time for penance."

During her lifetime, facing severe challenges, the noblewoman opened fifteen monasteries and seventeen convents throughout Spain. She also wrote a history of the movement. Four centuries later, in 1970, Teresa was declared a Doctor of the Church* for her writing and teaching on prayer, one of two women (the other being Catherine of Siena) to be so honored.

The Barefoots, whose members wore sandals made of rope, were a very strict order. Monks and nuns were required to sleep on straw, adhere to a meatless diet, and be supported entirely by alms.

All of this was to be modeled by Elena Cornaro.

Veneration of saints who were portrayed as rulers was popular with seventeenth-century nobility. Like Elena, Teresa in her childhood was fascinated by stories of martyrs. The Spaniard also subjected herself to excessive self-punishment, scourging herself with whips repeatedly and wearing haircloths that inflicted the most intense pain. Teresa was known for her kindness to the poor, especially impoverished women. And whenever she could, she gave away her money. Elena also did each of these things in secret.

In her own time, Elena was surrounded by religious figures of austerity and altruism who impacted her life and values. The esteemed Fr. Fabris led a very modest and simple

---

* "Doctor of the Church": a title bestowed since the Middle Ages upon known Christian theologians of exceptional merit and saintliness.

life in spite of his prominence. He constantly was serving others. Her close friend and teacher, the distinguished Rabbi Shalma Abbroff, was known to be extremely generous to his people and was also recognized for his work with the area's destitute, going personally to them to give aid. He fasted often and for extended periods of time.

As early as age five, Elena chafed at the luxury of her palace life. But outwardly she was required to conform. Despite her longing to be a nun, this holy vocation was disallowed by her unpersuaded parents. And, at numerous times, her pastors suspected that she was fasting too much; they continually admonished her to desist. At one point she sought a renowned Benedictine exorcist for guidance.

As a Cornaro, Elena showed dutiful loyalty and concern for the Republic, but she had an overriding desire to retreat. Amidst this desire, she was also greatly troubled by her total resistance to both parents' marital aspirations for her. Her complete opposition greatly conflicted with her sense of filial duty to obey, yet, throughout her life, Elena would shrink in utter horror at the very thought of marriage. Many times, turmoil and deep anguish consumed the gentle maiden.

Her physical health and her studies began to be affected. Scurvy was her first major illness. Now known to be caused by a prolonged lack of ascorbic acid (vitamin C) in the body, scurvy is characterized by weakness, anemia, spongy gums, bleeding from the mucous membranes, and other serious health problems. Elena's prolonged fasting is likely to have precipitated the disease. And when she was sent to the summer palace at Padua to recover, the intensity of her academic work temporarily waned.

She soon returned to Venice, where a woman of vision and enlightenment became a best friend. She was the Abbess Maria

Felice, foundress of the Capuchines on the nearby island of Santa Maria della Grazia. In a century marked by the establishment of many orders of nuns, the followers of Sister Maria took vows of strict poverty, derived from the rules of the Franciscan order. Over the years Elena would bring other women to the nearby island on retreats to hear the saintly abbess, a woman much admired for her exemplary life. Many of the attendees were persuaded to renounce vanities and opulent living.

Ironically, Elena's desire for the religious life was not always supported by the religious in her life. Quite opposed to her desire for the convent was her Confessor, the Jesuit Carlo Boselli. And it was Sr. Maria who dissuaded Elena from seeking another convent after her discouragement over the atmosphere in her first convent experience. The abbess told the young Cornaro that the future held greater things for her. With inspiring words, Sr. Maria told Elena that she was "to shine amidst the darkness of the world as a great beacon of evangelical perfection."

From the perspective of Elena's father, it was now time for his spectacularly intelligent and elegant prodigy to be prominently positioned in the public square. But the devoted daughter, now entering womanhood, had a strong will of her own. Not wanting any recognition for herself, she was utterly determined to lead a life of quiet sacrifice and humility.

These disparate perspectives over how Elena's life should be lived inevitably led to a tragic conflict between father and daughter. It was a conflict that caused such deep agony for the young Cornaro that it would ultimately lead to her undoing.

7

ON INTERNATIONAL DISPLAY

... Venice with its "liquid streets," the most glorious and heavenly show upon the water that ever any mortal eye beheld.

LONDON DIARIST THOMAS CORYAT
ON FIVE MONTH'S JOURNEY OVER EUROPE
RECORDED IN *CRUDITIES*
1611

This Mayden Republic... Touching Her View, She is taxd all the World over for the Latitude of liberty She gives to Carnall plesure.

ENGLISH HISTORIAN JAMES HOWELL
1651

THERE WAS NOTHING MORE VENETIAN than a brilliant social life, and the Cornaros had the daughter to adorn it. Elena was developing into an exceptionally beautiful woman, delicate and graceful in bearing, just over five feet tall, with elegant features in the classic mold.

The young Cornaro was graced with a pleasing soprano voice which she was called upon to display after palace dinners. She was also trained in the art of canto, reciting long passages of poetry. It was difficult not to spoil the young star.

Frequently, Elena would be called upon by her father to perform with music and conversation in an afternoon palace party, or to exhibit her rare talents at an evening banquet. Gianbattista craved an audience to entertain and Venetian society yearned for the spectacle.

As his daughter grew older, these festivities became Gianbattista's vehicle for displaying Elena's accomplishments. Carefully he planned and staged the events and, with characteristic Italian hospitality, created colorful mosaics of leading political, academic and religious figures representing most segments of the Republic.

Prior to widening the venue for his stellar attraction, Gianbattista first assembled relatives to hear her. They gathered from the five branches of the family, named for the Venetian parishes in which they lived: San Cassiano, San Maurizio, San Paolo, San Samuele, and his own San Luca.

Typical of the nobility of that era, the Cornaros were a cohesive clan, assisting one another in various ways when needed. Many proudly shared the same coat of arms, with some of the Cornaro clan even writing stipulations in their wills that their offspring marry another "Corner."

They flocked to support Gianbattista's presentations.

One noteworthy relative attending the festivities was the much touted Federico Cardinal Cornaro. The cardinal had recently commissioned the celebrated artist Gianlorenzo Bernini (1598–1680) to design a chapel in Santa Maria della Vittoria in Rome. The chapel project began in 1645 and was completed in 1652.

Bernini, known for his unique Roman Baroque style of sculpture, was greatly admired in Venice and had produced several monuments there. The Cornaro Chapel in Rome was considered one of his masterpieces, combining sculpture, painting and architecture in a complex, highly-charged theatrical setting. It displayed mostly sixteenth-century Cornaro family figures (a doge and cardinals) seated in boxes, idealized in white Carrara marble. The Chapel entrance featured a central, shimmering statue of the popular saint, "Teresa in Ecstasy," depicted in a mystical dream where she was being struck repeatedly with the golden arrow of a beaming seraph.

With the increasing successes of Gianbattista's family auditions, Elena's father next invited personal friends to the palace. Among the invitees was the affable and elderly Doge Domenico Contarini, accompanied occasionally by the Dogaressa. Other guests included ranking procurators and, most notable for Elena, her tutors: Rabbi Abbroff, Fr. Vota and, almost always, Professor Rinaldini. Many dignitaries, accustomed to socializing with men of letters, arrived at the Cornaro Palace from far and wide. Heads of noble houses were there: the Giustiniani, Pesaro, Morosini, Sagredo, Grimani, Tiepolo and Farsetti neighbors next door on the Grand Canal.

Perfecting his agenda, Gianbattista then arranged meetings with the prominent heads of Venetian learned societies, precursors of the area's academies. Invitations were eagerly sought. In attendance were members of the Dordonei and Pacificii in Venice, and the Ricovrati in Padua. Soon notables from across the country were arriving at the Cornaro Piscopia Palace parlors: scholars from the Erranti in Brescia, the Intronati in Lucca, and the venerable Infecondi in Rome.

One prominent guest was the Florentine bibliophile, Antonio Magliabechi. A self-educated goldsmith, Magliabechi would one day bequeath his substantial book collection to the grand-duke of Tuscany, whom he served as librarian. The duke, in turn, was to donate it to the city of Florence.

From Genoa came the General of the Jesuits, Gian Paolo Oliva, a skilled peacemaker among the monastic orders, whose reach stretched across Europe in settling delicate disputes between royalty and the clergy and among missions. It was Fr. Oliva who sent the sculptor Bernini to work in the court of King Louis XIV. Over his years of association with the Cornaros, Fr. Oliva became Elena's friend and frequent correspondent. He gave her ancient relics, including the skull of the virgin-martyr Santa Faustina from the Catacombs in Rome. Elena treasured these ritual objects, placing them reverently in her private chapel.

To his delight, Gianbattista's guest list of prominent dignitaries gracing his palace grew steadily. Eventually appearing on the list was the nobleman and scholar, Gregorio Barbarigo, Bishop of Padua and Chancellor of the Theological Faculty of the great university there.

The conversation of these eminent guests was serious. With Elena often at the center of rigorous discussion, some of the most advanced theories of the day in a variety of subjects would be examined. Despite being painfully modest in demeanor, Elena's filial duty overrode any resistance, and she submitted to her father's demands to participate.

When requested—and to the astonishment of the assembled guests—Elena would instantly improvise eloquent discourses in a wide range of topics, including geography, mathematics and art. A favorite of hers was astronomy.

As one of her early biographers, Antonio Lupis, described it, discussions of astronomy with palace guests revealed the young woman's startling contemporary knowledge of the movement of the planets, the path of constellations, the study of spheres, and the dynamism of the stars.

Word spread about the shining star in the Cornaro palace. At Gianbattista's invitation, luminaries from other countries eagerly travelled to hear Elena. The French Benedictine monk Jean Mabillon visited from St. Germain des Près in Paris, where he was editing nine volumes on the Benedictine saints. An outstanding scholar from the eminent literary center of the Maurists, Mabillon was to become famous for his most distinguished writing in Latin, *De re diplomatica* (1681), the first work to record standards for authenticating medieval manuscripts. His deep loyalty to monastic life and its accompanying customs greatly endeared him to Elena.

Gianbattista's gatherings were garnished in lavishly baroque style. His wife Zanetta, who had the reputation among some Venetian socialites for being frivolous and highly extravagant, became comfortably accustomed to supervising preparation of refreshments and arranging for entertainment in the grand manner. Under her direction, a variety of coffees, flavored liqueurs, crystallized fruits and pastries arrived on cue for palace visitors in the afternoon. In the evening, they enjoyed imported wines and even more elaborate trays of sweetmeats. Increasingly, an invitation to a Cornaro palace function was a highly prized achievement in the Republic.

Being part of a Republic described as "one of the most musical centers in Europe," the Cornaro palace was rarely without special music at these illustrious gatherings. The Cornaros carried on the Republic tradition of music on a grand scale, with carefully chosen selections of contemporary works often climaxing Cornaro parties.

New music was burgeoning in the 1600s all over Italy, and most of it was printed in Venice. The early years of the

Seicento saw the beginnings of opera and ballet. Ten opera houses were built in Venice during the period from 1637 to 1690, some entirely financed by noble families. No expense was spared to obtain the finest singers.

But the creation of glorious baroque music had its darker side. Emasculating boys—in order to prevent normal vocal change and preserve their treble voices—was commonly practiced then. *Castrati* were among the most admired celebrities throughout Italy in the seventeenth century.

The composer Claudio Monteverdi, a pioneer in the fresh genres of opera and oratorio, served as organist and choirmaster at St. Mark's for thirty years, beginning in 1613. In the Republic's vibrant musical life, St. Mark's served as the focal point. Monteverdi completed a number of stage works and sacred music pieces for Venice which are now lost. Later, after becoming a priest in 1633, the prolific musician created two major operas there: *Il ritorno d' Ulisse in patria* (The Return of Ulysses to his Homeland) in 1641, and *L'Incoronazione di Poppea* (The Coronation of Poppea), first performed in Venice in 1643, the year he died.

A year later, Monteverdi's pupil, Francesco Cavalli, produced an opera masterpiece, *L'Ormindo* (The Prince of Tunis), for Venice. During Elena's lifetime, Cavalli became organist at St. Mark's in 1665 and choir director from 1668 to 1676. Prefacing modern opera, he introduced solos and set pieces in his work.

Composers Monteverdi and Cavalli blended the serious and comic in new operatic art forms, staged previously only in courts and salons, now performed in popular theaters before audiences of women as well as men. Cavalli wrote over forty operas, some for the inaugural performances in these new

Venetian houses. As a result, Venice became firmly established as the leading opera center of Italy.

As an upper class woman in the Cornaro family, Lady Elena was thoroughly immersed in these groundbreaking cultural events. Her father, in his role as procurator, oversaw music at St. Mark's, including its renowned choir *Cappella Marciana.*

Although early biographers differ as to the instruments played at the Cornaro Piscopia Palace, all agree that Elena studied music theory with the assistance of her organist-companion Maddalena Cappelli, as well as the nuns who were known to compose both choral and instrumental pieces.

The harpsichord, an instrument on which Elena excelled, was introduced in 1611 and became very popular during the *Seicento.* Also during Elena's lifetime, Venice gained notoriety for its exceptional violin craftsmanship. The Venetian violins were made according to new and higher standards established by the Amati of Cremona, who served as teachers of the Stradavari and produced instruments yielding increased power for larger opera halls. Enjoying the music produced by the finest violinists of the Republic, Elena herself showed unusual skill on this cherished instrument. Later, Antonio Vivaldi (1678-1741), a priest born in Venice as the son of a violinist at St. Mark's, composed chamber music that would be used widely by string ensembles performing in country villas such as those owned by the Cornaros.

As early as 1663, the composer and choir director Carlo Grossi created a sacred cantata, *Sacre ariose cantate,* to be sung especially by the seventeen-year-old Elena. Grossi's cantata was an extended devotional work for voice in six movements. On its dedication page, the composer wrote, "I admire, undoubtedly as miraculous gifts from Heaven, the Glorious Talents of Your Very Illustrious Lady."

Three centuries later, the cantata dedicated to Elena would be performed again in Padua in her honor. Grossi wrote four operas for Venice between 1659 and 1677: *Romilda, Artaserse, Giocasta* and *Nicomede.*

When requested by her father, Elena would sing for guests in many different languages at the palace's numerous performances. She added her own embellishments, reflecting the prevalent convention of improvisation in baroque music. To the delight of her audiences, she also included her own favorite "folk songs" of western Europe. Occasionally, she added native melodies from the mountains of Greece.

Ceremonious gatherings were another Cornaro tradition, as Gianbattista persevered in his quest to thoroughly involve his socially reluctant daughter.

One prominent Cornaro ancestor whose name surfaced repeatedly was Caterina, Queen of Cyprus. Through the writing of the scholar-prelate Pietro Bembo, and through her father's extemporaneous accounts, Elena well knew the history of the family's most storied relative and only reigning monarch. Caterina presided over a glittering fifteenth-century court when in exile at Asolo. Her great beauty—captured by the renowned Renaissance painters Titian, Tintoretto and Veronese—as well as her wisdom and her tragic life enthralled her countrymen for generations. Her legendary story would echo in the life of another Cornaro several centuries later.

Queen Caterina was the daughter of a very wealthy nobleman, the merchant cavalier and ambassador Marco Cornaro. Her mother was the Greek princess Donna Fiorenza (Fiorini), whose father was the Duke of Naxos and whose grandfather was the Turkish Emperor of Trebizond. Caterina was born into enormous family wealth, including large Aegean estates owned by her mother.

Caterina's father Marco had made a fortune in flourishing trade with the Levant as well as mining in Cyprus in the early fifteenth century. Over time, powerful western mercantile Cornaros had built up monopolies in shipping and in importing salt and slaves.

Marco and his brother Procurator Andrea became friends of the King of Cyprus, James II de Lusignan. For the Cornaro traders, Cyprus was strategically located forty miles south of Turkey, in the eastern Mediterranean. Over the years, Marco had accomplished several delicate diplomatic missions for the king. As a result of his ambassadorial and trading skills, Caterina's father obtained vast lands on the island of Cyprus. With two other Venetian families, the Cornaros controlled a large part of the island in land holdings. According to Cornaro family legend, it was "Uncle Andrèa" who suggested that King James of Cyprus consider Caterina, with her dark eyes and "deep reddish-gold hair," as a bride.

The Cornaros' Piscopia name came down through the Lusignans of Cyprus. Soon after English monarch Richard the Lion-Hearted bestowed the kingdom of Cyprus on the Knights Templar, they sold it to the French crusader Guy de Lusignan in 1192. At this time, there also developed close business ties between Italy and Cyprus. Venetian merchants, with the Cornaros in the lead, exported fruit and wine from Cyprus and became involved in the silk and cotton industries on the island. Guy's successor, Peter Lusignan I, was a renowned king who was greatly admired in Venice for his help in aborting a Cretan rebellion. He was handsomely entertained in Venice in 1362, again in 1365, and finally in 1368, a year before he was assassinated.

Caterina Cornaro, Queen of Cyprus, is one of the most illustrious women of the Renaissance. In this portrait attributed to the Venetian master Titian, the storied beauty is shown in a regal jeweled robe and crown, with a shield bearing the Piscopia coat of arms. As the only reigning monarch in the Cornaro family, Caterina was a source of great family pride.

(Galleria degli Uffizi, Florence. By permission of the Minister of Culture and the Environment)

At the request of Pope Innocent VI, King Peter stayed at the Grand Canal palace of Elena's ancestor, Federico Cornaro. Known to be the richest citizen in Venice, Federico's fortune was largely derived from sugar plantations operated on Cyprus' slave economy of the 1360s. Federico and his brothers Fantino and Marco established better methods for cane production to meet the increased demands of European markets. Their success brought great wealth to several Cornaro Piscopia family members. Federico lent the visiting Cypriot king 60,000 gold ducats for his journey to the papal court at Avignon to seek French aid to defend Cyprus against the Turks.

Unable to repay his debt, Peter thanked his Cornaro host by bestowing on Federico his hereditary knighthood, the Order of the Sword, originally instituted by Guy. The king further granted to the Cornaros the fiefdom Piscopia (now Episkopi) in southern Cyprus as well as a castle there. The Cornaros planned to make the location a major trading post between eastern and western nations.

Along with the helmet crest of Cypriot knighthood, the Lusignan royal coat of arms was then added to the renamed Cornaro Piscopia Palace in Venice. And it was this Piscopia title, the Order of the Sword, that was to be unsuccessfully sought as rightful inheritance by Gianbattista to use during his lifetime.

In the fifteenth century, young Caterina Cornaro became a political pawn in the hands of an ambitious and rising Republic that wished to annex Cyprus. "She walked as a puppet moved by Venetian strings," wrote the nineteenth-century biographer Edward McCurdy in *Essays in Fresco*. As later orchestrated for her descendant Elena, Caterina was chosen by the Senate for an arranged marriage to royalty. In Caterina's case, the arrangement took place in 1468 and the chosen marriage partner was the dashing Cypriot, King James II. With the marriage agreement, the Senate created a new title for Caterina, "Daughter of the Republic," and settled upon her a 100,000 ducat dowry. She was fourteen years old.

Fresh from St. Ursula's Benedictine Convent in Padua and never having seen her fiancé, the lovely young maiden was actually wed by proxy on July 10 in an elaborate ceremony in the Ducal Palace. Four years later, after a formal ceremony in the Basilica of St. Mark on September 19, she sailed to the Lido to begin a four-month journey, accompanied by forty noblewomen and seven galleys. As the four Venetian and three Cypriot ships set sail, Caterina and her seasick maidens encountered storm-driven waters on their long journey to eventually meet the maiden's husband and see Caterina officially crowned as Queen of Cyprus, Jerusalem and Armenia.

About to enter the "cosmopolitan Mediterranean society," Caterina's departure was led by the new Doge Nicolo Tron on the Bucentaur. The departure scene was recorded for posterity in a painting by Gentile Bellini, "Miracle of the Holy Cross," now in the Accademia in Venice. Caterina Cornaro is depicted with her crown and jeweled robe, kneeling at the head of a resplendent row of noblewomen attendants aboard ship and ready to embark.

James de Lusignan, Caterina's husband, was the extraordinarily good-looking son of King John II and his mistress Marietta. With the help of the Sultan of Egypt, James had ousted his sister Charlotte from the throne of Cyprus in 1460. He would be the last of the Lusignan line to reign.

To strengthen his position, James sought Venice, then a major naval power, as an ally through marriage. An eager Venetian Republic responded, issuing its enthusiastic decree formulating the alliance. Young Caterina's wedding was finally solemnized in Famagusta at the fourteenth-century Cypriot Cathedral of St. Nicholas. Three days later, she was crowned in a cloth of gold in the Cathedral of St. Sophia at Nicosia amid jubilant islanders.

The union happily became a genuine love story, though sorrowfully brief. A year after their wedding, King James died in August, just prior to his thirty-third birthday, probably from malaria (then referred to as a fever). He had been on a hunting expedition near Famagusta with his court. Upon his death, James left behind a grieving wife, seven-months pregnant. A year later, Caterina's son, James III, died. He was only eleven-months old.

Although she remained as queen, her reign in Cyprus was a tragically difficult one, filled with more sorrow and added intrigue. She often "melted into tears," and it was rumored that she considered suicide. Her husband's will had a "large treasure" he had amassed. But it could never be traced. And some suspected that the Queen's husband had been poisoned. The suspicion was long uttered, but never resolved.

To add to the tragic chapter, Caterina's Uncle Andrèa and cousin Marco Bembo, prevented from leaving by locked palace gates, were cruelly murdered by conspirators. Their bodies were thrown into the palace moat beneath the Queen's windows. Also killed were Caterina's physician and chamberlain. Later, a palace guard—while being interrogated on the rack about the locked gates—confessed that he had been involved in the conspiracy.

Zarla, an illegitimate daughter of the late king, and other rebels arose to usurp the throne. The Queen was imprisoned for several months on the island of Cyprus. But, with the help of her father, Caterina was freed when a Venetian fleet of ten ships under Captain-General Pietro Mocenigo arrived to protect her.

The coastal people admired their benevolent queen; but Cypriot nobles greatly resented Venetian domination. The noblemen heard of a reported plan to marry the widowed Caterina to Alphonso II, the illegitimate son of the King of Naples. They suspected that the Queen was willing to accept this plan—a scenario totally unacceptable to the Cypriot noblemen.

Venetian leaders, fearing an attack by the Turks, recalled the queen through her brother Giorgio and forced her to abdicate her throne in 1489, ceding Cyprus that same year. She returned to Venice in sovereign style, magnificently dressed in black velvet with veil and jewels. And, despite the tragic end of her queenship in Cyprus, Caterina was now happily surrounded by much celebration in her native city. Accompanied by parades, banquets and jousting tournaments, she was welcomed warmly with drum and trumpet salutes. In the midst of the celebration, Doge Antonio Barbarigo, ancestor of Bishop Gregorio, navigated over the lagoon on the Bucentaur through a severe squall that erupted during Caterina's June fifth arrival.

In her honor, the Republic granted Caterina the dominion of Asolo and its castle for life. There the deposed queen set up a mini-court. Thirty-three miles from Venice, Asolo is near Trevino in northeastern Italy and is now the site of an international chamber music festival, *Festivale Internazionale di Musica da Camera di Asolo.*

The Asolo setting was an idyllic one for Caterina, with 4,000 courtiers and servants in attendance, including a personal secretary, a German doctor, and a favorite dwarf (a questionable royal custom of the day!). Caterina's court was a magical world of visiting scholars, poets, artists, and titled European travelers, encircled with dancing greens, madrigal music and costly feasts following the chase. All of it was permanently praised and romanticized by the queen's kinsman, Pietro Bembo, in *Gli Asolani* (1505), his eloquent Arcadian love dialogues dedicated to Lucrezia Borgia. *Gli Asolani,* set in the queen's country estate gardens, offered a description of aristocratic values that would influence Count Castiglione in his widely circulated *Book of the Courtier.*

For nearly twenty years, the queen lived at Asolo and her splendid Barco villa built nearby, fully establishing herself there until her death in 1510. Returning to her homeland often, she spent time at her family palaces in Venice and Murano. In her will, Caterina left the family's Venetian palace, *Palazzo Cornaro della Regina,* to the papacy.

The legendary pride of all Cornaros, Caterina's dramatic story would be reenacted on international stages in several operas over subsequent centuries. The most well-known renditions were *Catarina Cornaro Königin von Cypern,* written by Franz Lachner in 1841, and Gaetano Donizetti's *Caterina Cornaro,* first performed in 1844, four years before the composer's death.

Emerging from the Renaissance that transformed Europe, the Venetian Republic of the *Seicento* continued to exemplify some of the earlier period's creative genius and enlightenment. This momentum continued for a hundred years, having begun with the great Venetian victory against the Turks at Lepanto (1571)—where so many Cornaros became heroes. Venice's government remained a model of intelligence and organized efficiency. The diplomatic skill of its ruling nobility, including Gianbattista's, was highly admired; its charity to the poor and tolerance of the foreign-born were widely applauded.

In this Later portrait of Caterina Cornaro, the Queen of Cyprus is shown in a subdued court dress and veil, reflecting a sadder era in the sovereign's life, following the tragic losses of family and throne. Entitled "Cornaro Katalin," the painting is by Gentile Bellini and is one of the earliest known female portraits in Venetian painting *(circa 1500).* The indistinguishable rectangle in the Upper left corner of the portrait features a Latin inscription noting Bellini's high station.

(Szépmüvészeti Múzeum, Budapest)

Besides the advancement of new music, Venetian artistic aptitude was evident in seventeenth-century architecture and in burgeoning and brilliant theater. The outstanding Venetian theater would serve to ignite the genius of the French dramatist Molière.

Scientific inquiry was encouraged at the illustrious University of Padua under the Republic's jurisdiction. The western world's first botanical garden, designed in 1545, was nurtured there. The cosmopolitan workshops of Venice—with artisans representing many countries—crafted superior products in leather, metal, and glass, and the finest editions in printing, engraving and bookbinding. The Republic's mosaicists, wood-carvers and stuccoists were being sought by other nations, and Venetian art would inspire the coming masters of Holland, Germany, England, France and Spain. This island Republic, so rich and dynamic in history, contributed greatly to founding the best that would arise in Europe over the next century.

And also the worst.

The "Merchant City" that had given the world the courageous medieval mariner Marco Polo—whose *Divisament dou monde** ("Description of the World") would later inspire another Italian explorer, Christopher Columbus—was embarking on an age of "acquisition and display." It became a seaborne society so prosperous and carefully regulated that it unwittingly steered the natural vitality and exuberance of its people toward unrestrained, excessive living. Gregorio Barbarigo called the entire century so "truly extrava-

* Marco Polo's work, first published in French, was later called *Il milione.*

gant... that for the curious there could not be anything more curious."

This era of extreme self-indulgence was spawned during Elena's childhood and was matched by extremes of religious asceticism. Monastic life, especially in the newly founded orders, differed sharply from the showy entertainment that generally prevailed and was supported by the government. Although the Republic experienced much progress in basic knowledge and literacy, this progress in seventeenth-century Venice was counterbalanced by an increase in superstition and a significant rise in crime. In the view of most historians, these weaknesses were actually no more prevalent in the Republic than in the rest of post-Renaissance Europe.

Venice thoroughly embraced the baroque in its philosophy, literature, and art. This was also true in Venetian architecture, seen in the sumptuousness of its public buildings and in many of its 200 private palaces (a number belonging to Cornaros).

As in other states, this structural adornment of the Republic tended to be overdone by the end of the *Seicento.* And there were other signs of indulgence and moral decay. While passing very democratic laws to welcome people from other lands, the powerful Senate of 120 men also placed under curfew all of its Jewish settlers and confined them to a restricted area. The high-walled Jewish ghetto of Venice was set up in 1516. However, despite this ominous and unjust move, the governors of Venice did protect Jewish people and property, honoring many of their rights.

Venice continued to imprison criminals in dungeons, cruelly hanging some in prominent places and torturing others on the notorious rack. The crime of counterfeiting brought the severe punishment of cutting off the offender's right hand.

And women who illegally "coined" during that era actually had their noses sheared off. The nobility was not completely immune. One Contarini was beheaded for wounding a doge on the nose!

In a city that nurtured 150 churches and monasteries, gambling was widespread. The first gaming house, *Ridotto,* was opened in 1638 in a Venetian palace, and gambling came under state control that year. Flagrant prostitution also thrived at this time, with rampant syphilis the shameful price.

On the other hand, one of Venice's shining accomplishments of this era was that it maintained the largest and best endowed hospitals for public use anywhere in the world.

Amidst the luxury, refinement, ease and "unimaginable wealth" of rulers like the Cornaros, the mundane and toilsome life of the lower class Venetians was enlivened by a number of extravaganzas throughout the year. These special festivities included the Carnival and the Regatta, as well as marriage feasts and church festivals. While these extravaganzas offered excitement for all Venetians, the celebrations masked the underlying decadence of the time.

Yet the corrosion was not universal. "Besides profound corruption," Swiss historian Jacob Burckhardt reminds us, "appeared men of nobility and artistic splendor, giving luster to life."

Despite the decadence, leading Venetians were expected to maintain both high personal standards and exemplary public service. Gianbattista abided by this standard during his mature years as *Procuratore de supra.* His daughter, whose seriousness and piety naturally set her apart in this pleasure city, considered Venice's overstated, baroque expression suffocating, its baubles fleeting and its excesses increasingly intolerable. But, having been taught to be a loyal Venetian, she dedicated herself to contributing to the city's social betterment, in the best Cornaro tradition.

Born in this ancient city of majesty and frailty and paradox, Lady Elena reflected both its contradictory complexity and its fragile splendor.

8

SOCIALITE OR SCHOLAR?

There are two things equally difficult to find: a crow of lily-white feathers, and a young girl not taken by the vanity of clothes.

FR. MASSIMILIANO DEZA,
ELENA'S FIRST BIOGRAPHER, 1686

ELENA'S STUDIES were accelerating in a variety of subjects, including mathematics, physics, astronomy, geography and dialectics. In her late teens and early twenties, she was increasingly interested in linguistics, logic, and rhetoric—areas of learning which provided her the needed insights and polished skills for serious discussions of spiritual beliefs, especially with other scholars.

Carlo Rinaldini, after a year as Chairman of Philosophy at the University of Padua, published a mathematics book in Latin, centering on sophisticated problems of geometry: *De resolutione et compositione mathematica.* He wrote the book, issued in Padua in 1668, for twenty-two-year-old Elena.

Upon the death of Elena's first teacher, Fr. Fabris, in November of that year, Rinaldini's personal relationship with his young pupil strengthened. Considering Elena a daughter, he called her his *Minerva, Dea del Sapere* ("Minerva, Goddess of Learning"). She returned the sobriquet, referring to him as *Il Padre della Sua Cultura* ("The Father of Her Culture").

Rinaldini offered Elena a strong background in the entire course of philosophy, in preparation for theological studies with the Franciscan Provost Felice Rotondi, who had been teaching at the University of Padua for three years. Rotondi greatly advanced her concentration in theology in the fall of 1668. He expressed utter amazement at how quickly she grasped each concept.

The following year, Elena took on the task of translating from Spanish into Italian the aforementioned book, *Colloquy of Christ,* by Carthusian monk Giovanni Lanspergio. She dedicated the translation to her close friend and confessor Fr. Gianpaolo Oliva, General of the Jesuits. A publishing success, the small volume was issued in five editions in Venice from 1669 to 1672.

Elena was being hailed continually throughout the community for her intellectual prowess. Local academies, some of which had her father as patron, were competing to have her join them. She made her choices carefully as she moved among these academic circles.

Elena began to address learned societies of the Republic which were traditionally bastions of male membership. In 1670 the *Accadèmia dei Pacifici* (Academy of the Peaceful) in Venice installed her as president. Beginning that same year, she also gave a series of speeches about the social and political problems of the Republic.

By all accounts, her days were remarkably disciplined and thoroughly exemplary. When "The Morangona," the great bell of San Marco, was rung each morning at dawn, Elena would go into her private chapel or attend early Mass. Daily she sought to closely adhere to a discipline of many hours of morning prayer, then intense study during long afternoons, accompanied by as strict fasting as possible while she was unobserved. Carrying out her family's tradition of public service, Elena also would often take time to work in one of the four hospices in Venice.

Historically, patricians and commoners alike shared pride in their Republic, with "an overriding sense of civic community," according to historian Paul Grendler. The ruling class passed many laws benefiting the underprivileged; workmen who made up trade guilds *(scuole)* helped feed the poor. Women in Venice were vigorous patriots, in times of war often contributing their jewelry and even their hair for galley rope!

The four charitable Venetian conservatories then were the Incurabili, Mendicanti, Ospedaletto and Pietà—hospitals named for patient specialties. The oldest of these, San Lorenzo de Mendicanti (Beggars), was a church-hospital complex designed in 1601 by the architect Vincenzo Scamozzi, a pupil of Andrea Palladio. An exclusive stable of horses was kept there. Today, Mendicanti is incorporated into a section of the city's major medical center.

Foundling hospitals in Elena's day took in orphans: boys who learned crafts, and girls who joined choirs and orchestras. Composers were recruited to teach them; concerts performed by the children drew large audiences and substantial contributions. Mendicanti girl choristers were trained to sing and play sacred music, screened off from their audiences by fancy, carved latticework. Elena first went there to hear music, and at the hospice closely observed some of the area's needy.

From then on, Elena spent many hours, especially at Mendicanti, bathing and feeding abandoned babies and reading to the impoverished elderly. Beggars and "Girls of Sin"—

young prostitutes particularly—were ministered to by the compassionate noblewoman. She saw to it that as many as possible were given food, care, money, and spiritual counseling. She also sought priests to say prayers for their salvation.

Courtesans lured cash and the curious to Venice over many years. Throughout the city there were hundreds of prostitutes, operating with a government whose reputation for tolerance encouraged and actually protected them.

Informally classified on several levels, these women ranged from the cultured, court courtesans (the most expensive anywhere)—who operated out of their own houses and were often bedecked with the beautiful and sophisticated adornments of the wealthy—to the often desperate and starving harlots working in brothels. They were from quite diverse backgrounds—from established Venetian families to refugees and slaves—and some were children as young as eight years old.

"Ladies of Pleasure" were seen everywhere: on the Piazza, in gondolas, at the opera, and at masked balls. Their liveries were well known. A few became quite influential. Thomas Coryat mentions a Margherita Emiliana as the founder of an Augustinian monastery, and in 1611 she was in a portrait with Coryat in *Crudities.* There was Alvina the "Curtezan" in Thomas Otway's play *Venice Preserved,* written in 1682. Another was the storied Attila, the mistress of Casanova at the beginning of the next century, when courtesans' prevalence had actually diminished.

In the increasingly permissive environment of seventeenth century Venice, a Society of the Publick Courtesans developed to control prostitution. Some expressed concern about moral decline, and the courtesans were taxed and restricted in small ways. They were not allowed to have houses on the Grand Canal, or wear floor-length white veils, the traditional covering of unmarried ladies in Venetian aristocracy. And their gondolas could only be propelled by one oarsman! Their legal badge was supposed to be a mandatory yellow handkerchief. But many courtesans cheated on the rules; they also had freedoms not allowed the protected noblewomen in Elena's circle. "Famoused over all Christendome," the Venetian courtesans were glamorized by such master artists as Giorgione and Carpaccio, and some of the subjects are now believed to have been noblewomen!

A sixteenth-century poet, Pietro Aretino, described their alluring attire: "the murrey-coloured [from the purple-red mulberry] dress of taffeta sewn with gold, the sleeves of purple velvet embroidered in silver, the coif of green silk with gold design." He averred that "Stellina, who is only fifteen, has eyes that stab."

One historian has suggested that the prevalence of professional courtesans in seventeenth century Venice was partly due to the "enforced bachelorhood" practiced among nobility in order to safeguard family fortunes. The number of celibate men from the Republic's upper class increased during the seventeenth century by an astonishing sixty percent.

In his earlier years, Gianbattista and his playboy set were well-acquainted with the principal cultured courtesans. Now as *Procurator de supra,* he abided by the higher standards expected of a leader of court society, and he was well-respected by his family and fellow citizens in that regard. His wife Zanetta, unfairly accused of being a prostitute, remained a loyal wife throughout their marriage.

During holiday times in Venice, including the favorite *Carnivale* (Carnival), Zanetta showed herself to be an energetic, vibrant woman and a rather inveterate pleasure seeker, reveling in the festivities and exuberant crowds. Thousands were lured to the island city for the ten-day, pre-Lenten *Carnivale.* Masqueraders in counterfeit beards and noses, their faces wine-stained with mulberry juice, prowled the alleys. There were jousting tournaments, serenades, and street fairs everywhere. Bridges crossing canals were wrapped in silver-spangled, scarlet drapery, lined with turquoise silk. Banners adorned each window, and torches and candelabra illuminated every lane.

All of Venice sparkled.

Private dinners and festive masked balls were held in palace drawing rooms. In full gold and royal blue regalia, the ducal floating palace, the Bucentaur, led a flotilla of flower-filled boats along the waterways. From beautiful baskets, filled with eggs carrying perfumed waters, fishermen tossed confections called "sugarfish" up on every balcony overlooking the canals. And gallant gondoliers provided the poor with free rides to places of celebration.

Gondolas, those flat-bottomed "sedans," were as much a part of the Venetian landscape as the winged lion of St. Mark. Of compulsory black and their bowsprits embellished with polished hammer work, gondolas would curve out of the water at each end in silent, thirty-foot sweeps. They so impressed King Louis XIV that he had several shipped to France to dazzle the guests at his garden parties in Versailles!

Cornaro gondolas were outfitted with carved decorations; special gilded boats were used for the holidays. Each one was outfitted with velvet-lined sedan chairs and silk coverlets, pierced brass lanterns and an arched awning of rich fabric and needlework. The gondolas were open at both ends and fringed with white tassels to furnish protection from the pervasive sun.

Their graceful navigators were the best of the famed Venetian gondoliers, two per boat in Elena's day. These men were highly skilled oarsmen who could maneuver the long, colorful Cornaro crafts smoothly around sharp turns on narrow canals. When Elena was their entrusted passenger, they greatly appreciated her courteous and considerate manner, and willingly kept silent about her many journeys alone in the dark to help the area's needy.

During Elena's lifetime, there was always a special surprise to delight the crowds at the annual Carnival. The patron "Pantaloon," in medieval costume, teased them from his throne near St. Mark's Square. The crowd watched intently from all over the Procuratorie building.

Dancing around Pantaloon in satirical parade were actors wearing fantastic monster masks, poking fun at prominent dignitaries. Courtiers in theatrical wigs, shell peddlers, and mountebanks, showing off serpents and selling drugs, were also there. If the weather permitted, the Piazza became a vast and picturesque outdoor ballroom with brilliant firelights, tables in the center, and brass bands for dancing under the stars.

Silver-eyed and happily flouting the Senate's austere dress code, Zanetta would prop her elbows on a large oriental carpet that was hung over the lower balcony of the palace. From that position, she could comfortably watch morning holiday preparations. She was a shimmering figure in pale green watered silk brocade. A comb of lustrous pearls swept back her hair, well-bleached from many hours of drying in the sun. She cheered and waved to early party seekers with her new eye-catcher: a ruffled point lace fan.

Noble ladies and their attendants spent many hours needlepointing, often the day's main task. The finest and newest work was Venice point lace made by a few talented women in Burano, six miles from Venice. Their unique work was first spawned from fishnet mending. Hand sewn in high relief, their lace featured varied petal patterns, overlaid with the most delicate flowers in full bloom, all joined in a network of intricate stitches. It was highly prized by the Venetian upper class women, who sought to adorn their sleeves and garnish their exposed bosoms with this fine lace.

Fan in hand, tickling her troop of fashionable little dogs, Zanetta sampled the sorbet, comfits and preserves to be served at a huge supper party that evening. She plucked at her embroidered petticoat to reveal high pattens, those infamous wooden clogs originally designed for rain gear.

Decorated with leather straps, pattens sometimes elevated wearers as much as two feet, encumbering them so that they wobbled along, supported by attendants clutching them on either side! "'Tis ridiculous to see how these ladies crawle in and out of their gondolas by reason of their 'choppines,'" noted one nineteenth century account, "and what dwarfs they appeare when taken down from their wooden scaffolds."

It was perhaps this absurd style that prompted a group of testy senators, the Sumptuary Board, to seek several times to impose detailed laws limiting fancy dress and other extravagances in Venice. Their goal was to delineate every detail of acceptable dress, as well as what ladies might eat, and how they should furnish their dwellings.

Sumptuary Board lists were lengthy, prescribing each accessory, from length of ball gown trains to the number of silken sheets allowed. They forbid palace guests from consuming more than one-and-a-half pounds of marzipan per banquet. The board even proposed the burning of false bosoms!

These strictures were largely ignored, and merchants engineered a black market to sell lady customers ribbons and trimmings on the sly.

Doge Contarini's two daughters were among the first to abandon the practice of wearing pattens. Zanetta merely scoffed at the official dress code, for she was a lover of lavish, expensive clothes and copious jewels, and Carnival provided the perfect backdrop. She insisted upon the proper finery for her children. Little did she know that beneath one of her daughter's sumptuous dresses—hidden by heavily embroidered cut velvet and beaded and tasseled embellishments—was at all times a white or black scapular, and a monk's simple habit.

Outwardly, with her curled hair and ornate gowns, Elena was compliant, wearing the fancy attire befitting her station. But underneath she could rebel against the ostentation of her mother's chosen costumes and cosmetics. Elena used any excuse to avoid fancy clothes, pleading with her mother that she was ill, or insisting that it was too warm in summer or too cold in winter, or that she was too busy studying.

In spite of Zanetta's urging, Elena also disliked watching Carnival's boisterous burlesque. But from a young age, she was required to attend. Observing from her palace balcony as the far and famous poured in for the fanfare, the tenderhearted girl questioned the holiday's validity, bothered by its excesses. Early accounts say she would ask her mother why so many people could be engrossed in such superficial, idle pleasures—what she described as "nothing-things." And she retreated in tears to her little oratory, asking forgiveness for them and for herself.

As Elena grew older, her persistent mother kept pressuring her to socialize and conform both in manner and in dress.

Elena often sought to withdraw, journeying to the nearby island of Santa Maria della Grazia, to seek the counsel of Abbess Felice. After her oblation, she had begged her father to allow her to join the convent of the *Vergini di Castiglione* (Virgins of Castiglione) near Brescia. Elena's much-admired Jesuit Luís Gonzaga was born in Castiglione, and his three nieces—the princesses Cynthia, Olympia, and Gridone—had set up the convent.

As noted earlier, it was Elena's confessor Carlo Boselli who intervened, opposing the move. He cautioned Elena about the serious effect it would have on her parents, and Elena abandoned any immediate plans. She told her father that eventually—after their deaths and with his permission—she wished to enter the Dimesse women's order in Padua. And from this time she made it a custom to attend at least two retreats a year at Grazia, where she would abandon all studies and any visits from public officials, and briefly live as she wished, as a nun.

Once again, her mother was relieved that Elena had postponed her desire for the cloister. Zanetta often dreamed a mother's dream of a fashionable wedding for her daughter—an event which was then the ultimate goal for most Venetian maidens of high birth.

As historians have noted, Venetian weddings in the seventeenth century tended to be truly wondrous affairs. The typical celebration of a wealthy family often involved an alliance of prominent families, beginning with the bride's dowry. The dowry was an important arrangement for the bride because it was the only fund she would control.

In Venice, as elsewhere in Europe, many nuptial conventions were followed, from financial arrangements to feasts and trousseaux. By the beginning of the seventeenth century, customary visits to convents by brides on their wedding days were no longer observed, but grooms would salute fiancées beneath their windows several times before the celebration.

The marriage festivities could last for two or more days. After the church service, the first senators and procurators and family relatives would assemble at upper story galleries in the bride's home. The young bride, adorned with garlands of flowers in her hair, would be escorted by a black-robed attendant, (often her dance teacher serving as master of ceremonies), to kneel on a velvet cushion in her parents' great hall. A prayer of blessing was offered by the priest.

Great sums of money were spent on elaborate clothes and jewels for these affairs. After the priest's blessing, wedding dresses of white silk and linen would be exchanged for gem- and lace-encrusted robes for dining on pyramids of partridge and pheasant. Then followed dancing minuets, accompanied by string music. The wedding celebration continued well into the night and usually lasted several more days. And as only a Venetian scene could be enacted, uniformed gondoliers with red satin sashes and caps stood at attention holding large, ornamental candlesticks on either side of palace staircases. For the entire evening, they provided a formal escort of radiant light from the canal water's edge up into festive halls.

During the first year of marriage, mothers would present perfectly matched pearl necklaces to their wedded daughters in additional ceremonies witnessed by friends.

Zanetta continually longed for all of this for Elena. But her daughter shrank from it—from marriage or the limelight—finding distasteful the growing public admiration surrounding her life. The young Cornaro strongly preferred anonymity and quiet study. It was this embodiment of gentle simplicity that endeared her to many...even a German prince!

Little is known of Elena's suitors, not even their names. But several of her early biographers, including those who knew Elena or her parents, recorded that the suitors were numerous; several specifically mentioned a German prince.

The prince had crossed the Alps to visit Venice for Carnival and, probably at the invitation of Zanetta (ever the hopeful mother!), he appeared among guests at a Cornaro Piscopia Palace party. After dinner that evening, Elena recited and sang in six languages. The prince, whose name remains unknown, was apparently mesmerized. He sought her hand, and Gianbattista enthusiastically granted permission. Little did he yet realize how deeply heartfelt was his daughter's aversion to marriage. Elena firmly said no, begging to be excused from further entanglements.

In addition to rejecting suitors, young Elena had to deal with vexing health problems. After a several-week bout of dysentery at the age of twenty-five, the very weakened maiden became ill with "red fever," either scarlet or rheumatic fever. This is now known to be a respiratory streptococcal infection, a condition not completely understood until the beginning of this present century. It is a highly contagious bacterial disease characterized by a sore throat, fever, and rash.

Although old medical and historical records were often incomplete and lacked correct details, recognition of symptoms was early recorded, noting epidemics in crowded housing conditions. When working among many ill people, an increasingly frail Elena was exposed to disease constantly.

To deal with "red fever" in Elena's time, various methods were employed. One of the more primitive practices was bloodletting; other methods included broths, herbal medicines, bed rest, and application of cold compresses and leeches to reduce fever.

By all accounts, Elena suffered the classic symptoms of the disease: high fever, sore throat, and crimson skin rash. Her prolonged illness continued for a month. Increasingly concerned over her deteriorating condition, her father sent Elena to recover at the summer palace in Padua—complete with a physician in residence, servants, carriages and companions.

9

RECOVERY IN PADUA

If a nobleman or private gentleman wishes to know how to build in a city, let him come to the Cornaro Palace at Padua; there he will learn how to construct not only a superb portico, but also the other parts of sumptuous and comfortable buildings. If he wishes to adorn a garden, let him take, as a model, the one you have arranged....

– Editorial dedication to Luigi Cornaro by Venetian publisher Francesco Marcolini in the celebrated *Il settimo libro d'architettura* (The Seventh Book of Architecture) of Bolognese Sebastiano Serlio
June 1, 1544

The light of early morning against aged stucco walls reflected over stone walkways, accentuating the shade beneath an allée of pleached European hornbeams. Arbors of fragrant roses and brilliantly colored flowers in urns relieved the formal embroidery of tightly clipped boxwood hedges. In the central rondel was a marble fountain tiered in arabesque, its sculptured, gamboling putti dabbling their feet in the lower basin.

The whole expanse was bracketed by vineyards and an orchard of apricots, figs, pomegranates, and citron. In a prominent place near the entrance gate—planted precisely to focus across the main parterre—stood a stately, twenty-five-year-old cypress, Elena's birthday tree. Its tapering branches gently swept sun away from wooden benches and terraces.

Tranquility pervaded the summer palace gardens.

Removed from the social and family pressures in Venice, a weakened Elena chose for her recovery the quiet and protected left wing of the Odeon Palace at Padua, across the front carriageway. Living in the summer palace, she could gradually distance herself from others and remain unnoticed. It proved to be an ideal retreat for the contemplative Elena.

The Cornaro palace complex was situated in Padua near *Il Santo,* the pilgrimage church dedicated to Saint Anthony of Padua (1195 to 1231), the city's Portuguese patron saint who is buried there. With its arcaded streets and quaint squares, its vast basilicas and early frescoed chapels, Padua claimed to be the oldest city in northern Italy. The Bacchigilione River, in two branches, curves through it.

From Padua's origins as a fishing village in the fourth century B.C., it grew to be recognized as the wealthiest town in the region. The town flourished in Roman times—eventually bulwarked by medieval walls and archways—and it emerged as a thriving commercial, academic, artistic, and religious center. Twenty-eight miles west of Venice, the city was administered after 1405 by two Venetian nobles, one a military captain and the other the Podestà overseeing civilian affairs. This arrangement remained until the end of the Republic in 1797.

Down the lanes of Padua walked the great Italian masters still revered today: Dante Alighieri and Petrarch, Luís Gonzaga, Mantegna, Giotto, Bellini, and Donatello. The town's history

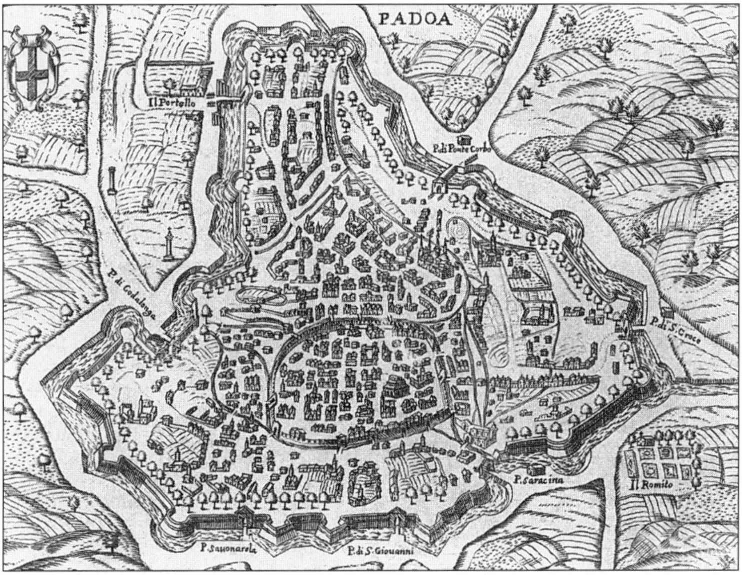

PADUA, THE "CITY OF DOMES," IS THE SITE OF THE ANCIENT UNIVERSITY WHICH AWARDED ELENA HER DOCTORATE IN PHILOSOPHY ON JUNE 25, 1678. HER PRIMACY FURTHER ENHANCED THE UNIVERSITY OF PADUA'S WORLD RENOWNED STATUS.

(Itinerario D'Italia Di Francesco Scoto. Padua, 1659. Special Collections, Vassar College Libraries. Photograph by Charles Porter)

was influenced significantly by the famous lords and families of the Este, Carrara and Cornaro.

The Cornaros were established in Padua in 1406 after the fall of the politically powerful and enlightened Carraras, who were in control for nearly a century. In that year, Francesco Cornaro acquired large land holdings confiscated from the Carrara family. Another of Elena's ancestors, Luigi (Alvise in Venetian dialect) Cornaro, also left family discord in his native Venice to begin a new life in Padua.

The son of Antonio and Angeliera Cornaro, Luigi became an extraordinary humanist, philosopher, and Renaissance health advocate who lived from 1464 to 1566. As he was approaching forty, Luigi became seriously ill with intestinal disorders, fever, and gout from an overrich and dissolute life.

Vowing to reform—as he saw himself completely excluded from public affairs—Luigi moved to Padua. There he studied law and, for many years, served as volunteer administrator of the bishopric.

While in Padua, Luigi began a strict and novel fifteenth-century fitness regimen of moderation, diet, and exercise. His success story was described in a remarkable best seller, *La Vita Sobria (The Temperate Life).*

The first and most popular edition of Luigi's book was written when the author was eighty-three years old! Another version followed at eighty-six, a third at ninety-one and the last at ninety-five, seven years before the author's death at the age of 102. Published from 1558 into the twentieth century and translated into five languages including English, *La Vita Sobria* earned senior citizen Luigi Cornaro the title "The Apostle of Senescence."

In a letter to the Right Reverend Barbaro, Patriarch Elect of Aquileia, ninety-five-year-old Luigi wrote, "I endeavor, as much as in me lies, to convince all mankind, that a man may enjoy a paradise on earth even after the age of fourscore." And he later illustrated the point by leaping up on his horse!

The spirited four treatises in his book told of his youthful love of "Heady Wines" and "High Sauces." He listed his personal illnesses caused by imprudent living in his younger years, including colic and gout, sciatica and rheumatic pains. Recommending a virtuous and abstemious routine, Luigi described the meager diet he adopted that restricted him to twelve ounces of solid food and fourteen ounces of wine a day, eventually limited to one egg as the daily main portion.

Having been revitalized in middle age, Luigi married the patrician Veronica di Spilimbergo. She came from a city near Udine named in honor of her family. When Luigi was fifty-three, the couple had a daughter Chiara (Clara) who was wed in 1537 to a Cornaro Piscopia named Giovanni, Fantino's son. Giovanni and Chiara produced twelve children, eight boys and four girls. One of their girls became a Paduan nun and wrote about Luigi's happy experiences with his grandchildren; her reflections were included in the third edition of *La Vita Sobria* in 1722. Elena Cornaro was directly descended from this robust branch.

Luigi Cornaro was a learned man, as well as a liberal patron of the arts, called a sixteenth-century Maecenas.* For much of his long life, Luigi surrounded himself with a celebrated cadre of talented people, including painters and sculptors, architects, dramatists, and musicians who represented the flowering of the Renaissance in Italy. He commissioned

* In the first century B.C., the Roman statesman Gaius Maecenas was a patron of Horace and Virgil. Elena's father, Gianbattista, was also called a Maecenas.

The Paduan palaces built by Luigi Cornaro in the sixteenth century included Odeon *(right)*, Loggia *(rear)*, and the Mansion (now destroyed). Elena summered and studied in the Odeon Palace, and died there in 1684.

(Photograph courtesy of the United States Committee for the Elena Lucrezia Cornaro Piscopia Tercentenary, Pittsburgh)

the eminent Veronese Giovanni Maria Falconetto (1458–1534), whom he met through Pietro Bembo, to help him design his notable complex near the present-day Via Melchiorre Cesarotti. "In the pleasantest Parte of Padua" and named for a local poet who was one of the founders of Italian Romanticism, the complex contained a mansion on the left near the street that faced the *Odeo Cornaro* (Odeon Palace). In between was Falconetto's famous *Loggia Cornaro* with its pillared portico. The Odeon Palace, believed to be designed by Andrea della Valle, was where Elena would spend the last few years of her life.

Luigi and Falconetto became intimate friends, and these commissions from Luigi enabled Falconetto to devote himself fully to architecture. Around 1500 the two went together to Rome, where Falconetto had studied earlier, to review buildings and antiquities and to learn from established masters. What resulted was a lifelong interest in rediscovering classicism. This interest was inspired especially by exposure to the works and writings of first-century Roman Marcus Vitruvius, and to structures planned and restored in the fifteenth century in Rome and Florence by the Venetian humanist Leone Battista Alberti.

Luigi and Falconetto were the first to bring these concepts of architecture to Venice and Padua. Luigi subsequently wrote his *Scritti sull'architettura (Treatises on Architecture).* The Cornaro Paduan palaces, occupied by Luigi in winter and summer, were all strongly and classically Vitruvian in influence. Luigi's favorite Loggia formed the back of the complex at the far end of the broad entryway. It was conceived by Falconetto and referred to as a garden house.

Constructed between 1522 and 1524, the Loggia anchored the entire design and surrounding flower beds. It was used for entertainment, including popular theatrical and musical performances, sponsored by Luigi. These special events made use of the two-story stone building which featured the open loggia with frescoed ceiling, divided by six Doric columns that unified five bays on the lower floor. Originally the columns were decorated with two bas-relief figures, representing Victory, over spandrels of the central arch.

The Loggia's upper story contained a banquet hall and grand stairways designed by Luigi. The facade was patterned with theater masks and Ionic pilasters separating the alternate design of windows and niches with sculptured figures of Apollo, Diana and Venus by Zuan Padovano. Luigi had provided an invigorating environment, especially for beginning performers.

In the middle of the long, right side of the carriageway was Elena's retreat, the Odeon, a small but courtly palace completed in the early 1540s, after Falconetto's death. It was modeled after the great imperial Roman houses and was sometimes referred to as the "Music Mansion." A double vine-covered arcade connected the Loggia to the Odeon. With its bay front, it also was two-storied, featuring a central octagonal music room that was surrounded by beautiful, frescoed and white stuccoed smaller rooms. These had vaulting in shell pattern and were decorated in the style of Raphael's Loggia in the Vatican. On either side of the front entrance were Padovano's statues of Acteon and Diana. Luigi's mansion is no longer standing. Viewed as as proud national monuments, the Odeon, now called the Giustinian Palace, and the Loggia were both restored by the Italian government at the end of the twentieth century.

Architect Falconetto stayed at the Cornaro compound, where he was helped by his sons with the stucco work. He also

THE COMPLEX OF LUIGI CORNARO'S PADUAN PALACES INCLUDED THE LOGGIA *(rear)*, DESIGNED AS A PERFORMING ARTS CENTER BY HIS FRIEND AND PROMINENT ARCHITECT GIOVANNI FALCONETTO. THE VITRUVIAN BUILDINGS, LOGGIA AND ODEON, WERE RECENTLY RESTORED AS NATIONAL MONUMENTS BY THE ITALIAN GOVERNMENT.

(1784 engraving courtesy of Father Francesco Ludovico Maschietto, Basilica of San Giustina, and Editrice Antenore. Padua, 1978)

headquartered there for his other city projects, including elaborate gates and archways, some still standing. During a thirteen-year period from 1533 to 1546, Falconetto helped complete the city gates—San Giovanni, Savonarola, the Loggia della Gran Guardia, the Triumphal Arch, and the Grand Cappella del Santo. The Loggia Cornaro, Falconetto's masterpiece, and his drawings and plans influenced another younger member of Luigi's illustrious circle, Andrea Palladio (1508–1580). The social and witty Palladio—admired by others of world renown, especially Goethe—designed the celebrated Rotonda Capra villa at Vincenza in 1570. Palladio's classical concepts, transcribed from the imposing buildings of early Rome, were carried throughout the world to determine the design of such monuments as Whitehall in London by Inigo Jones. Palladio's other designs of rural architecture and his writing have had an international impact down to the present day. He, too, had studied in Rome (under the patronage of Count Trissino).

Returning north, Palladio designed numerous churches in Venice, most notably the Redentore (1577–1592), built in gratitude for the city's deliverance from plague and finished strictly to Palladio's plans after his death. His first masterwork there was San Giorgio Maggiore (1565–1583, completed by Lorenzo Scamozzi), attended by Elena; it was the church where she would officially become a Benedictine oblate.

The young architect's reputation soared, and he was commissioned for palatial houses along the Grand Canal and for many country villas. Palladio was also summoned by Pope Paul III for consultation on the completion of St. Peter's Bascilica.

Angelo Beolco, another of Luigi's coterie and recipient of his patronage, was a Paduan playwright popularly known as *Il*

Ruzzante, the name acquired from a peasant character in his first drama, *Pastorale*. The play was one of a large number of comedies he wrote in the rustic dialect of Padua.

Beolco put together one of the first Italian acting troupes. And it is believed that Luigi's association with Ruzzante stimulated the elder Cornaro's interest in building theaters. Some of these talented men and their performances were supported financially by Luigi Cornaro, who established a summer school for them at the Loggia.

Ruzzante, Falconetto, Palladio, Bembo and the printer Aldus Manutius were among Luigi's friends who belonged to the *Accadèmia degli Infiamatti* (Academy of the Enflamed), a literary and theatrical society organized around Luigi. Collaborating with leading artists became a Cornaro custom.

In addition to artistic endeavors, the gentlemen involved had delightful times hunting and attending evening intellectual gatherings in the sophisticated Cornaro gardens, a tradition carried on by Gianbattista and his sons. Around the time Luigi's *La Vita Sobria* was being released, the world's first teaching botanical garden—then called The Simple Garden and later known as the *Dell'Orto Botanico* (The Botanical Garden)—was established by the University of Padua in 1545. It was near the Cornaro complex and would always influence area plantings. Venice chose its superintendents and assigned the permanent gardeners.

When Elena lived in Padua, the important botanical research center was directed by Giorgio Della Torre (1619–1681). Andrea Moroni from Bergamo, who also helped design the sixteenth-century Basilica of San Giustina near the garden, was its architect. Orto Botanico's enclosed beds were planted primarily then with herbs for instructional purposes by the

A TRUE "RENAISSANCE MAN," ALVISE (LUIGI) CORNARO WAS AN ARCHITECT, LAWYER, ARTS PATRON, PHILOSOPHER, AUTHOR, AND HEALTH AND DIET CENTENARIAN. HIS BEST-SELLING AUTOBIOGRAPHICAL BOOK, *LA VITA SOBRIA,* IS STILL IN PRINT. THE PORTRAIT SHOWN HERE *(c. 1565)* IS BY VENETIAN PAINTER JACOPO TINTORETTO (1518–1594).

(Palazzo Pitti, Florence. By permission of the Minister of Culture and the Environment. Photograph courtesy of the University of Delaware Library, Newark, Delaware)

medical faculty of the university, who were consulted and attended an ailing Elena.

An apothecary's shop was annexed to the garden. Early specimens grown there included the familiar anise, licorice, camomile, digitalis, marjoram and rue and the rare *Platanus* orientalis (Oriental Planetree) and *Vitex angus-castus* (Chastetree), acquired in 1550. Lilacs were introduced there in 1565, jasmine in 1590, woodbine (Virginia creeper) in 1649 and locust trees in 1662. The Goethe palm *(palma di Goethe: chamaerops humilis)* was recorded in 1585 (the tree that inspired the German poet when he visited the garden in 1786 to form his ideas on the metamorphosis of plants). Along with an herbarium and library, the Botanical Garden's original design is still maintained and open to visitors.

Luigi Cornaro was an early conservationist. His mansion was to be replaced by a larger palace and the plans supposedly were abandoned to save the original frescoes. He was concerned with preserving the lagoons of Venice and the extensive lands around his country villas at Este (designed by Falconetto) and Codevigo where Elena would vacation. He wrote about his engineering projects, draining marshes and creating farmlands. (His *Treatise on Waterways* [1566], along with Pietro Bembo's *Gli Asolani,* were called by historian Jacob Burckhardt writings of "classical perfection.")

Much as Elena would be, Luigi was a greatly admired and modest figure. The elegant Tintoretto oil portrait of Luigi, displayed in the Pitti Palace in Florence, reflects the centenarian's spirit of enlightenment as well as his gentle humanity.

Surrounded by the nourishing setting of well-designed buildings amidst the city where the Franciscan miracle worker St. Anthony (The Hermit) died and was venerated, the summer palace provided the ideal environment for Elena's charitable, domestic endeavors. Able to be alone, she often waited on her servants, cooking their meals herself and actually serving them. They testified that she would have scrubbed floors and swept the mansion if allowed.

When they objected to her attending them, Elena would counter, "Who am I more than you, dear sisters?" Stories were prevalent about Elena's sense of goodness, displayed as a young teenager. When her favorite personal maid Lorenza ("Nonnina") was in her sixties and ill, Elena, in a quite tender and uncomplaining manner, took care of her for many weeks before she died. Nearly every night, the young girl got up numerous times to help her dearly loved "Grannie" Lorenza.

"My own Lorenza," she asked, "do you want nothing that I can do for you?" In response, the loyal servant said, "Ah, my little lady, I do not want you to deprive yourself of your rest for me." But her mistress pleaded, "My dear Nonnina, I have no suffering except the fear that you will not tell me what you want."

Another story came from the beggar Victoria, a frequent daily visitor seeking bread at the summer palace kitchen. She fell down a stairway one night, hitting an iron railing. Secluded in her oratory, Elena was informed of the accident and of the woman's critical head injury. Immediately, the young Cornaro and her servants carefully lifted Victoria and gave her a bed in the palace.

Thinking Victoria had died from the wounds of her severe fall, Elena and the palace staff prepared her for burial. Elena herself requested water and proceeded to wash the beggar's feet. She also sent for a priest and began funeral arrangements.

Miraculously, Victoria rallied under this care and survived for years to tell of Elena's kindness.

The most revealing tale of Elena's deep and abiding commitment to others was told about the Cornaros' old servant, Angela Codeviga, who had smallpox. Very disfigured and abandoned, Angela's body exuded a foul odor and crawled with maggots. Elena was the only one, including the servant's own relatives, who would come to her rescue, heroically washing, feeding and tending her until she was gone. Touched by Elena's compassion, Zanetta exclaimed, "My daughter, you are indeed brave to have done such a thing." Elena answered humbly, "We are bound to help our neighbours as ourselves... ."

When in Padua, Elena regularly attended the sixteenth-century Benedictine church, San Giustina (St. Justina), a source of vital importance in her life. Abbot Codanini had gone there from San Giorgio Maggiore, and many of its monks were drawn from the University of Padua. The church was cradle and center of the Cassinese reform. Consecrated in 1606, the solemn and spacious eight-domed basilica had a complex history.

The sixth-century original structure, built on location of an oratory where the virgin-martyr Giustina was buried, was destroyed by an earthquake in 1117. The next edifice was dismantled for a more grandiose one, begun in 1502 and completed after an eighty-year effort. It overlooked a marshland on the site of a Roman theater that now contains the striking eighteenth-century promenade, Prato della Valle, surrounded by a canal that is crossed by four marble bridges and adorned with seventy-nine commemorative statues. The local Andrea Briosco (1470–1532) designed the basilica, begun by Friar Girolomo of Brescia in 1502; it was later modified by Matteo da

Valle in 1520. Further construction was supervised by four other architects and builders and it became one of the largest basilicas in Italy. Andrea Moroni completed San Giustina in 1532, without a finished facade, as it is today.

In 1562 the body of St. Giustina and that of St. Luke the Evangelist, which was originally brought from Constantinople, were taken to the new church from the old site. The tomb of St. Luke was erected in the left transept of the basilica. Three hundred monks from the Cassinese congregation and twelve abbots escorted dignitaries from the College of Doctors carrying St. Luke relics and city magistrates bearing those of San Giustina in an elaborate procession winding through Padua.

The first bishop of Padua, St. Prosdocimo (A.D. 48-141), who was believed to have been converted by St. Peter, reportedly buried St. Giustina there, at the location of the present building. Little is known of Giustina, a patron saint of Elena's two cities, Padua and Venice. She was thought to have been the daughter of a noble family and, at the age of sixteen, was stabbed to death for refusing to worship pagan gods.

Elena knew the Basilica of San Giustina and its traditions intimately, at a time when the building was in pristine condition. It was decorated with rich marble columns and devotional art in the form of paintings, mosaics and exquisite choir stalls of delicately carved inlaid friezes depicting the Old and New Testaments. She prayed at the main altar beneath a highly colored, implicitly spiritual canvas—the dramatic "Martyrdom of San Giustina" by Paolo Veronese (1575)—showing Giustina captured by soldiers and in chains. Elena also often sought the remote solitude of its Romanesque-Gothic St. Luke's Chapel, treasured by the Benedictine monks who would be buried there.

And so it was, within the orderly garden setting of the Odeon Palace, that Elena Cornaro regained her health. In the beautiful San Giustina sanctuary, her indomitable spirit was renewed.

LADY GARDENER GATHERING HERBS WITH ANCIENT HORTICULTURAL IMPLEMENTS. THIS ILLUSTRATION IS FROM AN EARLY PLANT CATALOGUE OF THE UNIVERSITY OF PADUA'S BOTANICAL GARDEN, *ORTO BOTANICO.* THE GARDEN WAS A SIGNIFICANT INFLUENCE ON THE NOTED CORNARO GARDENS AND AREA PLANTINGS. THE OLDEST BOTANICAL GARDEN IN ITALY, ITS BEDS ARE STILL MAINTAINED IN THEIR ORIGINAL FOUR-PART DESIGN OF 1545. THE GARDEN IS OPEN TO THE PUBLIC.

(L'Horto de i semplici di Padova. Venice, 1591. University of Delaware Library, Newark, Delaware)

10

IN PURSUIT OF A PH.D.

What? Never! Woman is made for motherhood, not for learning.

GREGORIO CARDINAL BARBARIGO
BISHOP OF PADUA, 1677

...If the Procurator of San Marco insists, I am willing to modify the point and let his daughter become a Doctor in Philosophy.

CARDINAL BARBARIGO
1678

BACK IN VENICE, a refreshed Lady Elena embarked on an even more strenuous lifestyle, with a grinding, daily schedule of intense disciplines. She had grown from a passive maiden to an articulate, conscientious and mature young woman who would politely reprimand an irreverent priest or quell noisy congregants. She pressed her professor, Rinaldini, toward scientific research and publishing. Much sought after, she could discuss controversial public policy with diplomacy and authority, and would raise a dissenting voice in legal disputes, reportedly with justice and grace.

The story was told of Elena's dismay over the continual, loud chatter of two ladies in church at Padua. When she spoke with them about it, they found Elena to be so gracious and courteous that that they apologized profusely. At other times, the lack of decorum by some priests during Mass so offended Elena that she would confront them afterwards and, in a respectful way, remind them of proper church behavior.

Seven of the most important academies in Italy and abroad had invited Elena for membership. Many academies carried ludicrous names that purposely obscured their importance. In *Curiosities of Literature*, Isaac Disraeli (1791–1834), father of British prime minister Benjamin Disraeli, wrote anonymously an amusing chapter entitled, "On the Ridiculous Titles Assumed by Italian Academies." In it, he observed that the academies "burlesque themselves" with their "denominations of exquisite absurdity." Disraeli noted that their members adopted totally unrepresentative names for their literary groups "to rid the air of pedantry" and chose misleading "sportive relaxations" to conceal their intellectual preoccupation. One academy in Naples was called *Degli Ozio* (Of the Lazy). There was also a "Sleepy" in Genoa, and among Siena's academies were the Insipids, the Blockheads, and the Thunderstruck!

Most of the Republic's societies actually were beneficial to its cultural life. Paralleling private meetings of intellectuals in noblemen's salons and modeled on standards at monastic libraries, Venetian academies were first formed in 1484. The printer-editor Aldus Manutius founded the influential New Academy (1500) whose members were required to speak Greek. It met weekly to consider texts for publication, assign reading and engage in literary discussion. Some academies possessed book collections and even printing presses. Members supported projects of the needy and talented among themselves, and also contributed to the community's poor in an effort to encourage education.

Elena presided over several academies, meeting to debate scientific, theological, and philosophical theories. On her aforementioned inauguration as President of the *Accadèmia dei Pacifici* in Venice, she addressed the body on qualities required of ruling princes, suggesting that the powerful should be both learned and selfless. She then praised her predecessor, Francesco Santinelli, contrasting his talents with what she claimed were her own "foul imperfections."

In a more poetical speech to the distinguished Academy of Gli Infecondi ("The Unproductive Ones") in Rome where she was named "The Inalterable," she used snow to symbolize the light of reason ("illumination of thoughts").

When she was twenty-three, the German press enthusiastically reported Elena's improvised discourse on astronomy before an audience of knights and literary men. Another account cited a public debate featuring Elena, Fr. Francesco Caro, the prominent young philosopher, Giovanni Gradenigo (Luigi's son), and Fr. Giacomo Fiorelli. The debate was widely hailed for its erudition, and at the end, Elena graciously thanked her opponents in Greek. Her reputation as a rhetorician was firmly established.

While in her middle twenties, Elena made many public appearances, but she shrank continually from the accompanying adulation. Her less-than-robust health actually allowed her to withdraw completely once more. Records show that she was suffering from nephritis (inflammation of the kidneys). We know now that there are numerous causes of this disease, among them infection and malnutrition, which often afflicted the young Cornaro.

For a cure Elena journeyed to the *Fonte della Vergine di Monte Ortone* (Springs of the Virgin of Mount Ortone). This was a famous shrine on the outskirts of Padua. Pilgrims visited the site for its miraculous waters in which an image of the Virgin Mary was supposed to have appeared. There, it was reported, Elena passed three kidney stones, easing the nephritis. She subsequently recovered and returned by boat along the Brenta River to Venice.

Social demands and requests for her scholarly presence continued. During this period of Elena's life, Zanetta sought to have a portrait painted of her daughter. Portraiture was popular among aristocratic families then, but, characteristically, Elena balked at the idea.

"Saints should have their features handed down to future generations," she pleaded, "and not sinners like myself." Gianbattista insisted that the painting be done, with its subject in elaborate court dress. It was the first of many portraits commissioned during Elena's lifetime, and the painting is now part of the Cornaro Piscopia Collection of the Museo Civico in Padua.

As Elena's remarkable academic progress continued, her main tutor, Carlo Rinaldini, became more fully convinced that she should concentrate on the requirements necessary for a degree from the University of Padua. Appreciating the political advantages of this accomplishment for a woman, Professor Felice Rotondi quite agreed, explaining to twenty-six-year old Elena the unique honor it would bring to family, city and university.

Rinaldini consulted with Gianbattista, recommending that it was the appropriate time to seek university recognition for Elena. Gianbattista eagerly arranged all means of support to gain this unprecedented, final goal. To facilitate the plan, and upon the advice of physicians that the moist climate of Venice was contributing to Elena's frequent illnesses, the family again moved Elena to Padua in 1672.

As soon as she had settled in Padua, her father invited twenty-six Venetian procurators and various senators to hear her. Family friends were also enlisted to enjoy a merrily impressive evening of music and poetry. Gianbattista continued to set the stage for his daughter's academic triumph.

And Padua was perfect. The place was burgeoning with international artists, scholars, and ideas — still enjoying a time of cultural efflorescence. The Renaissance had reached Venice through Padua, and its intellectual environment had formed very early. The famed Roman historian Titus Livy was born in Padua in 59 B.C. and retired and died there in A.D. 17. Generations of scholars flocked to the Veneto village. The permanent university, a renowned *Studium Generale,* was founded in the heart of town in 1222.

The second oldest in Europe, the Paduan university was chartered by Pope Urban IV in 1261. It was originally established at the suggestion of Jordanus, Bishop of Padua, who urged Bolognese Professor William of Gascogne to teach there. The University of Bologna was the earliest, tracing its roots by official decree to 1155. (Some records even assert that its origins go back to 1075, and 1088 for its law school.) University students in Bologna migrated to Padua to make up some of the first classes there, predominantly in law. Over the years, the two schools developed into traditional rivals.

In 1611 Coryat recorded that Padua, over its 350-year history, had acquired the reputation as the most cosmopolitan of all universities in Europe. Young men from Hungary, Poland,

Germany, France, and England were among its 1,500 students then . Today it is one of the largest universities in Italy, with a total enrollment of over 65,000.

The Paduan university of Elena's era had a rather expensive tuition, with one source listing the cost at 30,000 ducats per year, a very significant sum then. As a result, its students were mostly from the upper class, with some poorer scholarship students supported either by the city or by private individual sponsors such as Rabbi Abbroff. Many students enrolled at sixteen. They were expected to be of the Catholic faith, with the bishops serving as chancellors awarding the degree certificates, but this was broadened, especially for foreign students. Underclassmen were forbidden to study elsewhere.

Padua's historic roster of faculty and students over the centuries is truly extraordinary. Albert Magnus, the famed teacher of the great medieval theologian St. Thomas Aquinas, was present at the university's beginning. Marcantonio della Torre was anatomy instructor to Leonardo da Vinci in the fifteenth century. Galileo launched a new era in science and literature while teaching mathematics there from 1592 to 1610.

The experimental method of research with actual observations began at Padua with Galileo. During this time, he also increased the power of the new Dutch telescope to discover quite distant stars and to view uncharted planets. His simple wooden lectern still stands, carefully preserved in the Room of the Forty, an anteroom of the university's Aula Magna.

The earlier Polish astronomer Copernicus studied at Padua, as did the martyred religious reformer Girolamo Savonarola (1452-1498), and the multitalented Leone Battista Alberti (1404-1472), a Venetian who designed important buildings throughout Italy, restoring the ancient style to much of its architecture. Moreover, the legendary Franciscan

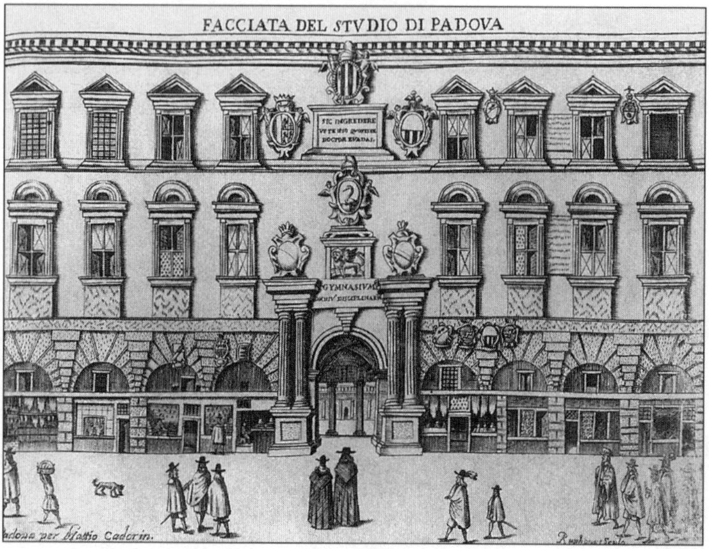

FACADE OF *IL PALAZZO DEL BÒ,* THE ORIGINAL CLASSROOM BUILDING OF THE UNIVERSITY OF PADUA. THE SECOND OLDEST UNIVERSITY IN EUROPE, PADUA CONFERRED ON ELENA HISTORY'S FIRST PH.D. TO A WOMAN IN 1678. "THE BO" IS STILL IN USE.

(Itinerario D'Italia Di Francesco Scoto. Padua, 1659. Special Collections, Vassar College Libraries. Photograph by Charles Porter)

friar Anthony (later canonized as St. Anthony of Padua) taught theology there.

The center of university life at Padua was and still is *Il Palazzo del Bò,* or The Palace of Learning, named for an ancient tavern with the sign of the ox *(bove)* that was located there until 1493. The tavern was converted to a palace and occupied by the Carraras, who largely financed the university. Later, the Bonarin family made substantial financial contributions to the school.

Several buildings at the Paduan university were designed by Andrea Moroni and erected between 1542 and 1601, one consisting of a two-storied Gothic cloister with Ionic and Doric columns and a central court surrounded by a series of rooms where classes were held. "The Bo" had vaulted ceilings, and its facade, entrance walls and the Aula Magna hall were decorated with frescoes and faculty and alumni coats of arms. The noted theologian Fra Paoli Sarpi as well as Girolamo Fabrizi were involved in its sixteenth-century reconstruction.

The pride of Padua's classrooms in "The Bo" was the Anatomy Theater, a laboratory opened in 1596, the first in Europe. It resembled a miniature Roman arena. Early dissecting operations and autopsies were performed there by its School of Anatomy, considered the most distinguished of the Renaissance. In order to prevent city officials from finding out, cadavers were brought in under the cover of darkness on the waterway beneath the theater. During Elena's lifetime, the English physician William Harvey (1578–1657) and others conducted significant medical research at Padua. While teaching there, Dr. Harvey developed his noted theory of blood circulation.

Beginning in the twelfth century, universities emerged in Italy, France and England. Some were rather short-lived. They started as self-governing teacher-student associations, modeled after town communities and guilds. Courses of study varied within each university, but a standard curriculum eventually developed covering liberal arts, philosophy, theology, civil and canon law, and medicine. Often arts and philosophy were elected as preparatory subjects; theology, law and medicine were separate disciplines leading to individual degrees awarded for each profession. The doctorate was the only degree conferred.

"Liberal Arts" in the Middle Ages meant the "trivium," or three learning branches — grammar, rhetoric and dialectic, and the "quadrivium," four mathematical paths — arithmetic, geometry, music, and astronomy. Mastery of these seven fields was considered necessary preparation for advanced studies in classical philosophy and Christian theology, studies that Elena was now pursuing in depth.

By the thirteenth century, European universities, including Padua, had become separated into arts, theology, law and medical faculties. As these departments developed over the next two centuries, the distinctions were further delineated. By the fifteenth century at Padua, one rector, elected annually, was in charge of each faculty department, and students took an oath to obey him. The rector of the arts university and his appointee were the authorities whom the Cornaros first approached for permission to have Elena defend her thesis for a degree. Arts faculties concentrated particularly on the trivium and quadrivium, and elements of this concept remain today.

Aristotle's ideal of "liberal studies" prevailed at Padua during Elena's lifetime with the rise of Renaissance humanism and rediscovery of classical literature and values. There was new expansion of grammar and rhetoric, replacing the

EIGHT ALLEGORICAL HANDMAIDENS OF LEARNING ARE FEATURED AT THE TOP OF THE MAGNIFICENT 22-FOOT-HIGH WINDOW *(right)* AT VASSAR COLLEGE, INCLUDING *(left to right from top)* PHILOSOPHY, MUSIC, ASTRONOMY, GEOMETRY, GRAMMAR, DIALECTIC, MEDICINE, AND THEOLOGY. THE PRODIGIOUS ELENA CORNARO MASTERED EACH OF THESE AREAS.

(Photographs by Charles Porter)

medieval emphasis on logic. The Aristotelian perception of a free man's broad and general liberal education rather than concentration on specific crafts and skills is followed today in many liberal arts colleges of the western world. It was believed that people in an open society who acquired knowledge through liberal studies could attain intellectual and moral excellence, and would be well-positioned to reason and judge values. The principle is clearly still relevant and meritorious.

Within the academic structure of Padua—with its great resources of eminent professors, ancient texts, and newly printed books in its library (founded in 1629)—Elena was intensely focused amidst these resources for the next six years. She immersed herself deeply in her advanced studies, as much as her strength would allow.

Having diligently learned all of the basics in grammar, dialectic, geometry, astronomy, philosophy, history and medicine, Elena's primary interest at Padua was theology. The School of Theology had been added to the university in 1363. There she persevered in her studies with Fr. Felice Rotondi.

Early records indicate that Elena's foremost theology teacher was Don Hippolito Marchetti, but the San Giustina scholar Fr. Ludovico Maschietto recently found that Marchetti was actually not on the Paduan faculty at the time. The existing evidence points clearly to Fr. Rotondi as the university professor who oversaw all of Elena's advanced religious studies. Prominent theologians teaching at Padua during Elena's time there included Giacomo Fiorelli and Francesco Macedo.

According to twentieth century historian Paul Oskar Kristeller and university scholars in Padua, there is no evidence of Elena actually having formally attended any classes there. At this point in her academic career, she was far too advanced in most fields for general course study. Her tutors were drawn from the university faculty, and she may have heard lectures on occasion. Much of her preparation was done in Venice. The one absolute certainty amidst the sketchy details of her studies at Padua is that Elena earned a degree from the university.

Within the university framework, the great bulk of her work was accomplished on her own. Elena learned additional Hebrew for further examining sacred texts. Her outstanding proficiency was acknowledged when she was later listed with the ranking Christian Hebrew scholars in Jewish biographical studies.

Padua's School of Philosophy had acquired an eminent European reputation in the fifteenth century. Elena's mentor Rinaldini saw to it that her studies were also directed toward philosophical areas that would broaden her in analytic and synthetic thinking.

As a humanist scholar, with a rare depth of knowledge in a broad range of ancient and modern languages, Elena progressed to examining moral philosophy and poetry, also acquiring a more profound sense of history. By 1676, Elena was thoroughly ready for every theological problem that might be presented by an examining board. In Rinaldini's assessment, the thirty-year-old scholar had completed all necessary preparation, had reached the summit, and was eminently qualified for a degree in either theology or philosophy.

As always, Elena was appalled at the idea of any personal reward or recognition. She begged her father to abandon the quest for permission to defend her thesis and fled in tears to her mother in Venice. Her face greatly flushed, the distraught daughter exclaimed, "I cannot do this because, after all, I am only a maiden."

Erected in 1552 by Andrea della Valle, the interior pillared courtyard of "The Bo" is decorated with alumni and faculty crests and carved lions. The University of Padua attracted male students from all over Europe in the seventeenth century.

(L'università di Padova. Venice, 1922. Courtesy of Monsignor Nicola Fusco)

Rotondi again appealed to Elena's sense of duty, and eventually the first petition was drawn up, addressed by Elena's father to the University of Padua's Rector of the Arts Faculty, Girolamo Basadonna, in 1677. Gianbattista's letter sought a degree in theology for his accomplished daughter. Enthusiastically, the rector and the examining commission of senators (*Riformati dello Studio),* known for their broad policies, endorsed the letter unanimously on November 18. Elena's close advisor Rotondi was designated to present her to the Sacred College when a date had been set.

Suddenly, the process halted. The Cornaro petition had been negated from Rome that same month by the final ecclesiastical authority for University of Padua approval, Gregorio Cardinal Barbarigo, the Bishop of Padua and former Chancellor of the Theological Faculty there. At first he was willing to give his consent, until he realized the specific discipline involved. Typical of the spirit of the age, the very idea of a degree in theology for a woman shocked his Eminence. "What?" he declared, "A female doctor and teacher of theology? Never!"

Accustomed to having his own way, Gianbattista remained undaunted. Over the winter months he pressed the issue, writing letter after letter to various officials of the Tribulan and the Magistrate of the Reformers, as well as to Cardinal Barbarigo. Gianbattista, although older than the cardinal by eight years, had met his match. It is instructive to consider their backgrounds. Both were Venetians, men of learning, with similar legacies. Both were noblemen from extremely distinguished families in the Republic's history. Both held powerful offices.

Barbarigo's father had served as a noted ambassador, and his son became the protégé of Pope Alexander VII, who served in the papacy from 1655 to 1667. Gregorio was born in 1625 and educated in law in Padua. When he was twenty-three, he was chosen to accompany Ambassador Luigi Contarini to the Congress of Münster in Germany, where the Treaty of Westphalia between Germany, France and Sweden was signed in 1648, terminating Europe's Thirty Years' War. There he met the apostolic nuncio, Fabio Chigi, who became the pope, a man of enlightenment, patron of arts and learning, and Barbarigo's mentor. It was Chigi who was responsible for sculptor Gianlorenzo Bernini's coming to Rome to work for fifty years, changing the face of the city.

Ordained in 1655, Barbarigo had already distinguished himself with a law degree from Padua. A year after his ordination, he was asked by Pope Alexander VII to oversee the Trastevere region of Rome, an area stricken by plague. His pastoral work so impressed the pope that in 1657 Alexander appointed him Bishop of Bergamo, where he fostered far-reaching church reforms laid out by the Council of Trent in the preceding century. Barbarigo was named a cardinal by the pope in 1660 and Bishop of Padua in 1667.

The new cardinal was a dynamic, cultured and scholarly man, as well as a linguist. He founded a college and reestablished the Paduan Seminary for young priests, with its own printing press and an exceptional library, containing books from all over Europe. Called a second Carlo Borromeo (the fifteenth-century saint of similarly energetic good efforts to improve the clergy), Barbarigo also donated large sums to charity and was broadly considered to be a serious and kindly man, especially to the distressed. He held strong reasons for his firm refusal of the Cornaro's request.

After Galileo had left Padua for Florence in 1610 and the subsequent plague had taken many of Padua's teaching physicians (especially from the School of Medicine), the university was significantly weakened for a time. Barbarigo, as its chancellor, had worked to strengthen the university and did not want to unleash any potentially unsettling projects. He knew granting a degree to a woman, no matter how qualified, had never before been undertaken anywhere. Females were simply deemed inferior.

Outside of convents, women were not allowed to teach and therefore needed no degree. Barbarigo expressed the concern that because they lacked theological background, women might misinterpret sacred texts. He firmly believed that giving women this academic support and acknowledgment would cause great controversy and bring adverse criticism to the school, where the well-paid faculty had always been allowed freedom in teaching. He was also sensitive to his church's position that had made necessary its reform movement, the Counter-Reformation in the sixteenth century. This movement attempted to stop the spread and minimize the effects of the Protestant Reformation, which spawned ideas that were still rife in Padua. And Cardinal Barbarigo did not want to undermine the new spirit that had entered the Roman Catholic Church nor lessen its influence.

Great tension existed between the two aristocrats over the winter of 1677–78: Gianbattista, a determined head procurator, and Barbarigo, the powerful prelate. Not one to accept failure easily, Gianbattista threatened to apply elsewhere for Elena and he went to great lengths to refute those who objected.

Gianbattista also made certain that all other affirming voices were heard. A doctor from la Sorbonne in Paris, Professor Ludivico Espiany de Saint-Luc, and French gentleman-scholar Carlo Cato de Court, had expressed their approval. Gianbattista promoted support of his daughter's consideration for a degree, especially from the academies. At the time, he was one of two "protectors" of the Delphic Academy, the social club that met in the palace of Venetian Senator Francesco Gussoni. Politically savvy, Gianbattista arranged for the entire Senate, in a motion adjourning a day's session of the Council of the Pregadi, to come to Padua to hear Elena in literary discussion. The motion was unprecedented for an academic candidate.

Back in Venice that same year, the French King Louis XIV sent his treasurer, the nobleman Emmanuel Teodosio Cardinal de Bouillon (1643–1715), to confirm his country's curiosity about the learned woman. The French cardinal found his visit to be a highly stimulating one, and he presented Elena with his portrait and established regular correspondence with her. In the welcoming party was General Grimani, representing Cardinal Barbarigo.

Significant exposure of Elena had resulted a year earlier from the publication by contemporary historian and biographer Gregorio Leti of his second edition of *L'Italia regnante* in 1676. It featured a thirty-nine page chapter written about Cornaro among the descriptions of "Illustri Signori" (Illustrious Men).

Encouragement for Gianbattista's aspirations for his daughter came from many, including Rotondi, who remarked, "If the women are permitted to study Theology, why must they be denied the doctorate in that subject"? The next year, Gianbattista again made application to the university for his now thirty-one-year-old daughter.

Cardinal Barbarigo may have witnessed and was surely cognizant of Elena's remarkable appearances before all the procurators and the entire Senate. Ultimately, and with some clearly expressed misgivings, the cardinal granted his permission for Elena to defend her thesis at Padua—not in theology but in philosophy, which was considered an equally prestigious degree.

"If the Procurator of San Marco insists," Barbarigo concluded, "I am willing to modify the point and let his daughter become a Doctor in Philosophy." This declaration cleared the way for Elena Cornaro to become history's first woman university graduate.

Gregorio Cardinal Barbarigo as depicted in the Vassar Window.

(Photograph by J.J. Sinnott)

LIFE PORTRAIT OF ELENA AT THE AGE OF 27. HER FAMILY INSISTED UPON THE PAINTING, NOT KNOWING THAT ELENA ALWAYS WORE A MONK'S WOOL HABIT BENEATH HER ELABORATE COURT DRESS.

(Giovanni Molinari. 1673. Museo Civico, Padua)

11

A UNIQUE ACHIEVEMENT

She was born to shine.

VITTORIA MARZOLO, 1925

THE HISTORIC EVENT took place in Padua on June 25, 1678. "It was like a coronation," Lupis tells us, conjuring up images of curious crowds gathering to greet an earlier Cornaro, the Queen of Cyprus. As a bell tolled, knights and nobles, clergy and students, city officials and representatives from other European universities assembled in Padua. They were gathered to witness the celebrated Lady Elena deliver her dissertation, the required public lecture in her specialty, leading to education's highest degree.

Gianbattista had pressed authorities of the University of Padua to declare a special convocation for the ceremony. His hope and plan was that it would be held in the Aula Magna on June 5, Elena's birthday. He knew that this date would have been during a time when hundreds of pilgrim visitors were drawn to Padua for the feast day of the city's patron, St. Anthony, on June 13. Elena, too, had anticipated the large number of people that would be there for this festival time of street fairs and music, bannered processions and special services in the basilica.

Not wishing to draw attention to herself or to detract from any church celebration, she pleaded with her father once again, asking him to desist, or at least to have the ceremony delayed. Gianbattista relented, and he sought a change of date. Cardinal Barbarigo designated the Saturday morning of June 25 to be the date for the occasion, and Aula Magna to be the place.

It was vacation time, and the university issued a notice to its entire faculty about the upcoming and unprecedented examination. Many guests were expected, especially from Venice, as well as other neighboring towns. Gianbattista had sent out personal invitations, undoubtedly to such noteworthies as the new doge, Alvise Contarini (1676-1684), who had succeeded Nicolo Sagredo after his one-year reign which followed the death of ninety-four-year-old Domenico Contarini in 1675. The elder Contarini was the doge who conspired with Gianbattista for Elena's marriage to his nephew.

Dignitaries from Bologna, Ferrara, Naples, Perugia, and Rome were also expected. Convening from the University of Padua were Angelo Montagnana, Prior; Marco Antonio Mussato, Provincial; and Gian Pietro Saviolo, Syndic. The Venetian rectors of Padua were there: Girolamo Basadonna, Podestà; Luigi Mocenigo, Prefect, and Cardinal Barbarigo's vicar, the Very Reverend Alessandro Mantovani; and the Vice Syndic, whose name is now lost. Seventy-two officials attending were listed in Latin in college archives of the Prince of the Accademia, dated June 25. The list also included Elena's sponsors (Promotores): Professor Rinaldini; Girolamo Frigimelica, the Count and Knight of Rubert; Angelo Montagnana and Ermenegildo Pera. Her science tutor Carlo Vota was in attendance, and Professor Rotondi presented her.

So many had accepted the various invitations that the Aula Magna proved to be too small. The location was changed

GREGORIO CARDINAL BARBARIGO SERVED AS THE BISHOP OF PADUA. A TOWERING FIGURE IN CHURCH HISTORY, HE WAS BEATIFIED IN 1761. CARDINAL BARBARIGO INITIALLY REFUSED THE CORNARO PETITION FOR A UNIVERSITY DEGREE, BUT THE VENETIAN NOBLEMAN EVENTUALLY BECAME ELENA'S ULTIMATE CHAMPION.

(Ragguaglio della vita... del Barbarigo. Padua, 1761. Annenberg Rare Book and Manuscript Library, University of Pennsylvania)

to the Cathedral of the Blessed Virgin of Padua (Il Duomo) on the Piazza del Duomo. Much to Elena's chagrin, the event had become a spectacular public event.

Renewed in the Renaissance, the cathedral sat on the site of a seventh-century church. It had been under the leadership of Bishop Stephen de Carrara in 1400, who served in a cathedral which was a twelfth-century Grecian brick building, originally designed by the architect Macillo. Its restoration during the Renaissance was attributed primarily to Michelangelo, Andrea della Valle and Girolamo Frigimelica. The edifice's plain, stark front awaited a stone facade that was never completed. Close beside the cathedral was the Romanesque-Lombardi Baptistry, its exterior frescoed and its interior dome and wall painting executed in 1376 by the Florentine, Giusto de Menabuoi. Overlooking the handsome square on the south side stood the Episcopal Palace of 1300.

The cathedral was chosen for this extraordinary academic affair because of its size and location, replacing the smaller Aula Magna. In addition to the religious lunettes and reliquaries that adorned the cathedral, it contained a valuable library *(Biblioteca del Capitolo)* of early manuscripts and printed books.

As the sun shone upon the cathedral that windy Saturday morning in Padua, Elena arose and received Holy Communion early. By mid-morning the wind had diminished, and it was smotheringly hot as the Cornaro carriages approached the cathedral. The diminutive thirty-two-year-old descended from her coach, accompanied by her father and personal attendants, and the "multitude of people" pressed closer. A hush settled over the assemblage inside as Elena made her way forward. Feeling faint and unnerved, she swayed, supported by Abbot Codanini who had come to her side.

A month earlier, Elena had hemorrhaged, "bursting a vein" thought to have come from her lungs. It was the first symptom in a series of prolonged attacks underlying the serious disease (thought to be consumption) that would increasingly debilitate her. The hemorrhaging was followed by several months of attempts at "strict cures" that resulted in general weakness and a sensitive stomach.

The oppressively hot June morning and the onlooking crowds made her appear to some as having lost control of her faculties. Fr. Codanini escorted her to the Chapel of the Virgin Mary. Kneeling, she prayed for strength to endure the rigorous ordeal unfolding before her that momentous day. Her mind then cleared, and her serenity restored, Elena was now ready.

Accompanied by choristers and a chamber orchestra, a procession of dignitaries entered and filled both sides of the cathedral. A special small pulpit or "raised chair" had been set up for Elena in the sanctuary near the altar. When she reached her chair, the commission of examiners then began its interrogation.

It was only the previous day that Elena had been allowed to choose the subject of discourse. In what seemed a tribute to her first tutor, Fr. Fabris, Elena elected to discuss the works of Aristotle. Random passages, chosen by lot without regard to the difficulties involved, were then assigned for her interpretation by the august and austere examiners. As it turned out, the passages were two *puncta* (philosophical passages) from Aristotle's *The Physics,* the popular name for natural science, and *The Posterior Analytics,* one of six treatises on logic.

For over one unrelenting hour in front of an audience of some of the most learned men in Europe, Elena animatedly expounded in classic Latin, answering the rigorous and probing questions "with a simple ease and dignity." Repeatedly, she

Gianbattista Cornaro, Elena's father, shown in official gold chains as Procurator of St. Mark. His Hands are clasped in wonder, witnessing his daughter's academic triumph. This depiction of the nobleman in Vassar's "Cornaro Window" is the only known extant image of Elena's father.

(Photograph by Charles Porter)

was interrupted by applause, especially from the many students attending.

By every account of that morning, there was utter astonishment amidst the congregation, as Elena Cornaro exhibited a profound and facile understanding of each difficult area explored. When she finished, Professor Rinaldini came forward. In what was described as an eloquent and scholarly speech, he reviewed for the listeners Elena's distinguished family background and the scope of her learning. He also praised her virtuous life, mentioning, in particular, her chastity.

Traditionally, a secret ballot was used to determine a candidate's success, and Elena urged that this be done. At the conclusion of her presentation, she withdrew. Vice-Prior Giovanni Domenico de Tessari received the election urns of all those gathered on the bench for voting. Suddenly he stood and proposed that the usual ballot be dispensed with entirely. This was a highly unusual request, subject to the vote of the entire college.

"This 'heroine' had borne herself so nobly and so well," he proclaimed, "demonstrating not only her philosophical but also her polymathematical learning." The idea of exempting Elena from any ballot was greeted by unanimous approval, and the decision was later confirmed by Cardinal Barbarigo.

Prominently seated in the front of the cathedral, Gianbattista and Zanetta watched as their daughter shyly reentered the room. As was the usual practice of the candidates, she approached Rinaldini with the request for a degree. He then pronounced her *Magistra et Doctrix Philosophiae* (Master and Doctor of Philosophy).

There was unrestrained applause across the vast cathedral, and even cries of "Bravissima!"

It was now time to present the traditional symbols of learning. Upon Elena's dark curls, Professor Rinaldini gently arranged the poet's crown of laurel, the "magisterial laurel." This ancient Greek, Apollonian emblem of victory was woven with native evergreen of Elena's land.

Fr. Rotondi handed Professor Rinaldini the mozzetta, a teacher's ermine cape, which he gathered around Elena's shoulders. A heavy gold doctor's ring, with the University of Padua seal, was then placed on her finger. Next, the customary symbolic volume of philosophy was presented. Rinaldini embraced her with the traditional words spoken in Latin, *"pacis osculum cum benedictione magistrali"* ("the kiss of peace with the master's blessing").

With his hands clasped in wonder, and nearly overcome with pride in his daughter, Gianbattista rose in triumph amid tumultuous acclamation. Carlo Rinaldini, Felice Rotondi, and Abbot Codanini, in academic and religious attire, stood around Elena, and as the entire assembly arose, joined the choir in a joyous "Te Deum." The red-robed Cardinal Barbarigo remained nearby the new laureate, who bore it all with quiet dignity and "silent suffering" as well.

This marked a defining moment in history. More than two centuries later, the scene was vibrantly portrayed in the great stained-glass window of Thompson Memorial Library at Vassar College. It was a scene that captured the imagination of a young American student from St. Louis.

12

FINAL ILLNESS

All literary Europe rang with the name of Helen Lucretia....

ABBESS MATHILDE PYNSENT, 1896

"LA PRIMA DONNA *Laureata nel Mondo*"—the first woman laureate in the world—was to be Elena's epithet. Following the cathedral ceremony that June day in 1678, a triumphal carriage procession, carrying family members on their way back to the palace for joyous feasts, passed through enthusiastic throngs of people in the streets roaring approval and cheering, "Viva Elena!" Many reached to kiss their countrywoman's hand. All of the Cornaros were relishing glory regained. One of their own members had achieved universal distinction.

"Such crazy behavior never seen in my experience," objected one taunting dissenter amid general public approbation. A university professor, Dr. Gaspare Cantu, in sarcastic commentary delivered heatedly to the examining committee, complained about the procedure that morning. There had been great confusion at the presentation, he claimed, with people shouting irreverently. No proper ritual was followed, and there was no secret ballot. Nor, he objected, had any money been deposited with the board of examiners. (In fact, the money was submitted, but the board had refused to receive it.) Furthermore, the critic Cantu added, the traditional gifts of gloves from Gianbattista for the bishop, the promotores and the doctors of the college were of cheap, inferior quality. They should have been of silk or chamois leather, he sneered. He called Elena's sponsor, Professor Rinaldini, *"il babuazzo"* (the simpleton).

Cantu's voice was little appreciated, and there was no other known opposition. Historians note that a seventeenth-century father of another young woman, the Countess Veronica Valeri from Reggio Emilia, attempted to get a degree for his daughter from Padua around this time. But no date has been found. Although she was Elena's "contemporary and correspondent," she was refused by the university. Along with her twin sister, Veronica became a nun at the Visitation Monastery in Modena, where she died in 1690. The debate over admitting women to the University of Padua continued for years.

After her degree was awarded, widespread esteem surrounded Elena. Her countrymen now affectionately referred to her as "The Cornaro." Among those who wrote about her, according to Giovanni Battista Fabri in *La Conchiglia Celeste* (Celestial Shell) in 1690, were Fr. Francesco Macedo, Don Giovanni Palazzi, Abbot Filippo Bonini and Giuseppe Fontana. Tributes poured in from all over Europe, including Utrecht, Lyon, Paris, Amsterdam and Leipzig. Frenchmen Monsieur de Court and the Abbe de Saint-Luc, who had previously supported her application, openly commended Elena and, most significantly, there was widespread praise for the university that had honored her. "The doctorate was for a man an achievement, for a woman a miracle," spread the popular belief.

Two weeks later, on Saturday, July 9, Elena was formally inducted in a convocation where she swore allegiance to the university and additionally was elected an examiner. Once again, it was by acclamation. She participated officially only once in this function, soon afterwards hearing two successful candidates for degrees (Antonio Orsato in medicine and Daniele Magnavini in philosophy).

Although her diploma has never been found, it may have been presented to her at the convocation. Seventeenth-century University of Padua documents were luxurious, illuminated manuscripts, works of art similar to those commissioned in the previous two centuries by nobility. Several issued by Padua in the early and mid-1600s are now part of the great Italian Renaissance collections of the Newberry Library in Chicago and the Pierpont Morgan Library in New York. They are hand-scribed in Latin and painted in resonant colors on vellum, high quality parchment (made from specially prepared skins of sheep, goats, or calves, rendering them durable and translucent). Each contained a description of the recipient's courses of study and was signed by examiners, the archbishop, and the chancellor of the university.

Padua's early diplomas contained four to six leaves (eight to twelve pages), sometimes illustrated with portraits of the awardees, their coats of arms and other heraldry, and included miniatures of the Virgin Mary with the Christ Child. Many leaves were adorned with initials and scrollwork borders of flowers and foliage interspersed with angels holding laurel wreaths. Pages were embellished in precious colors, including vermilion and ultramarine blue (made from crushed lapis lazuli). These were highlighted with paint of powdered gold.

Some of the University of Padua bindings in the Morgan Library collection are Venetian, modeled after the Persian style, in red and brown moroccan leather tooled in gold. These diplomas are silk-tied and corded with coral-colored wax seals of the Bishop of Padua, set in brass medallions. The Morgan collection includes a 1620 diploma, handsomely covered in the sunk-compartment binding of leather, patterned with inlays in rich tones of green, tan and golden velvet. Many of these intricate manuscript techniques were derived from illumination produced in monasteries.

In well-established Italian families, these valuable documents accumulated over the generations. Eventually, many of these artful diplomas which were not either donated to libraries or destroyed were sold by family descendants as highly prized pieces. Owners often tore out the first or title pages containing ancestral names, portraits and insignia, removing the personal identification. This may have happened to Elena's diploma from Padua. But in Elena's case, it is also quite conceivable that after her death the diploma was among her personal belongings taken as relics by various admirers who considered her a saint. However it was lost, her uniquely historic diploma regrettably did not make its way into a museum showcase.

Soon after receiving her diploma, another large celebration centering around Elena was held on July 15 in Padua with members of the Academy of the *Ricovrati* (Inmates) which she had joined in 1669. The meeting featured Elena in an improvised discussion of astronomy, focused on a newly discovered comet.* The academic portion of the celebration was followed by a concert featuring contemporary Italian compositions, and then a dance from which Elena, as usual, excused herself.

Officially, her degree was recorded on July 16, when the document was presented to the university authorities: Angelo

* Two centuries later, the discovery of a comet brought another pioneering woman to the fore. The story of Maria Mitchell (1818-1889), America's first woman astronomer and Vassar's first astronomy professor, is told in a classic biography by Helen Wright, *Sweeper in the Sky*.

Nineteenth-century half-length portrait of Elena, hair in pearled chignon with ermine mozzetta cape, symbol of teacher or Master (Magistra) presented to her at Paduan graduation in 1678.

(Venezia e la sua storia. Venice, 1838. Biblioteca Civica, Padua)

Montagnana, Prior; Giacomo Trento, Counsel; Carlo Mussato, Vice Procurator; and Gian Pietro Saviolo, Syndic.

The new laureate was finally able to return to Venice, where she remained for less than a year. After her degree, she immersed herself even more deeply in study, in theology, and in the reading of sacred works. Elena continued to correspond with various leaders and she regularly granted audiences.

In outward appearance, she refused "whatever was sensual and secular" among the accepted dress and social customs of the aristocracy. Elaborate clothes had become for her "the instruments of her martyrdom." She wore her hidden habit night and day, according to biographer Deza, with simple and even frayed robes, "like those of a poor townswoman." At her meals, she would use silver and fine linens only when her parents were present. In any weather, and often with stones in her shoes, she would walk beside her carriage with her footman rather than ride.

Elena's close friend, Sr. Maria Felice, the Capuchine abbess whose life of self-sacrifice she so admired, had set up one of the most austere orders at Grazia. Under her influence, Elena sought to follow this manner of living the life of a nun whenever possible, even in the palaces. As an oblate, she had taken a vow of poverty, and she begged alms for the poor and wrote appeal letters for them. She seldom called upon the palace servants available to her.

When Zanetta gave new underclothes to her companion Maddalena, Elena often gave the discarded ones to needy women. In the marketplace at Padua, where farmers from outlying areas came to sell their produce, Elena joined in, serving "the people with her own hands" and urging stable hands to "look after the tired animals."

At times Elena would remain for weeks in seclusion, becoming totally detached even from household staff, except for the evening meal, consuming herself in prayer and study for hours. Her mother was aware and often quite befuddled by some of this unusual behavior. Worried about Elena's withdrawal, Zanetta confronted her daughter one day, accusing her of becoming a hermit.

In September, 1678 Elena suffered another burst vessel in her lungs and vomited blood, signalling the beginning of more advanced stages of lung disease and probably gastric ulcers. After the prior attack, she never fully regained her health. For the next five years, her physical condition slowly deteriorated. Near the end of 1679, primarily because of increasing frailty, Elena moved permanently to Padua, with its more favorable climate. Zanetta and Maddalena went with her, and Gianbattista visited often to be with his wife and daughter.

Within the year after Elena's graduation, other female aspirants were discouraged from applying to the university. Padua's board had been duly warned about admitting women. One known aspirant was Carla Gabriella Patin, the older daughter of Carlo Patin, a respected French physician and Professor of Medicine there.

Savoring Elena's exalted position, Gianbattista endeavored to protect it against any contenders. He wrote at least one combative letter (dated February 27, 1679) to Rinaldini at Padua, opposing Dr. Patin's application for his daughter's degree. His caustic remarks smeared the whole family as unworthy, accusing Dr. Patin of being an idiot without virtue and Carla of being totally incomparable on cultural levels to Elena. Gianbattista won the dispute. Carla Patin was rejected.

Elena's fame continued to follow her throughout her remaining years, and curious admirers rarely left her alone again. One visit that attracted much attention was that of Cesar d'Estrées from France. Very soon after Elena became established at the Odeon Palace, on New Year's Day in 1680, King Louis XIV and his consort, The Infanta Maria Theresa, instructed their ambassador, Cardinal Estrées (1628-1714), to go to Padua and meet with Lady Elena. The cardinal was a Sorbonne theologian, able diplomat and member of the French Academy. He first went to St. Anthony's Basilica and then to the university to call on Cardinal Barbarigo.

Just before sunset, the cardinal arrived at the Odeon Palace, having first sought permission to visit. A cavalier welcomed him at the carriage door. Gianbattista, who encouraged and arranged all details of the visit, had gathered various Cornaro gentlemen and academic and religious leaders to provide an audience. Rinaldini attended.

From the private account of a family friend who was there, we have a wonderfully detailed record of the event. The account warrants quotation in full, as it thoroughly reveals the formality and demanding agenda so often endured by Elena.

> The Lady Helen Lucretia meanwhile presented herself on the top step of the stairs accompanied by many attendants, and when His Excellency appeared she moved with her people to meet him. But the cardinal begged her not to do so and having mounted the stairs himself, he paid her some compliments before he entered the hall and she replied in very apt terms. Thence they proceeded to the large Chamber prepared for the purpose.
>
> In company with His Eminence were four Princes, General Grimaldi, the Chamberlain of the Cardinal Barbarigo, many other Cavaliers, and two Religious, Doctors of the Sorbonne. At first no one entered the room except the Cardinal and Helen Lucretia. A large carpet covered the

whole pavement, and a smaller one was spread under the chair which had been placed opposite the door, out of respect for the high rank of His Eminence. He would not however sit upon it on any account, but retired to a smaller one nearer the door. This gave rise to many compliments, until at length the Lady yielded to the earnest request of His Eminence and took the larger chair and the place of honour. She did this, however, with a delicacy such as the Cardinal had not expected from a gentlewoman unused to the Court. She first drew the chair from off the carpet, and then seated herself. His Eminence then signified that he had come to salute her, attracted by the fame which had spread throughout the world of the rare gifts with which she was adorned.

She answered in terms of the deepest modesty, and showed the highest estimation for the greatness and dignity of the Prince. He continued the discourse in Italian, now and then interposing some word or sentence in French. The Lady who understood both languages equally well, answered with admirable quickness. After a quarter of an hour the Cardinal said: "I think that the Duke is outside and would have much pleasure in saluting you." He was very young and consequently shy, and upon his delaying to come His Eminence added: "Many other Cavaliers are desirous of doing you homage."

It was obvious that Elena's presence, however modest and unassuming her demeanor, was formidable to many.

After this the whole assembly were called together, and entered the chamber. When they were seated the Cardinal addressing them said that the lady was most affable, and that they might speak to her in French as she understood it perfectly. But no one dared to begin.

> His Eminence then said once more, that there were waiting outside two Doctors of the Sorbonne, men of great learning whom he thought it would be well to present to her. She answered that His Eminence could freely command, in the house of one of his servants, therefore these two other persons were also introduced. Then the Cardinal began to praise the Lady and to enumerate the languages and sciences which she had mastered. Whereupon a Doctor, a great friend of the family, said that if His Eminence and these gentlemen wished it, she would give some proof of her knowledge. Two salvers full of books and of musical compositions were therefore brought, but before the Lady was heard one of the Doctors took up a volume of [Greek orator] Isocrates and began to read.

Despite her reluctance to be the center of attention, Lady Elena's rare grace and learning brought continual pleas for an encore on this new day in 1680.

> The same book was then given to the Lady who continued to read it with so natural an accent, and with such correctness, that she was begged by His Eminence to continue, and quickly ran over another entire page. Then the Cardinal took first one book and then another, and, desiring in particular to test her knowledge of Hebrew, listened to her rendering of it with amazement, and asked who had been her master. The Rabbi [Abbroff] was then presented to him.
>
> They passed on afterwards to the trial in writing and singing of all those languages which she wrote and spoke perfectly, and sang in all but Hebrew, playing her own accompaniments to the entire satisfaction of everyone present.
>
> After this the Cardinal having praised the Lady, took his departure, absolutely refusing to let her accompany him, and not even allowing her to put her foot outside her own chamber.

The agenda for the day, as usual, was carefully orchestrated by Elena's father.

> His Eminence having left, the Lady went to the Accademia, where all had been arranged by order of the Procurator her father. She also repaired thither and was received by the Knight Lepido Zabarella and several others; after having been introduced, she seated herself after the Prince of the Academy, opposite the Canopy of His Eminence. As soon as she sat down the Cardinal came to compliment her, saying that this was a surprise very pleasing to him. Having returned to his place, music was now heard and afterwards Signor Rinaldini began to read. The Prince proposed a problem and two persons spoke. Then a sonnet having been declaimed by the Prince, the Lady began to recite the Eulogy in praise of His Eminence.

Her graciousness and diverse talents continued to awe the cardinal and brought enthusiastic applause and homage from the assembled crowd.

> When those present heard her unexpected voice a deep silence fell upon them. About two thousand persons were present, for after the Accademia there was to be a banquet. She recited with her usual correctness and was repeatedly applauded. When she had finished the Cardinal left his canopy and came to thank her, adding that he was going to make a demand full of vanity in asking for a copy of the composition made in his praise; nevertheless, he admired it so much that he was forced to make the request.
>
> She promised to grant it, asking time to transcribe the work into a better form. To this His Eminence consented and returned to his place. Afterwards Signor Secco recited a fine sonnet and the Accademia was concluded.

> The Lady, acting on the advice of Signor Grimaldi, retired without letting herself be seen by the Cardinal as she did not wish to assist at the festivity. It should be added that, when she began to recite all the people who had stood in the middle of the hall knelt down, and remained kneeling till she had finished, in order that the ladies and others might see and hear her. It will readily be seen how worthily she merited this honour.
>
> The Eulogy was copied on gilt paper, and she added beneath it two sentences, one in the Greek of Euripides, and one in the Hebrew of Samuel, signifying that she sent the composition only in obedience to the commands to His Eminence.
>
> At fourteen o'clock of the following day she went to present it, but the Cardinal had already left for Ferrara, so, in order that she might not fail in keeping her promise, she sent a messenger who found him at the Bridge of Lova. His Eminence in receiving it remarked that he considered it a great favour and would keep it as a gem of great price; then perceiving the Greek and Hebrew which had been added, he remarked that there was more than he had heard recited, and warmly enjoined the messenger to thank the Lady of whose marvelous mental gifts the whole world was witness.

Cardinal Estrées had spent the night at the Episcopal Palace as the guest of Cardinal Barbarigo before departing for Ferrara and Rome. Elena's reputation as a prodigy had already traveled to France and now even more so after Estrées' visit. Dominican Fr. Thomas Peyre in the Estrées entourage wrote to Fr. Giovanni Foresti that Elena's virtues and talents were greater than the accolades previously reported. King Louis XIV was informed and was very approving when he received through Elena a philosophical work of Professor Rinaldini's nephew Charles that was dedicated to him. Young Rinaldini was presented with a royal medal and elaborate gold chain for his treatise.

Elena grew increasingly exhausted by the demands of having to review so thoroughly for all these exacting discussions arranged continuously for her. But she soon wrote to her father:

> With the joy of my studies, the salubrity of the air, and the diligent care of the physicians, I feel much stronger; therefore, I hope that in the future I may resume my studies and thus rescue the name of our House from extinction and oblivion.

One retreat used during these stressful times—and for the family to escape both cities' summer heat—was their estate at Codevigo, four miles from Piove di Sacco. It was built on the bank of the Brenta River by Luigi Cornaro who used it as a country villa in spring and fall (he specified April, May, September and October). It was a huge farm property with a small but fine stone house designed by Falconetto in classical style with columned portico.

The structure, now a ruin, was situated in the center of a courtyard with fountains and gardens, orchards and vineyards. Tommasa Temanza, in his 1778 work on celebrated Venetian architects and sculptors *(Vite dei più celebri architetti)* described Luigi's villa which he had visited:

> A majestic doorway forms the entrance to the palace. It has two Ionic columns on the sides, a rich cornice, and a majestic frontispiece, which bears, carved in the center of its upper part, a large eagle with wings outspread. This

edifice has two stories; the first is vaulted, the second has rafted ceilings.

Codevigo would be considerably altered over the years. After draining marshes for arable land, building many houses for tenant farmers and a bridge over the Brenta, Luigi also had reconstructed an old church (dedicated to the prophet Zechariah) for this village of twelve hundred people. It is no longer standing. It was there that Elena taught Christian doctrine to residents and worked with the local priest so that lessons would continue in her absence.

Another Falconetta villa at Este, southeast of Padua at the foot of Monte Calaone (a spur of the lush Euganean Hills), had been developed by Luigi as a spring and fall hunting preserve. The hills—the storied land of the poet Percy Shelley—were profusely verdant. The splendid summits, with "red larch and the granitic and porphyritic [feldspar crystal] rocks abounding there" appealed to Luigi, who built the Cornaro estate on one of the hills outside of Este. For ten years (1650–1660), the estate was rented by Gianbattista to the Bishop of Padua, Giorgio Cornaro. When it was available, the Cornaro Piscopias enjoyed using the estate.

This Cornaro property, too, featured an enormous farm with a steward's house and palace located near a Capuchine convent. Around the mansion were glistening fountains, vine trellises and numerous lemon, orange and prickly-pear trees that created an extravagant overstory. It later became known as the Villa Benvenuti and belonged to the Farsetti family. An eighteenth-century palace inventory listed among its furnishings a painting of the Cornaro coat of arms, portraits of the Queen of Cyprus (whom Luigi would have known) and of Ruzzante, the friend of Luigi who gave recitations there on a moveable wooden stage.

In 1680 after the Estrées visit, Gianbattista dedicated significant time toward claiming the aforementioned ancestral Piscopia "Order of the Sword" title for himself. A glorious and highly coveted order of chivalry founded by the crusading knight King Peter I, it had been bestowed in gratitude for financial aid on his friend, Federico Cornaro. The custom was especially popular in both the fourteenth and fifteenth centuries among princes to attract faithful followers for religious missions. "C'est pour loyauté maintenir" (to maintain loyalty) was the patriotic Lusignan motto. Its badge was a silver cross-hilted sword on a blue field.

Despite his best efforts, Gianbattista was totally unsuccessful in getting his knighthood recognized. But he proudly preserved and sought to magnify the insignia and motto Federico had sculpted prominently on the front of the palace. He kept King Peter's royal coins (silver gros), impressed by the order's silver buckle, displayed with his art collection. His plight was met with empathy by his family, even from the daughter who rejected all publicity and self-acclaim. Elena wrote her father from Padua, "Inform us as diligently as possible about what you are doing for the honor of the knighthood and what you are going to do."

In spite of being lionized by the Republic, Gianbattista was never admitted to the order he coveted. He was denied the right to bear the arms of Lusignan, unable to wear the crimson velvet robe or the stole of gold, or follow his signature with a prestigious "K." Why? His marriage to Zanetta made it impossible.

In addition to his procuratorial duties, Gianbattista was also absorbed over these years in broad-scale preservation of his Venetian palace, which was reported to be falling apart. Enormous sums were spent on renovations ("fifty thousand ducati" on the interior), and it was said that he refined the palace superbly. Its "noble chambers" were rebuilt, widened and ornamented with fine cornices and molding, the library and exhibition hall extended, and the atrium decorated with sculptures by Orazio Marinali of Bassano to represent Apollo, Diana, geometry and prudence.

Modernization was a continuing project. Exterior capitals and columns throughout the portico and loggia were restored. Stuccoes and carved ledges were cleaned and embellished. On the second floor (the two top floors had been added in the 1500s), restoration work was done on the thirteenth-century frieze of animals in relief and old family insignia which heralded the honor Gianbattista never attained.

Carefully preserved items were the Order of the Sword with lions rampant incorporated into the family coat of arms and the crest and helmet of the knighthood of Cyprus. Featured was the Lusignan French motto, its inscription in Langobard (Lombard) characters. Some emblems remain partially visible today.

One of Gianbattista's unfulfilled plans was to extend the palace façade forward over the Grand Canal. He documented the wish in his will, requesting that his heirs attempt it.

It was during this time also that Elena attended the christening of her niece and namesake, the baby daughter of Girolamo and his wife, Dolfina Tiepolo Cornaro. Elena and her family also continued corresponding with the Jesuit General Oliva, especially during 1681, the last year of his life.

While Zanetta was in the palace in Venice, Gianbattista visited Padua in 1682 and attempted to have the treasured cypress tree taken down. He felt that it had grown so large and dark that it blocked his distant view and spoiled the symmetry of the garden. Elena begged him to spare the tree, pleading that it was her mother's favorite, softly adding, "Wait until this cypress withers away and dies of itself, and then the trunk of it will serve for my coffin." The tree was spared.

Sometime after the cathedral ceremony, Gianbattista's relationship with Cardinal Barbarigo improved. The Cardinal, who had gone to Rome, was an overnight guest at the Cornaro Piscopia Palace in Venice at least once during 1683. The two noblemen's differences concluded when Barbarigo was sought again for a degree in theology for Elena that year. The petition was too late.

Gianbattista, Rinaldini and Rotondi had never abandoned the idea of an additional degree for Elena. She, however, was quite unwilling to receive any further honor, and she was becoming too ill to care. For a year she was inflicted with severe uterine pain, sometimes with tremors and violent convulsions, vomiting and fainting spells, according to biographer Benedetto Bacchini. On two occasions she nearly died. To revive her, physicians administered smelling salts and cordials, the meager medicines of the day, and they tried to alleviate some of her lingering health problems. Elena would sometimes rally, but only temporarily. Amidst her frequent illnesses, Gianbattista was often misled by the temporary phases when Elena appeared to be better. And she rarely complained when her condition worsened.

From a sickbed, Elena was asked to settle a civil suit involving a prolonged trial and much money. One litigant was educated and a public figure, the other poor, but with written proof of his rights. Lying down, Elena listened to lawyers for three to four hours at a time for six days and, in well-measured opinions, pronounced sentence in favor of the less advantaged man. Meeting the losing party later, she reminded him that there could be no favors or friendship from the bench. In a court of justice, she explained, "it is not a question of comparing people with people but reason with reason and right with right." The case was widely discussed, and the resulting public recognition increased requests for Elena's help, which further depleted her strength.

Gianbattista came very often to Padua then, and he tried unsuccessfully to keep from Elena any serious quarrels with relatives in Venice to spare her from concern. Zanetta was more aware, being there to witness her struggle. By this time, Gianbattista finally realized that his daughter had compromised her health with overdedication. The next spring, in 1684, both parents knew that Elena was dying.

13

THE HEROINE'S FUNERAL

'Tis folly to shrink in fear, if this is dying:
for death looked lovely in her lovely face.

FRANCESCO PETRARCA (PETRARCH) ON THE DEATH OF LAURA FROM THE PLAGUE, 1348

THE WINTER OF 1684 was known to have been an unusually severe one for northern Italy, with "ice on houses" and "floods in March" noted. It was recorded that many trees in the area were lost, and harsh storms damaged the Cornaro cypress, which was thirty-eight years old. By late spring the tree was dying.

During Lent of 1684, Elena's excessive self-disciplines of prolonged fasting and frequent bodily punishments accelerated her final illness, according to her physicians. By then she was confined to the Odeon Palace, refusing any speaking invitations and struggling to complete correspondence. Zanetta remained there, along with ample staff provided by her husband. Maddalena slept in Elena's room to assist her during the night. Two University of Padua professors of medicine were also in attendance. Accomplished physicians of their day, Drs. Giorgio Calafatti and Domenico Marchetti described Elena's condition as cachectic, a wasting state, characterized by extreme deterioration of the body and progressive loss of weight and strength as a result of many serious and prolonged illnesses. Subsequent to his longstanding care for Elena, Dr. Marchetti became the family physician for the Cornaros.

In spite of intense suffering, Elena seemed undisturbed at the thought of approaching death, which she had foretold on several occasions. When her first episode of hemorrhaging occurred, Elena prophesied, "I shall lead a short life. Blessed be God."

When she first began to be seriously ill, Elena's old friend, Fr. Oliva, had come to comfort her and attested to her courage and patience. Abbess Felice was a frequent caller and surely witnessed the great effort involved when Elena was carried to one of the hospices to visit people with whom she had worked over the years. Not far from the palace was a monastery, known for its strict poverty practices, the Romite of St. John the Baptist. It was a convent of Cloistered Nuns whose Abbess, Anna Maria Zanolli, Elena had befriended. When the abbess became ill with dropsy,* Elena, then seriously ailing herself, made sure that clothes and food were sent to her friend. She also provided special luxuries to further bolster the sick woman, usually depleting her own supplies.

Elena's visitors during her serious illness also included her university tutors. Elena wrote Fr. Boselli in Venice a lengthy final letter requesting his permission to discipline herself twice weekly again as long as she could. When she was no

* "Dropsy" is an old term for what is now called edema, abnormal accumulation of fluid in body tissues, cells or cavities, resulting in swelling.

longer able to attend church, Elena heard prayers through a little window opening to the palace chapel.

Despite being bedridden, Elena was not too preoccupied to turn her attention to social concerns. Incredibly, one of her final social deeds resulted from her distress over the Turkish invasion of Vienna, the important Christian center under siege from July to September of the previous year. Hungarian subjects of Roman Emperor Leopold I [1640-1705] were revolting, and they sought aid from Sultan Mahomet IV. After invading Hungary in March 1683, the Sultan assembled a powerful army to attack Vienna. Leopold and his brother-in-law Charles, the Duke of Lorraine, attempted to defend the city with Rudiger von Starhemberg who held fast until John Sobieski of Poland heroically rescued him with German and Polish reinforcements. By September 12, 1683, the Pole John Sobieski routed the Turks, a victory that meant the beginning of the end of Turkish domination in the Balkans. It also marked the vanquishing of the Ottomans as any serious future threat to Christian nations.

With his political motivation overruling reason, Gianbattista pressed his daughter to compose *elogi* (praises) to the victors of the siege. Elena truly was appalled by most of Europe's indifference to the Hungarian citizens' ordeal during the war and by stories of children being taken into slavery. Desiring to please her father, she managed to write a tribute to Sobieski for King John III of Poland. She also composed panegyrics for Pope Innocent XI and the defenders, Duke of Lorraine and King Leopold. Her father arranged for them to be printed and forwarded to each, and she was sent "flattering replies" in return. Sobieski wrote the ill young woman a touching thank-you note. And a letter from the Pope, dated May 6, 1684, congratulated her on defending Christianity, and offered the papal blessing. Elena received these two encouraging replies in June, one month before her death.

In the final critical weeks of her life, during an exceedingly hot summer, Elena selflessly displayed her deep concern for the house servants, her parents and others. She had often worried about her father's "unbridled pride," especially when he distributed pamphlets extolling her. One particular evening, Maddalena heard Elena moaning and sighing while she slept. The Lady Cornaro had dreamed that her revered father, bound by chains in an iron coach, was being dragged by four wild horses to a precipice. She awoke weeping. "This vision she took as a certain sign that some grave tribulation was to fall upon him," explained one biographer. The nightmare continued to haunt her.

Because of the increased domestic tasks involved in caring for her sickly daughter, Zanetta obtained an additional maid to help at the palace. The new maid's unfaithful husband, a gambler and alcoholic, had abused her and the maid confided her troubles to Elena. Advising her of the power of prayer, Elena reassured the distraught woman that her husband would reform. In recounting the story after Elena died, the grateful maid told about the complete change in her spouse. She firmly believed that it was Elena's intercession that had determined his quick recovery. "I see miracles," she exclaimed, "I see miracles!"

As the end of her life drew near, Elena saw visions of the Virgin Mary, several early biographers report. She begged to be allowed to die "in humility" on a bed of straw on the floor—just as the saints she so admired had done. Zanetta, often dissolving in tears and rarely leaving her daughter's side, refused Elena's desperate plea.

The dying Cornaro also urged that there be bequests from her father for all the palace servants. She called them to her bedside to personally thank each of them for their service and loyalty shown her. Of Maddalena, who remained nearby as her intimate friend, Elena requested that all of her remaining writings be burned. She also urged that the many crude instruments of penance, hidden beneath the prie-dieu in her chapel, be destroyed.

Despite his dying daughter's request to Maddalena, Gianbattista rescued what little had survived of Elena's writing. And, contrary to the Lady Cornaro's direction, a bereft Maddalena would later exhibit Elena's tools of torture—some of the chains and hair shirts—so that others could visualize her sacrifice.

Ever faithful to her chastity vow and her modesty in preparation for her burial, Elena gave instructions to Maddalena to clothe her scarred body in the monk's tunic, asking that it be sewn over her feet. "You must sew my habit at the feet in such a manner as that it may not get displaced."

Several weeks before her death, Elena's doctors discovered a malignant growth ("bubo") adhering between the shoulder blades and "soon rupturing into an incurable and lethal wound." With Gianbattista praying for his daughter's release and Zanetta crying hysterically nearby, Dr. Marchetti probed the area, incising the tumor. Zanetta was incredulous that her daughter could endure "such pain in silence." With her kidneys affected and her lungs diseased, this final affliction signaled what is now known as multiple system failure. Elena was almost continuously comatose for nearly two weeks and hallucinating with religious visions.

As she had requested, the thirty-eight-year-old Cornaro was given the last rites of the church. The rites were administered by a Benedictine monk, Pietro Paolo Calderoni of Ravenna who was, appropriately enough, a man of letters. In the presence of her family, the priest, and the two women closest to her, Maddalena and Abbess Felice, Elena died on Wednesday, July 26, 1684, at six o'clock in the evening.

Her body was treated with aromatics and she was robed by Fr. Calderoni as the Queen of Cyprus had been in monk's dress. Caterina's shroud was Franciscan; Elena's was a complete Benedictine habit: tunic, scapular and hood with the hem stitched together carefully by Maddalena, as her beloved Lady had urged. There were numerous reports that Elena's body remained uncorrupted.

Accompanied by *gendarmi* in full dress, Elena was carried the next day from the palace library to the Basilica of San Giustina so that the people of Padua could pay their final respects. As she had requested of her father, her wooden coffin was of cypress from the palace birthday tree.

The glorious city of Venice mourned the loss of their splendid maiden. A crystalline and roseate atmosphere that permeated Elena's island home during summer had dimmed as if in tribute. It rained and was quite windy for three straight days over northern Italy. The usually lively scene at St. Mark's Piazza became hushed, relieved occasionally by the tolling of bells. Clusters of town folk spontaneously gathered in the Square in front of scattered flower stalls. Ordinarily profuse with flowers at that time of year, they were now covered. Sellers had roped them with branches of laurel, just as the ancient Greeks symbolized their sorrow.

"The saint is dead." "The saint is dead!" The mournful cry could be heard echoing in elegiac cadence along arcaded buildings and narrow lanes. Boatmen caught and passed on the cry across the early stillness of the lagoon, calling to one another as on the evening Elena was born. When citizens came together in mourning to spread the news the next day, candles were being lighted throughout the Cornaro Piscopia Palace and purple bunting was suspended over its facade. It was a misty morning on the Grand Canal.

Normally so self-assured, Gianbattista was overcome with grief. Records reveal that he could barely function. But his wife Zanetta, with heightened courage and verve amidst her painful loss, quickly emerged to handle the funeral arrangements. Seeking clergymen's help, she issued invitations to the entire college of doctors and philosophers at the university, who accepted by acclamation. She also enlisted city officials, both in Venice and Padua. The funeral service was scheduled at San Giustina for Friday, July 28. Befitting a Cornaro event, the commemoration was of royal dimensions.

On the day of the funeral, all the shops along the busy Merceria and the Rialto were shuttered in honor of Venice's distinguished daughter. Padua, too, joined in the mourning, suspending all affairs. Reminiscent of the crowded cathedral scene six years earlier at her dissertation, hundreds of people converged on the city, gathering in the streets leading from the palace to San Giustina. Over a monk's black habit, Elena's body was garbed in the ermine mozzetta cape, representing her doctorate. Her head was crowned with two wreaths: one twined with the poet's dark green laurel, the other of virginal white lilies.

Robed and stoled in full academic regalia and carrying candles, thirty-six university professors marched with the funeral procession that morning. The four flanking her coffin were Count Alessandro Boremeo, Dr. Calafatti, and two philosophy professors, Giacomo Bonzanino and Giovanni Cigala.

As a tribute to Elena, her portraits were added to the walls in the Academy Hall of the Barnabite fathers in Rome. In 1684, The hall was the site of a lavish memorial service for Lady Cornaro, hosted by fellow scholars of the Infecondi who called her "The Inalterable." The Pillars of the hall were also ornamented in purple and gold, with gems, coats of arms, and mythological and religious sculptures.

(Le Pompe funebri. Padua, 1686. Special Collections, Vassar College Libraries)

As everyone watched in respectful silence, the numerous dignitaries that had come from Venice were joined by members of various religious orders and associations. They were met by the abbot and the entire body of monks from San Giustina, attired in black. The long line of mourners came to the cathedral to pay homage at Elena's bier, which was placed in the middle and surrounded by hundreds of lights. Upon the bier were placed open books representing the various languages and sciences in which she had excelled. It was a scholar's honor once bestowed on the great Venetian publisher, Aldus Manutius, whose "first major publishing venture" featured Aristotle.

There was music during the service and a eulogy praising Elena. Composed by Fr. Francesco Caro Somasco, the eulogy was delivered in Latin by a young nobleman, twenty-seven-year-old Campolongo dei Campolonghi, who represented the University of Padua.

In keeping with the seventeenth-century sense of ritual, other universities and academies held elaborate memorials in the ensuing days. The cities of Padua, Siena and Rome joined in the tributes. In one of the first memorials, Count Alessandro de Lazzara, President of the Academy of the Ricovrati in Padua, gave a laudatory speech, followed by Carla Gabriella Patin, the physician's daughter whom Gianbattista had earlier tried to defame.

In Rome, solemn rites were held by the Infecondi at Academy Hall in the College of the Barnabite Fathers at St. Charles de Catinari. Elena had been one of the literary academy's outstanding members, and the ceremony it sponsored for her was a highly ornate affair, similar to state funerals of American heroes today.

"It was more like a triumph than a mourning," noted one observer of the affair in Rome. The program for the service was printed in many languages. With an escort unit of the pope's Swiss Guards welcoming arriving carriages, guests entered the college hall that had been transformed for the occasion by lavish decorations. Jasper columns were wound with golden foliage, and velvet hangings adorned with cherubs framed seascapes and landscapes that illustrated Elena's life story. Walls were covered with silk and fringed purple damask and sprinkled with precious gems.

"O passerby, look at the exuberant manifestations of Elena Lucrezia Cornaro Piscopia," began the epitaph beneath her sculpture, centered in a prominent place at the end wall. It was supported by a green marble base festooned with laurel that had been richly overlaid in gold. Muses crowned by stars and gilded, reclining lions were symbolically displayed around her statue. The memorial was directed by Michele Brugueres. Guests attending were the academy's patron Felice Cardinal Rospigliosi, and Pietro Cardinal Ottoboni, who would become Pope Alexander VIII five years later. Among the other mourners were the Bishop of Acquapendent and the auditor of the Spanish nuncio, Giovanni Febei, together with many prelates of the Roman curia.

A Venetian nobleman who knew Elena personally, Fr. Tommaso Farsetti, gave the funeral oration. "She appeared to be a girl genius," he said, and "posterity would have a difficult time believing there existed a young maiden endowed with such splendid qualities to exceed any man and become almost inimitable." An illustrated text of the Infecondi funeral, *Le Pompe funebri,* in a rare book edition of 1686 was purchased in London and given to Vassar College by the Class of 1912. It is now housed in Special Collections at the college library.

Even in her death, conflict surrounded Elena. A severe family controversy, involving the clergy, arose over choosing the most appropriate site for Elena's burial, planned for Saturday, July 29, 1684.

For his daughter's final resting place, Gianbattista sought St. Anthony's Basilica—where he was a benefactor of the Conventual Friars in charge, and where another Caterina Cornaro, who had died a decade earlier, was elaborately enshrined. (Her tomb can be seen today.) But the parish priest of the Church of St. Lawrence in Padua claimed his place suitable because Elena had been a parishioner.

Meanwhile, a feisty and fuming Zanetta, wanting the site to be the family vault in San Luca parish church in Venice, protested loudly against Elena's unprecedented personal wish to be entombed with the Benedictine abbots and monks in the mortuary of St. Luke's Chapel in San Giustina. "My daughter wanted no men in her life," she snarled, "and she is not going to be buried with them in death!" In the end, "Zanetta was silenced," and all three conflicting requests among the living were overruled in favor of Elena's.

Cassinensi monks of San Giustina were asked to prepare Elena's burial place in St. Luke's Chapel and to engrave the flat, plain, black marble tombstone. The inscription was composed by Vice Prior Tessari, Interpreter of Sacred Writ at Padua. He was the monk who had proposed the unanimous decision granting her degree at graduation.

St. Luke's was a small, fourteenth-century chapel that was built between 1301-1316 in San Giustina's east-west axis, near its bell tower. Having once housed the body of St. Luke, the chapel was a place of special reverence. Artist Giovanni Storlato had created the chapel's wall and ceiling frescoes in 1436, depicting the life of the gospel writer. Twenty years later,

San Giustina Basilica is the Benedictine abbey church named for the patron saint of Padua and Venice. Elena Cornaro is buried here in the former St. Luke's Chapel of the fourteenth century. This is the monks' mortuary, now called *Cappella Cornaro.* Restoration of the grave site was a gift of American women in 1978.

(Itinerario D'Italia Di Francesco Scoto. Padua, 1659. Special Collections, Vassar College Libraries)

Andrea Mantegna painted the chapel's panels and an altarpiece featuring the evangelist with other saints. When St. Luke's body was moved to the new basilica in 1562, the chapel became a monks' mortuary. Plague struck Padua two hundred years later, and its interior was covered with lime, destroying most of the panels and frescoes. Archaeologists eventually searched for additional Storlato frescoes, and the Mantegna altarpiece was later moved to Milan.

Surrounded by the solitude of this historic, remote chapel where she worshiped and adored her God, Lady Elena was laid to rest near the altar—in the sanctified ground that she desired, among the Benedictines she considered her brothers.

Following the funeral Mass of the previous day, a priest accompanying Cardinal Barbarigo, musing aloud, wondered who had ever given permission for a woman to be buried in the sacred male mortuary. Almost offhandedly the cardinal replied, "Sono stato io" ("It was I").

14

HER ENDURING LEGACY

Life, like a dome of many-coloured glass,
Stains the white radiance of eternity....

"ADONAIS," AN ELEGY ON THE DEATH OF JOHN KEATS, WHO DIED IN ROME OF CONSUMPTION AT TWENTY-FIVE.
PERCY BYSSHE SHELLEY, 1821

AFTERNOON SUN ILLUMINATED faces of figures, resplendent amid a panoply of colors in the stained-glass window at Vassar College. Standing at its base was a woman of great dignity, Ruth Crawford Mitchell. She was beaming. For her it had been a long journey. Now in her eighties, she had been a history student at Vassar six decades earlier, inspired to know the subjects of this artistic rendering. She savored telling the story of how the renaissance of its central figure, Elena Lucrezia Cornaro Piscopia, became her mission. As she spoke on this spring afternoon in 1978, the three-hundred-year-old legacy of the noble Venetian rose again from oblivion.

Ruth Mitchell was heralding people gathered from near and far—from Poughkeepsie, Pittsburgh, New York and Washington, D.C., and from Madison, Wisconsin and Berkeley,

Of the various areas of learning pursued by the scholarly Elena *(center panel)*, the two that were of particular interest to her were Philosophy *(left)* and Theology. Stained-glass panels are from the Vassar Library Window.

Inspired by the "Cornaro Window" at Vassar, Ruth Crawford Mitchell *(right)*, played a key role in the restoration of Elena's legacy in the twentieth century.

(Window photographs by Charles Porter; photograph of Ruth Mitchell by Herbert K. Barnett)

California—to celebrate the tercentenary of Lady Cornaro's achievement as the first woman in the world to receive a university degree. International gatherings of dignitaries from academic, religious and civic organizations were also being held in London, Vienna, Glasgow, and in Padua at the university that originally honored her. Because of the persistent efforts of this octogenarian American woman, Elena's story was alive. And no one celebrated that fact more delightedly than Ruth Crawford Mitchell.

Not since the years immediately following the Lady Cornaro's death had her legacy been so honored. Nine months after Elena's passing, on April 29, 1685, Gianbattista had invited a group of literati to the palace in Venice so that he, once again, could display his lost daughter's talents. The Benedictine Jean Mabillon was among the men of letters attending, and he wrote about it in *Museum italicum.* One of its chapters ("Iter Italicum") summarized Elena's life and accomplishments, and Mabillon sent a complimentary copy to biographer Bacchini. Among other items, including books, her diploma and sacred relics, Gianbattista had collected what was salvaged from her writing, the highlight of which was a personal *Ode al Crocifisso* ("Ode to Christ Crucified") [1680]. In her firm and persistent wish for obscurity, Elena had destroyed her most important correspondence with major figures. Her father showed guests all that remained.

Elena wrote three *elogi* in honor of Cardinal d'Estrées, Silvestro Valier (Procurator of St. Mark) and Angelo Sumachi, a Greek nobleman. The most notable surviving work was her aforementioned translation from Spanish of Lanspergio's *Colloquy of Christ.* In 1688, the University of Padua posthumously issued a small edition of her letters, sonnets, poems and eulogies written in various languages.

As it was the cherished custom in elite families to publish, Gianbattista encouraged any efforts to see his daughter's work in print. He and Zanetta also commissioned posthumous portraits of Elena, as well as ornate memorial stones. One of the stones was carved to go above a picture in the Cornaro Piscopia Palace in Venice; two were rendered for Padua. All three stones have since been lost.

Fifteen days after Elena's death, Gianbattista began what would be a five-year endeavor—as a last gesture of patriarchal pride—to erect a lavish and very expensive monument to Elena in the Basilica of St. Anthony, where thousands of faithful pilgrims have journeyed over the centuries. The location was suggested by the monks at San Giustina, who declined to have such a grandiose memorial in their church. The mausoleum was designed by Bernardo Tabacco of Bassano, a prominent sculptor from Rome who was educated in the Eternal City and greatly influenced by the Baroque architect, Francesco Borromini.

Biographer Massimiliano Deza visited the monument shortly after its completion. In his life of the Cornaro, Deza described the huge structure as "extending from a side pilaster almost to the very middle of the central nave," decorated with allegorical figures of Charity, Death, Faith and Purity, and sculptures of Aristotle, Plato, Democritus, Seneca and Timon. Centered above was a full-size, white marble statue of Elena in ermine mozzetta, entitled "Magistra et Doctrix." The monument commission, the biographer noted, cost over one million ducats.

There were many posthumous tributes to Elena in the form of essays, sonnets, national encomia, and eulogies from societies and dignitaries in France, Germany, Poland and Swit-

THIS LIFE-SIZE STATUE OF ELENA WAS CARVED IN WHITE CARRARA MARBLE FROM TUSCANY. IT IS NOW AT THE FOOT OF THE COURTYARD GALLERY AT THE "CORNARO STAIRWAY" NEAR THE ENTRANCE OF "THE BO," THE UNIVERSITY OF PADUA CLASSROOM BUILDING. THE STATUE WAS COMMISSIONED BY ELENA'S FATHER TO CROWN A HUGE TOMB IN ST. ANTHONY'S. IT WAS DONATED TO THE UNIVERSITY BY A WEALTHY COUNTESS IN THE EIGHTEENTH CENTURY.

(Sculpted by Bernardo Tabacco of Bassano in 1686. University of Padua, Italy)

zerland. Articles in religious and biographical references kept her name known for a time.

Elena's ability to foretell things was widely discussed, and there were numerous testimonies to the public's admiration for her. Several accounts chronicled efforts initiating canonization of Elena, in the hopes that she would be officially declared a saint of the Church. No documents have been found supporting the movements, and the efforts ceased with the deaths of Gianbattista in 1692 and Cardinal Barbarigo in 1697.

In the wake of his daughter's absence, Gianbattista dedicated the rest of his life almost exclusively to beneficent civic duty. A year after she died, he became a patron of two academies, the Delfici of Venice and the Ricovrati in Padua, where his daughter had been known as "The Humble One."

Zanetta, whom Gianbattista described as often "suffering from gout," was his heiress. "The lady procuress," he had written in his will of August 5, 1690, "being a woman of value which is known to everyone... I ask my children and heirs to love her."

Master politician and publicist that he was, Gianbattista left funds for his survivors to preserve the Grand Canal palace and, particularly, its chivalric decoration. Yet he also included in his final papers a clause requesting that he be buried *senza pompa* (without pomp) in the family's parish church. Zanetta died five years after her husband, at the age of 81. Elena's companion, Maddalena, continued to reside at the palaces for seven more years after Elena died. The dear friend and instructor of Elena stayed with the Cornaros for a total of twenty-seven years.

Of others surrounding Elena in her lifetime, the revered Abbot Codanini, who had initiated her devotion to the Benedictine Order, was placed in charge of the Monastery of St.

Faustinus at Brescia. He died in 1685, the year following the death of his close young friend. The beloved Rabbi Abbroff died in the summer of 1694 and was buried in the ancient Jewish cemetery at Lido. At his request, his body was later moved to the Holy Land. His son, Jacob, who became Rabbi of Venice, published his father's most famous writing, *The Word of Samuel,* in 1702. The Cornaro family confessor Boselli died three years after Elena.

Among Elena's sponsors, Rinaldini remained at Padua and died in 1699 at the age of eighty-four; Rotondi, who headed the Academy of the Ricovrati, died in 1702 and was buried at Il Santo in Padua. His grave is preserved there today. Carlo Vota was sent to Vienna and Moscow as Pope Innocent XI's emissary the year Elena died, and then to Warsaw until 1710. He died in Rome in 1715.

The influence of Cardinal Barbarigo—who played a pivotal role in Elena's doctoral pursuits—continued to be both immediate and far reaching, extending into the present century. In 1690 he wrote *Regulae Studorium* and modernized the curriculum of the Paduan Seminary he refounded there, and enlisted highly competent teachers to instruct the seminarians. The Seminary's innovative printing press contained lead types in Latin, Greek, Hebrew, Syriac, Persian and Slavonic languages, producing information for Christians in Moslem countries. Barbarigo participated in five papal conclaves and was a candidate for the papacy in three (most prominently in 1691). He generously aided leaders of the Eastern Orthodox faith, and it was said upon his widely mourned death in 1697 that their reunification with Rome lost a key proponent.

The cardinal's guidance was evident in two younger Barbarigos who also became outstanding cardinals: his nephew Giovanni Francesco and a distant relative, Marc

Antonio. The nephew served as ambassador to the court of Louis XIV of France and became a learned Bishop of Padua. He gained distinction there for his charitable work, his publishing, and his promotion of education. Marc Antonio accompanied Gregorio Barbarigo to Rome for the conclave electing Pope Innocent XI, and the younger Barbarigo remained there, eventually going to the sees of Corfu, Montefiascore (1678) and Corneta (1687). Another Barbarigo who was a much admired advocate of education, Marc Antonio founded an institute for the care and training of underprivileged girls: the *Scuole e Maestre Pie* in Montefiascore. And the elderly Cardinal Barbarigo, whose life had so dramatically intertwined with the Cornaros, was buried in the Cathedral of Padua, *Il Duomo,* where Elena had prevailed with his eventual blessing nearly twenty years earlier.

In the twentieth century, nobleman Gregorio Cardinal Barbarigo was the model figure during seminary days of Angelo Roncalli, who later became the universally admired and heroic Pope John XXIII. The seminary which Roncalli attended in Bergamo was founded by Carlo Borromeo, Archbishop of Milan. Roncalli, a humane and pastoral man from a simple, sheltered background, was elected to the papacy in 1958, at the age of seventy-seven. Within five years he had improved international relations with Soviet Russia with his encyclical *Pacem in Terris* (*Peace on Earth)* [1963], and he summoned the Second Vatican Council, resulting in church liturgical reform and a sweeping ecumenical movement that resounded around the world. Forty years later, another pope, John Paul II—who has energetically continued Roncalli's ecumenical efforts—recently praised the very type of scholarship which Lady Elena had pursued.

"Study is a precious gift," explained Pope John Paul II to a group of university students in Rome, "especially deep and systematic study. So as to bear fruit for the benefit of the person and their brothers and sisters who have [this gift], it must be enriched by charity, without which it is useless to possess all knowledge." To the aspiring scholars gathered with him in the Eternal City in 1998, the seventy-eight-year-old pontiff offered a description which thoroughly fit Elena Cornaro. And the Venetian prodigy would have undoubtedly applauded his further comments to the students.

"Charity," the philosopher-pope noted, "is accompanied by simplicity of heart. ...This does not consist in the superficiality of life and thought, neither in the denial of the real problem of reality, but in knowing how to discover the nucleus of all questions and in knowing how to redirect it to its essential meaning and its relationship with the ensemble. Simplicity is wisdom." Pope John Paul II concluded his comments by expressing the hope that the ecclesiastical university students gathered with him would "mature in the knowledge of the truth, which is the vocation and destiny of all people." It is a vocation and destiny that the Lady Cornaro had lived remarkably well throughout her brief life three centuries earlier.

And what of this young noblewoman whose life direction had been so affected by decisions of an earlier church leader, Cardinal Barbarigo? According to twentieth-century historian Paul Kristeller, Elena Cornaro "set a precedent of great significance in the history of women scholars." With her impressive scholarship and vast erudition, she helped enlighten and refine a European culture that was vehemently opposed to the advanced education of women.

Mastering most of the available and significant ancient and contemporary resources, Elena Lucrezia Cornaro Piscopia was the first female to surmount all barriers to the highest academic achievement. While there were other women of letters in Venice and Padua during the fifteenth, sixteenth and seventeenth centuries, no woman had reached the breadth of her scholarship and knowledge. In fact, Italians today refer to a woman with scholastic superiority by exclaiming: *"È una Piscopia!"* ("She is a Piscopia!").

A Renaissance woman in learning with a medieval spirit, living in the baroque era, Elena could function in an opulent seventeenth-century Venetian court, be active with convents, remain at home and yet thrive in the intellectual environment of the University of Padua! Being born in a multicultural Republic with wealth and the legacy of power necessary to course uncharted and forbidden ways, Elena had been further endowed with a mind that Bacchini described as "adept at everything, penetrating, versatile, quick." Her love and loyalty to her family and an abiding community awareness thrust her, albeit unwillingly, into public view. Studying Elena's life three centuries later, Vassar librarian Joan Murphy observed, "One marvels at the eclecticism of the woman, the range and variety of her scholarly world."

Addressing a gathering of scholars in Padua for tercentenary celebrations of Elena's graduation, Dr. Patricia Labalme provided context for the life of the seventeenth-century prodigy. "It was her sense of belonging to the great clan of the Cornaro which defined her commitment," noted Labalme. "It was her position as a woman which gave that commitment its particular shape."

Despite early documents replete with florid phrases and adulatory praise characteristic of much baroque writing (e.g. "Her intelligence was full of life, celestial life; her heart was full of fire, divine fire"), the enormous range of Elena's scholarship was not exaggerated. Of her membership in seven of the most important European academies, University of Padua authorities attested:

> [A]s such she was part of, and at times presided over, profound but brilliant debates, primarily on scientific, philosophical and theological subjects. At her homes in Padua and Venice she frequently met with famous scholars and other people of renown who gathered there to discourse on recondite and abstruse problems.

Directed by learned and powerful men, Elena's accomplishments were truly her own. And the remarkable legacy of her life begs a question: were her academic accomplishments actually a result of extreme paternal pressure to purge the tarnish from a celebrated name, or were they due to her natural superior abilities and love of learning? Both interpretations are valid, concluded twentieth-century Benedictine scholar Fr. Ludovico Maschietto.

During Elena's era, there was little achievement allowed women outside the circles of family and religious endeavors. As in medieval times, the two primary paths for a woman of seventeenth-century Europe to follow were being a good wife or serving as a nun. Despite being endowed with astounding intellectual ability, Elena was restricted by personal and public demands in an age tempered by its prescribed limits for women.

Elena's study covered both conflicting paganism of Greek and Roman eras, as well as medieval Christianity. In spiritual matters, according to Deza, she had considerable understanding of divine wisdom. She could converse eloquently on the efficacy of grace, freedom of will, the knowledge of church fathers, the mystery of the Holy Trinity and the essence of God.

Clergymen and nuns from a remarkable panoply of monastic orders, as well as a rabbi, a musician, and an English advisor, helped shape both her intellectual and spiritual development. During her life, Elena derived the most satisfaction from listening to religious leaders. The Jesuits, the Franciscans and Capuchines, the Dominicans and Augustinians, and especially the Benedictines, were of profound influence and a major source of enlightenment for Lady Cornaro. She was familiar with both traditional and contemporary forms of worship, preferring the former. Elena held an orthodox point of view in a humanistic time which followed the blind faith prevalent in the Middle Ages. And she faithfully followed her Benedictine vows of poverty, chastity and obedience.

Deliberately reclusive by imposing her own strict enclosure, Elena sought to be treated as a poor person. "Few saints of our times," wrote Abbess Pynsent, "could unite learning and holiness to so eminent a degree." Following the saints' example of Christian virtues, sometimes in a hostile secular setting, Elena attempted to live in cloistral seclusion. Hers was a gentle voice in a boisterous period.

Along with great gifts—"the royalty of intellect" for one—this self-transcendent noblewoman lived with great burdens. There were the demands of a nakedly ambitious father who, current interpreters suggest, exploited her talent, seeing it as a distinct political advantage and a boost to his own pride.

Gianbattista unashamedly drove Elena to succeed! Having a socially unacceptable marriage himself, the father resolved to surpass all illustrious Cornaro tradition and have a daughter who would excel in unparalled fashion. Elena was frail and yet she was not discouraged in considering the robust requirements of convent living. Her piety and great sensitivity to others were ingrained, but she endured dashed hopes of being allowed to be a nun. The devout maiden seemed often obsessed with her own worthlessness and was continually going to confession. Elena sought to please but, in spite of her father, wished no honor. Becoming quite renowned at a very young age, she was constantly surrounded by adoring crowds and did violence to herself to overcome the intrusion of celebrity. Her beauty and her scholarship served the state, as well as the Cornaros. Most tragically, she was subjected to intense suffering, and her life ended far too soon.

"From her face she would spread grace with the demeanor of a queen, full of majesty, nobility, gentleness and devotion," we learn from biographer Deza, and Fr. Maschietto concurred. "Royal stature, surely," explained Deza, but she preferred to walk the common way, trying to pass through life unobserved. With deep gratitude, Elena considered any ability she possessed to be small and simply a gift from God.

One day in Venice, a celebrated Dominican priest preached about Elena at the Church of Ss. Peter and Paul before his large congregation. During his sermon, the pastor praised her, extolling her marvelous accomplishments. Unfortunately for her, the Lady Cornaro was present at the Mass and felt overwhelmed with shock at this public recognition. Fleeing in embarrassment, she never attended his services again.

With a glittering heritage to uphold, Elena's defiance of lavish living and her lifelong chastity were considered by her contemporaries to be sanctified behavior "to rid herself of a restrictive stereotype." Hers was a dual heroism. Nearly worshiped by some Venetians for her scholarship, this young Mother Teresa-like figure was also greatly admired by fellow citizens for her spiritual virtues. Elena's deep compassion and

IL SANTO, THE BASILICA OF ST. ANTHONY IN PADUA, IS WHERE ELENA'S FATHER HOPED TO HAVE HIS DAUGHTER BURIED. IN THIS PILGRIMAGE CHURCH, HE ERECTED A MONUMENTAL TOMB IN THE NAVE, BUT IT WAS NEVER OCCUPIED.

(Itinerario d'Italia Di Francesco Scoto. Padua, 1659.
Special Collections, Vassar College Libraries.
Photograph by Charles Porter)

humility were as highly esteemed as her unprecedented academic achievements.

Stories circulated about the "miracles" involving the Lady Cornaro, and there were several willing witnesses. It was also well known that she salvaged one priest from scandalous living.

Motivated by social commitment and her illustrious name, the Lady Cornaro, by correspondence, sought welfare reforms through the church, petitioning the Vatican, approaching state officials, and enlisting her father's help. "... An exceptional woman," remarked Dr. Labalme, "she was also a thoroughly Venetian exceptional woman."

Elena's triumph can be perceived in a rare and noble life of beneficence and achievement that graced the nations of Europe and was to enrich ours in the twentieth and twenty-first centuries. Her courage transcended centuries. The accompanying tragedy is that she would surely have been a more enduring force of classical genius and sacred inspiration had she not died prematurely.

Would this very human and complex person have held a wider role had she lived longer? Would she have been allowed to achieve her full potential as a scholar, philosopher, teacher, jurist, writer, linguist, arbitrator or leader in other public service? Less easy to foresee is the awareness of her genius by future generations. Will they know of this important figure, so emblematic for the educational, historical and women's studies spheres? Will they recognize her great gift to women and to all of humanity? Will her life, again, be considered for sainthood? What would Elena say to us today?

Epilogue

HONOR, OBSCURITY and REVIVAL

. . . ad perpetuam rei memoriam (. . . may render her memory ever living in future ages).

University of Padua announcing
the coining of a medal to honor
Elena Lucrezia Cornaro Piscopia
January 11, 1685

For the first time in the university's history, the Prior and Bench of the Sacred College of Philosophers and Physicians at Padua ordered a bronze medal struck in tribute to a woman laureate. The unique medal was produced six months after Elena's death, and marked an extraordinary moment in the school's history. Never before had such a tribute been awarded to a woman. And for more than three centuries, it has remained a singular honor at the esteemed University of Padua.

After awarding Elena a degree in 1678, the University of Padua was widely praised throughout Europe. Perpetuating her memory seemed only appropriate following her death a mere six years later.

There was keen interest among the nobility of the seventeenth century in metal work. Portrait medals were a popular Petrarchian expression, enthusiastically regarded as a durable and proper reward for personal accomplishment, especially in Italian courts, termed "The Currency of Fame." The tradition carried over from the early Renaissance with the influence of the Veronese painter and medalist Antonio Pisanello (Pisano, 1395-1455), considered the master sculptor in this medium. The talented Pisanello also collaborated with Gentile da Fabriano on frescoes for the Ducal Palace in Venice (1415-1422).

Gianbattista suggested that Padua's commemorative medal for his daughter be executed by Francesco Neidinger, whom he commissioned to mint a special gold version for the university. On the obverse was an effigy of Elena, in mozzetta cape and a crown of laurel *(see previous page)*. The reverse was impressed with a seascape, showing clouds parted above rain showers, falling on waves that held an open shell in the act of receiving celestial grace *(right)*.

All elements symbolized the laureate's gifts of learning and piety coming from heaven to earth and returning to God. *"Non Sine Foenore"* ("Not Without Reward") was imprinted on the perimeter. An original of the portrait medal honoring Elena is now in Padua at the *Museo Bottacin*, annexed to the

Civico Museo. The medal appeared in many publications; three hundred years later, it was minted again for a cadre of international celebrants honoring the Lady Cornaro.

Three years after striking the original medal, the University of Padua published the remaining collection of Elena's writings. It was a small volume that included an introduction of her life by Benedetto Bacchini in Latin. Elena's works preserved in the publication—in Latin, Greek and Italian—were academy discourses on the Republic, political problems and resolutions, the tributes to Cardinal Estrées, the Kings of Poland and Hungary, Emperor Leopold and the Duke of Lorraine. Featured, too, were epistles written to Pope Innocent XI, Cardinal Bouillon and General of the Jesuits, Paolo Oliva. There were also printed epigrams concerning Christ, the spirit, humility, obedience, language and the family. This sampling of her literary papers, "all harmonious and original," reveal Elena's characteristic charm and idealism.

The massive *Il Santo* mausoleum that Gianbattista had built between 1684 and 1689 for his daughter was never occupied; because of its size, the huge structure actually obstructed the view of the high altar. With the approval of Elena's brother, Girolamo Baldassare, and at the urging of St. Anthony's, the mausoleum was dismantled forty years later. Girolamo then had it replaced with a portrait bust of his famed sister, positioned in a niche high in the central nave above the site of the sarcophagus. The handsome marble sculpture of Elena, depicting her with hair curled and a jeweled cross around her neck, was rendered by Giovanni Bonazza in 1727 and remains there today.

Of the surviving Cornaro Piscopias, Elena's younger brother and sister had no children. Francesco died in 1690 and

SCULPTED BY GIOVANNI BONAZZA (1695-1730), THIS CLASSICAL MARBLE BUST SHOWS A MATURE ELENA WITH CURLED HAIR AND A JEWELED CROSS. THE BUST WAS PERMANENTLY PLACED IN THE NAVE OF ST. ANTHONY'S BASILICA ON A HIGH NICHE OVER THE SITE OF THE SARCOPHAGUS BY HER YOUNGER BROTHER GIROLAMO AFTER THE TOMB WAS DISMANTLED IN 1727.

(Biblioteca Civica, Padua)

Caterina Isabetta (also recognized for her language ability and charity) died in 1707. Her brother Girolamo had two daughters, both named in honor of his famous sister: Elena, who married Sebastiano Foscari in 1702, and Lucrezia, wed to Giovanni Loredan in 1703. The family's Venetian palace became the "Loredan Palace" when it was left to Lucrezia, and the Codevigo mansion was renamed "Foscari Palace." Girolamo died in 1734, marking the end of the Cornaro Piscopia line.

The year 1761 brought to prominence one of Elena's key advocates. On July 16, the Catholic Church celebrated the beatification of Gregorio Cardinal Barbarigo by Pope Clemente XIII. This sacred church honor, preceding sainthood, entitled him to public veneration. Barbarigo had earned universal admiration for his unification efforts with the Eastern Church, his interest in education, and his great pastoral charity.

A decade later—a century after Elena had received her degree—a wealthy Venetian countess, Lady Caterina Delphina, paid tribute to Elena. She donated to the University of Padua the life-size statue of Elena that surmounted the disassembled catafalque in St. Anthony's. It was later revealed that this act of generosity was undertaken by Lady Caterina in an effort to overcome her own reputation for licentious living. Ironically enough, it was a fallen countess that had paid tribute to a symbol of purity!

Originally commissioned by Gianbattista in 1686, the statue had been sculpted by Bernardo Tabacco of Bassano. It was an elegant, classical goddess rendition in Carrara marble, portraying the university's laureate in ermine mozzetta.

Donor Countess Delphina was the wife of Andrea Troni. It was this second marriage to a much older, very wealthy and ranking nobleman that entitled her to preside over Venetian society in her celebrated salon at San Giuliano. Her husband's titled position as Procurator of St. Mark and "Knight of the Equestrian Order" was carefully inscribed at the base of the statue—no doubt to be admired by the literati whom the clever countess collected. Under Elena's name was the epitaph, *"Unico Exemplo"* ("Without Precedent"), a phrase to be used on Vassar College's window 130 years later.

The Countess's gift can be seen today in the university's "Il Bo," at the foot of the Cornaro stairway leading to the second floor gallery. Hundreds of students swarm by it daily, most not aware of Elena's legacy.

Following the acquisition of Cyprus through Queen Caterina Cornaro in 1488, which marked the peak of Venetian power through its maritime possessions, the Republic's political and economic influence gradually declined over many years. The Republic came to an end with the French Revolution. And by the close of the eighteenth century, the legacy of Elena was thoroughly forgotten.

The French Emperor Napoleon Bonaparte, who had been born of Italian parents in Ajaccio, Corsica, invaded Italy at this time, conquered it and made himself "Master of Venice." There he transferred the old Library of St. Mark to the Ducal Palace in 1812. Entering Rome, his forces sacked the pontifical palace and sold many volumes of the Vatican Library. Exiling monastic orders and looting churches, Napoleon held the elderly Pope Pius VII a captive at Fontainebleau in 1813. With its monks dispersed, San Giustina Basilica in Padua was taken over by the state for military purposes. The basilica lost its Benedictine artifacts after the last abbot had escaped to Avignon during the French invasion. By 1816 sacred books in the basilica's collection had been sent to libraries in Venice,

Padua and the state archives. St. Luke's Chapel deteriorated and the Lady Cornaro's grave site disappeared.

Napoleon met his Waterloo and died in exile. In 1866 when the Prussians defeated Austria, Venice was incorporated into ancient lands of "Italia," forming the United Italy. The Cornaro Piscopia Palace, then called the Loredan Palace and connected by an overpass to the Farsetti Palace next door, was taken over by the Municipal Meeting and designated its current title, *Municipio* (City Hall), in 1867.

A great pioneering venture began in America at this time that would bring the Cornaro legacy to the New World. In the Hudson River town of Poughkeepsie, New York, Matthew Vassar had become a wealthy man through his brewery manufacturing. In 1861 he founded the women's college that carries his name, explaining, "It occurred to me, that woman, having received from her Creator the same intellectual constitution as man, has the same right as man to intellectual culture and development." On February 26, his Board of Trustees was presented with a small tin box (and the key) containing deeds and securities that totaled $408,000, "one half of his entire estate." Vassar Female College became Vassar College by decree February 1, 1867. One of the college's early trustees was Frederick Ferris Thompson, the wealthy son of a founder of the Chase Bank. Frederick served as a Vassar trustee from 1885 to 1899.

On both sides of the Atlantic, the "long period of silence" in Elena's story was broken at the turn of the twentieth century. In Europe, the breaking of the silence began in Rome in 1895. Italy had become a popular resort for the British, and a Benedictine monastery for English nuns was established in Rome under the supervision of Abbess Mathilde Pynsent. Educated at St. Scholastica's Convent in Teignmouth, Devonshire, England, Abbess Pynsent was keenly interested in seventeenth- and eighteenth-century Italian writers. She became particularly intrigued by documents about the Benedictine oblate, Elena Cornaro, including graduation and funeral records and a diploma. The abbess located the Cornaro documents in various places in Padua and Venice, including the archives of the Paduan bishop, the University of Padua, the *Civico Museo,* and San Giorgio Maggiore and the Library of St. Mark's in Venice.

With the permission of Pope Leo XIII, Abbess Pynsent went to San Giustina to verify the existence of the burial site of the first woman laureate. She and two other nuns found their way to St. Luke's Chapel, called the Chapel of the Confraternity of the Blessed Sacrament, open only during monks' funerals. By the Sunday evening of September 8, 1895, the sisters had located Elena's grave on the Epistle side near the altar. They were barely able to decipher the few remaining words on the cracked, black marble marker.

Red-robed priests, assembled there for a basilica procession, held torches and tapers to assist with light. The abbess described in a private letter the colorful scene accompanied by great excitement, when the grave was found, as eight tower bells rang to signal the start of the procession. Seeking the priest in charge, Abbess Pynsent offered to replace the grave's broken stone. She also approached the bishop's representative, who supervised sacred relics, to confirm the burial site.

With the consent of the Vicar General and an official committee present—including the rectors of the Scots College in Rome and the University of Padua, as well as authorities from San Giorgio Maggiore in Venice and from the city of Padua—the tomb was opened on Wednesday, September 11. Those present saw in the old cypress coffin the thick black cowl, the habit of the monks of Subiaco which Elena had requested. Its plaits and even the threads where it was stitched together over the hem by Maddalena were nearly perfectly preserved. Measurements found Elena to have been five feet, 1-1/4 inches in height. Leaves of the laurel wreath that had been placed on her brow two centuries earlier "were quite soft and almost fresh." Roses had been scattered there, evidenced by a small branch with thorns still intact.

An engineer named Brillo measured and recorded the size of the entire grave. After the new coffin was closed, a large wreath of laurel and lilies, in which a florist had intertwined oak leaves and acorns, was placed on the cover. Abbess Pynsent's special gift was a replica of the original marble marker.

At the last minute, Fr. Marino Frattin, a priest from San Giorgio Maggiore (where Elena had become an oblate), arrived unexpectedly. He offered the absolution, praying for the forgiveness of sins. Those attending signed their names on the lid of the coffin: Abbess Pynsent and another nun, Mother Maurus Watson; James Austin Campbell, rector of the Scots College in Rome, and Carlo Ferraris, rector at the University of Padua; a parish priest, Domenico Puller; from the city, Gaetano Varda; and Giovanni Campeis, special delegate from the Episcopal Chancery. Abbess Pynsent described the scene in a small biographical volume published by the order in 1896 titled *The Life of Helen Lucretia Cornaro Piscopia.* It was based on the writings of Deza, Lupis and Bacchini, and has long been out of print.

By the turn of the century, Vassar College was well-established and expanding. Vassar trustee Frederick Thompson and his wife Mary Clark Thompson had no children. After he died in 1899, his widow continued their annual custom of providing scholarships for four boys and four girls to attend college. In her husband's name, Mrs. Thompson donated an endowed library to Vassar.

The Frederick Ferris Thompson Memorial Library was completed in 1905, a "companion in elegant detail" to the Vassar Chapel. The next year a magnificent, 22-foot-high stained-glass window was installed in the library's west wing depicting Cornaro's graduation scene at Padua. It could not have been a more appropriate theme for this pioneering college for women. But precisely how Elena was chosen as the window's central figure remains a mystery to this day.*

"This promises to be a splendid work," wrote Caryl Coleman, President of the Church Glass Company of New York to John Hardman Studios in Birmingham, England. Coleman's enthusiastic letter was written early in 1903. Three years later, a column in a local Poughkeepsie paper (unearthed seven decades later by a Vassar student) described the completed window:

> The subject is very appropriate for the Vassar College Library as it represents the triumphal festivity of the woman pioneer of learning. The central figure is seated on a throne, all about her are other figures doing her homage. The coloring of the group is deep and rich. Dark purples and reds are predominant, throwing a subdued quiet light over the library. (*The Poughkeepsie Daily Eagle,* February 2, 1906)

During the months prior to the window's installation, numerous transatlantic letters, cables and drawings went back and forth between the U.S. and England. Much of the discus-

---

* Further discussion about the origin of the Vassar window can be found in the Epilogue Appendix (pp. 261-265), offering various possibilities regarding the choice of the window's theme.

sion dealt with details of the window's composition as well as wrestling with delays and duties at Custom House. The donor, the architect, the two glass firms and Vassar were all involved in the communiqués. Records show that Mr. Coleman sent Mr. Hardman "a tracing of the architectural structure of the window measured to scale."

"We have kept all the detail renaissance to harmonize with the costumes of the figures, rather than gothic to harmonize with the architecture," explained the New York manufacturers to Vassar administrators. In addition to preferring that gold be introduced in Elena's cape and on marble, Mrs. Thompson advocated that some of the reds be toned down.

Suggestions and revisions abounded from all quarters. "There is too much purple in the figures in the foreground," advised the New York company to Birmingham. The plain cross "will not do." "The cushion on the throne is too pronounced..."; "...it must be quite secondary...." For the setting, the Cathedral of Padua (where Elena had defended her thesis) was seriously considered but rejected.

Architect Francis Richmond Allen proposed that the central cherub display a Cornaro coat of arms: two Greek crosses and two red lions rampant with gold crowns. In his communications, Allen exhibited a keen sense of humor, discussing with the Birmingham company treatment of a background figure: "But no man ever had an arm that could do the 'stunt' that is indicated in the drawing: either one long enough or crooked enough." He also noted that "the cherubs in the lower foreground are exquisite."

At Mrs. Thompson's suggestion, the subjects were kept secular rather than religious to emphasize the educational dimension of the historic scene. "...[H]istorical subjects are always expensive things to do," claimed John Hardman's. "Our allowance to you on this window is $2,750.00," replied Mr. Coleman of Church Glass in New York. "Be very careful to follow the portrait of Helen… ." "…Let us have a likeness, as near as it is possible to have one." "Mr. [Dunstan] Powell is giving it his personal supervision from first to last."

Finally, at the end of December 1905, thousands of "jewel-toned pieces," each carefully numbered, traveled by Cunard steamer and railways in three huge crates to be assembled on the Poughkeepsie campus. "An inscription for the ribbon at the base of the window…will tell the spectator exactly what the scene represents," explained the manufacturers. *"In Laud[e] Helenae Lucretiae Corneliae Piscopiae Laurea in Philo[sophia] Patav[ino] Gymn[asio] unico exemplo Donatae"* ("In praise of Elena Lucrezia Cornaro Piscopia as the first instance of the doctorate in philosophy awarded [to a woman] at the University of Padua"). The wording mirrored what was incised on the university's statue at Padua.

In what was considered one of the finest stained-glass works of art in the country, the Lady Cornaro had arrived in the United States. It was, as the *Daily Eagle* had noted, a "very appropriate" home for the pioneering laureate.

As she studied beneath the new window several years later, Ruth Crawford puzzled over the cherubs' bordering banderole. She pored over a pamphlet about Elena which Church Glass had sent to Vassar in 1906. Soon enough, the story inspired her sufficiently that she would pursue its theme for more than fifty years.

The first decade of the twentieth century was a time of great change in America, with large cities and industry growing significantly. Immigration soared, and Ruth became an early champion of the foreign born. After graduating from Vassar in 1912 and making two trips around the world, Ruth

Three of the "exquisite cherubs" in the Vassar College library window noted by architect Francis Allen and admired by Ruth Crawford Mitchell. As reported by a Poughkeepsie newspaper in 1906, the window featured the "woman pioneer of learning."

(Photographs by Charles Porter)

then received a Master's Degree from Washington University in St. Louis in 1915.

That same year, Vassar celebrated its fiftieth anniversary. In "The Pageant of Athena," written by undergraduate Edna St. Vincent Millay, students reenacted the library window scene, with Cornaro reading a passage from Aristotle, responding to questions from her examiners, and then being invested with the insignia of her doctorate. Amid trumpet flares, "we reproduced the original ceremony exactly," according to a student reporter, "and the long discourses in Greek and Latin were relieved only by the excitement of Helena's swooning just before her examination.... [T]he procession of dignitaries got tangled up when it came to the rostra..."

Meanwhile, Ruth went on with her career, serving as National YWCA Secretary, working on Ellis Island during some of its busiest years, and in New Jersey and New England, helping young immigrant women adapt to new lives in the United States. During World War I she headed a team with 1912 Vassar classmates Mary Hurlbutt and Elinor Prudden, making a social survey of Prague for Dr. Alice Masaryk, President of the Czechoslovak Red Cross. The group was the nucleus of the International Migration Service. And in 1919, Ruth Crawford realized that monastic orders, including the Benedictines, were being permitted to return to Italy.

A decade after her graduation from Vassar, Ruth had been appointed as lecturer on the history of immigration in the Department of Economics at the University of Pittsburgh. Now married, she left her teaching position after several years to begin work on nationality classrooms. Begun in 1926 in the university's skyscraper-style Cathedral of Learning, the classrooms' authentic interiors were individually designed to represent different countries. Ruth also helped establish the university's cultural exchange program.

Over the next thirty years, nineteen nationality rooms had been successfully completed in Pittsburgh. The Italian room (opened in 1940) depicted a fifteenth-century Tuscan monastery, in honor of Italy. In the surrounding Allegheny County, Italians represented the single largest foreign-born group.

Wishing to share Cornaro's story, Ruth suggested to the Italian Room Committee that a dedicatory painting of Elena be rendered for its wall mural. Giovanni Romagnoli, a leading Bolognese portraitist, was commissioned for the work, and the mural was unveiled in 1949. The statue of Elena at the University of Padua served as a model. While Romagnoli was lettering an inscription on his imported painting, a long-time friend, Fr. Nicola Fusco from New Kensington, Pennsylvania, came to see him.

As the Italian-born Benedictine priest gazed at the new painting of the lovely laureate — showing her surrounded by the learning symbols of her day (books, musical instruments and a globe)—it rekindled in him an old curiosity, aroused more than a decade earlier. Fr. Fusco had conducted some research in Rome and at the Benedictine Archabbey of St. Vincent College near Latrobe, Pennsylvania. Subsequently, he wrote an article about Elena published in 1949 in *La Lucerna,* an Italian cultural magazine. The University of Pittsburgh's copy went into the Italian Women's Committee files, where it emerged twenty years later.

As a young man, Nicola Fusco left his native Formicola (a village between Naples and Rome) to join his parents in Pittsburgh in 1906. Six years later — the same year Ruth Crawford graduated from Vassar — Fr. Fusco finished his reli-

TWENTIETH-CENTURY MURAL SHOWING ELENA SURROUNDED BY SYMBOLS OF LEARNING, LOCATED IN THE ITALIAN INTERNATIONAL CLASSROOM AT THE UNIVERSITY OF PITTSBURGH. THE LIKENESS OF ELENA WAS TAKEN FROM HER MARBLE STATUE AT THE UNIVERSITY OF PADUA. PAINTED IN BOLOGNA BY GIOVANNI ROMAGNOLI AND DEDICATED AT THE UNVEILING IN PITTSBURGH IN 1949, THE MURAL WAS A GIFT FROM ITALIAN WOMEN IN THE PITTSBURGH AREA. IT IS FEATURED IN ONE OF TWENTY-FOUR ROOMS REPRESENTING VARIOUS WORLD CULTURES IN THE UNIVERSITY'S CATHEDRAL OF LEARNING.

(Photograph by Thomas C. Pears III)

gious studies at St. Vincent and became pastor of the Church of Mount Saint Peter in New Kensington, a parish with a largely Italian membership.

While Ruth was busy developing the Nationality Rooms in Pittsburgh, Fr. Fusco headed a pilgrimage to Italy in the summer of 1936. It was then that he first saw Elena's statue at the University of Padua. *Who was this woman,* he wondered, *the only female figure among many famous men portrayed there?* No one he asked seemed to know anything about her. But over the next four decades, Fr. Fusco would come to know her unique story well.

In 1953, Angelo Roncalli, the Bergamese priest just installed as Cardinal of Venice, visited the Cathedral of Padua. He celebrated Mass at the altar of his hero, the Blessed Gregorio Cardinal Barbarigo, a former Bishop of Bergamo and key advocate of Elena Cornaro.* Two years later, Ruth Mitchell went to Padua on a cultural exchange program and discovered that the Italian government was conducting extensive excavations at St. Luke's Chapel. The work was undertaken in the hopes of locating fifteenth-century frescoes, painted by the Venetian Giovanni Storlato, beneath the monks' mortuary.

Because of vital rehabilitation work needed on older parts of the basilica following World War II, nothing had been done in the chapel by the Benedictine fathers for many years. Ruth Mitchell found Elena's coffin resting in a "gloomy cellar" beneath the chapel, she later noted. Both the original gravestone and Abbess Pynsent's replacement were severely fragmented.

---

* Angelo Roncalli became Pope John XXIII in 1958. Two years later, his seminary idol, Gregorio Cardinal Barbarigo, was canonized as a saint of the Roman Catholic Church on June 17, 1960.

Distressed by the poor condition of the chapel and Elena's grave, as well as the neglected Tabacco statue stored away at the university, Ruth resolved to stimulate interest in restoring St. Luke's Chapel. Armed with a photograph of the statue, she arranged for the disregarded work to be cleaned and relocated. When she returned home, she found Fr. Fusco's *La Lucerna* article about Lady Elena and met its author, who lived only thirty miles away!

After retiring from the University of Pittsburgh in 1956, Ruth was able to devote herself full-time to a Cornaro renaissance. She faithfully pursued her mission in the United States and Europe over the next decade. Engaging foreign governments, enlisting ambassadors and college presidents, and enlivening international committees became regular fare for the St. Louis native.

For her remarkable international efforts, Ruth was decorated by four governments (Italy, France, Yugoslavia and Czechoslovakia) and given an honorary Doctor of Humanities degree from the University of Pittsburgh. In 1969, she was invited to Padua by San Giustina's new abbot, Innocenzo De Angelis, to plan international celebrations for the three hundredth anniversary of Elena's 1678 graduation. The abbot had organized a group of oblates there to foster the renovation of the mortuary. Funds for the project had already been raised from the citizens of Padua, but the renovation would be a long and complicated process.

At the 1969 meeting in Padua, Ruth Mitchell, an active Episcopalian, was ceremoniously named an honorary oblate of the Benedictine order of San Giustina. Fittingly, the Benedictines gave her the name "Elena Scolastica."

One key development of the 1969 Padua gathering was the formation of two large Cornaro tercentenary committees, one based in Italy and the other in the United States. Ruth Mitchell was chosen to chair the U.S. committee; Dr. Maria Tonzig the Italian group. Members of both committees embarked upon the project with vigor during the years leading to the 1978 tercentenary. Many involved in these efforts were people in their seventies and eighties. All were volunteers.

Among the nearly fifty international honorary committee members were university presidents and chancellors; college professors; ambassadors; cardinals; archabbots; heads of Benedictine orders; superintendents of monuments, arts and letters; bank chairmen and museum heads; and the mural painter, Professor Giovanni Romagnoli. Two influential members of the *Celebrazioni Centenarie Elena Lucrezia Cornaro Piscopia*, Padua's International Tercentenary Committee, were Professor Paolo Sambin, Director of the Institute of History at the University of Padua, and Dr. Tonzig, philosophy and art scholar.

Beginning in 1971, rigorously documented research was conducted by University of Padua authorities under Professor Sambin to establish Elena's primacy as the first woman graduate. Dr. Tonzig investigated 114 universities around the world that were in existence in 1678. The study took three years and the results were published in *Quaderni,* the Paduan university periodical. Elena's primacy was declared official and, in 1974, it was publicly announced at the 750th anniversary of the founding of the University of Padua. "*La Prima Donna Laureata nel Mondo*" ("First Woman Graduate in the World") became her modern title (introduced in writings of the 1970s by the Jesuit Domenico Mondrone).

Dr. Tonzig's research revealed that, after Elena Cornaro, the next woman to be awarded a doctorate was from the University of Bologna. Maria Catarina Laura Bassi, also an Aristotelian scholar, became a Doctor of Philosophy in 1732, more than fifty years after Elena!

Few women earned college degrees anywhere before the twentieth century. It was nearly 200 years after Padua's ceremony for Elena when Boston University awarded the first Ph.D. to a woman in the United States. The laureate in that case was Helen Magill, daughter of the president and an alumna of Swarthmore College, who received her degree in 1877.

The United States Cornaro Tercentenary Committee, headquartered at the University of Pittsburgh, represented a wide spectrum of organizations across the country. Delegates from the American Association of University Women, the YWCA, the National Council of Catholic Women, Zonta International, Kappa Gamma Pi and the National Council of Administrative Women in Education were among the participating members.

Because there was almost no information in English about Elena, the publication of her profile by Nicola Fusco was of prime interest. Tragically, only two days after delivering his story to Ruth Mitchell in 1971, Fr. Fusco was killed in an evening automobile accident on a rainswept highway near Latrobe, Pennsylvania. His paperback was subsequently revised and expanded as a small memorial volume, issued in a limited edition of 1,000.

Located in Fr. Fusco's parish in New Kensington was a large fabricating plant of ALCOA, the Aluminum Company of America, headed by Roy Hunt. His wife, the noted bibliophile Rachel McMasters Miller Hunt, had been a close friend of Fr. Fusco, both rare manuscript collectors. His book, *Elena Lucrezia Cornaro Piscopia 1646-1684,* was published in 1975 in memory of Fr. Fusco (1887-1971) and Rachel Hunt (1882-1963) with a grant from the Hunt Foundation to the University of Pittsburgh.

A blue ribbon panel was assembled to accomplish the publication. Gabrielle Forbush, a Vassar classmate of Ruth

Mitchell, revised the text. Forbush had written numerous magazine articles on Cornaro. She had also served as correspondence editor at the White House for President Franklin Roosevelt. Agnes Starrett, Director Emeritus of the University of Pittsburgh Press, edited the volume. Dr. Tonzig and John Halmaghi, Bibliographer of the Hillman Library, compiled a scholarly bibliography. The book was case-bound in Venetian red linen with the commemorative medal from Padua stamped in gold on its covers. The first 500 were individually subscribed during 1975, each given to the donor's selected library. Proceeds were designated for the Paduan Cornaro Restoration Fund to renew the grave site in St. Luke's Chapel, as Fr. Fusco had wished.

In that same year, through the successful distribution of the book by the American committee, the $10,000 goal was reached and sent to Padua, ensuring restoration of the Lady Cornaro's burial site.

At last, Elena's life story was introduced through international reference and public libraries, including specially bound, white leather copies for the Vatican, Windsor Castle and the White House. Book Number One, subscribed for by the Class of 1912, was assigned to Vassar College.

In 1977, at Ruth Mitchell's request, E. Maxine Bruhns succeeded her as national chairman of the United States Cornaro Committee.* Director of the University of Pittsburgh's

* In honor of their exceptional contributions to society, both Ruth Mitchell and E. Maxine Bruhns were named "Distinguished Daughters of Pennsylvania." They are also the only two individual women to be granted the David Glick Award, given annually by the World Affairs Council of Pittsburgh to a citizen who has made "a distinguished contribution to the understanding of world affairs."

Nationality Rooms and Intercultural Exchange Programs, Maxine Bruhns had been very active as Vice-Chairman of the Cornaro committee since its inception. The tercentenary became an intense focus. Both American and Paduan committees communicated with colleges, universities and organizations around the world involved in women's education and invited thousands of people to participate in anniversary tributes.

The response was tremendous! There were over 135 observances across the U.S. and Europe throughout 1978. Fifty-two Benedictine Priories held commemorations. Descendants from branches of the Cornaro family surfaced from as far away as Iran.

In the spring of 1978, one of the first celebrations was held in a Washington, D.C. series by the Italian Cultural Society, the American Italian Bicentennial Commission and Georgetown University, the first Catholic university in the country. A large reception was given at the Italian ambassador's residence; architecture and baroque music lectures, panel discussions on women's education, an address by the Archbishop of Washington and an early opera were scheduled.

Typical of the illustrious tercentenary celebrations was the three-day public symposium held in April at Vassar College with major guest scholars in history, philosophy, music and art. Under the chairmanship of Professor Benjamin G. Kohl (who succeeded Lynn Bartlett as Vassar's committee chairman in 1976), the symposium featured a comprehensive library exhibit and included high Mass in the college chapel.

In a fitting highlight of the festivities at Vassar, Ruth Mitchell spoke to the celebrants in front of the sunlit window which had served to introduce her to Elena Cornaro seventy years earlier. She basked that evening in the knowledge that her lifelong mission of restoring the Cornaro to her rightful place of worldwide honor was now thoroughly accomplished.

Monsignor Fusco's Pennsylvania parish of Mount St. Peter held a special observance. At the University of Pittsburgh, ceremonies stretched over the tercentenary year and were coordinated with academic events at Carlow College, Carnegie Mellon University and Duquesne University. At Pittsburgh's Heinz Chapel on June 25 (Elena's graduation day), the United States Committee held a service that included a eucharistic liturgy, Renaissance and Baroque music, and a reception in the Cathedral of Learning in the great Gothic Commons Room near the Romagnoli mural.

In the fall, a university lecture series was held with distinguished speakers on early women scholars and artists, climaxed by a gala Venetian banquet in the Henry Clay Frick Fine Arts Cloister. Departments at the University of Pittsburgh were asked to incorporate aspects of the Cornaro and her seventeenth-century culture in their curricula. Led by the university, academic scholarships were established by schools around the country in Elena's name. The mayor of Pittsburgh, Richard Caliguiri, declared a Cornaro Day in October. And across the University of Pittsburgh's campus, students sported T-shirts with Elena's portrait, while at Swarthmore, undergraduates wore T-shirts with an image of their own Helen Magill.

Padua's celebrations were truly spectacular. With Benedictine oblates attending from all over the world, two major commemorations during a week-long celebration in September were conducted by the University of Padua, the Borough of Padua, the Benedictine order and San Giustina. Co-chairmen were Abbot Innocenzo Negrato of San Giustina and Professor Aldo Stella from the University. All events were provided with simultaneous translations in English, German, French and Spanish.

The academic program (September 3-6), opened at the main university building, "Il Bo," with the rector welcoming Italian and foreign delegations. There followed a commemorative address, reception in the Aula Magna, and visit to a permanent, historical Cornaro exhibition. The Town Council presented Carlo Grossi's Sacred Cantata, dedicated in 1663 to Elena. A roundtable discussion was held, with scholarly talks by representatives from Padua, London, and the United States. The Paduan celebration also included a tour of principal city monuments (the Loggia, Odeon Palace, and the Virgin Mary's Chapel in the Cathedral of Padua) and was highlighted by an organ recital of late seventeenth-century music at San Giustina the next day. On Wednesday, celebrants departed for Venice to visit Cornaro historic locations.

The Benedictine program (September 6-9) began in the afternoon with a Mass of concelebration at San Giustina. Thursday's schedule included the presentation of monastic delegations, a visit to Elena's tomb and the university, a discussion on "The relationship between science and spirituality," an address by Fr. Francesco Maschietto, and vespers in the basilica before another Grossi cantata performance. There were additional church services on Friday, an oblates' roundtable and an organ recital. The program was brought to a close on Saturday with visits to Venetian places of significance to Lady Cornaro's life, and a Mass at the Basilica of San Giorgio Maggiore.

For the tercentenary, the University of Padua restruck the beautiful bronze medal of Elena and published a scholarly biography in Italian, *Elena Lucrezia Cornaro Piscopia, 1646-1684, prima donna laureata nel mondo* by Fr. Maschietto. The well-documented, illustrated work contained an extensive bibliography and analytical index.

When the United States committee met for the last time in 1979, there had been other important developments in the Cornaro renaissance. Padua made plans to renew the national historic sites, the Odeon Palace and the Loggia. Dr. Tonzig was compiling the Paduan celebrations and the primacy records in an Italian book, *Elena Lucrezia Cornaro Piscopia, Prima Donna Laureata Nel Mondo, Terzo Centenario Del Dottorato (1678-1978),* issued by the university and San Giustina in 1980. An arcade near the center of the city was named for Elena. On the Venice street wall near the palace where she was born, an engraved brass nameplate was installed with Elena's name, graduation date and the twentieth-century appellation: *"Prima Donna Laureata nel Mondo."*

Through the efforts of the Department of Antiquities and Fine Arts of the Italian government over many years, St. Luke's Chapel had been renovated to its 1301 distinction. The flooring was replaced and windows, lights and a new altar installed. With funds provided by the Superintendent of Monuments in the Venetian area, stonework in the high vaulted ceiling and the remaining Storlato frescoes on the walls and ceiling were restored. Paduan businesses, private individuals and the Benedictine order all contributed to the architectural rehabilitation.

In tribute to the interest of her citizens and the renowned scholar buried there, Italy renamed St. Luke's Chapel, *Cappella Cornaro* (Cornaro Chapel). It was officially dedicated on June 25, 1978, in a ceremony which included church, university and civic authorities. Elena's tomb was decorated with fresh lilies and laurel from Ruth Mitchell. (Ruth died six years later, having seen the fruition of her lifelong efforts in reviving the legacy of the Lady Cornaro. Fittingly, Ruth's death in 1984 also marked the tercentenary of the death of her heroine.)

With funds raised from Fr. Fusco's profile, Elena's grave, originally constructed by the monks, was repaired. Fragments of the first gravestone were placed on a nearby chapel wall. Installed on the pink marble floor was a classical replica of Elena's original, simple, black marble stone with the 1684 inscription. On its frame were incised the seals of the Benedictine order and San Giustina, the crest of the University of Padua, and, lastly for Elena, the Cornaro Piscopia coat of arms with the crusading knight King Peter's Order of the Sword in the center. Once again, she was returned to her final resting place in consecrated soil.

During the final stages of restoration work, the leaden plate was found which had been carefully put back by Abbess Pynsent in a simple coffin, encasing the one of ancient cypress. Engraved on the tablet were these words:

> *Here rests Elena Lucrezia Cornaro Piscopia, a Venetian Noble Woman of Famous Name.... Her Surviving Parent, Gianbattista of San Marco, Mourns Her Most Sorrowfully.*

ACKNOWLEDGEMENTS

IT WAS THE SHEER SPLENDOR, the suffering and complexity of this important, yet obscure, historical figure that attracted me. Determining my way was the magnetism of Ruth Crawford Mitchell who discovered "The Lady Cornaro" at Vassar College, our alma mater. For nine years, I served as Promotion Chair of the United States Committee for the Elena Lucrezia Cornaro Piscopia Tercentenary, organized to honor the Paduan laureate in this country and abroad in 1978. The trail has taken me to numerous research centers from Chicago's Newberry Library to the Vatican's extensive collection.

The core of my research was made possible by invaluable contributions provided continually over the years by two scholars at West Chester (PA) University: the Venetian Erminio Braidotti, Professor of Foreign Languages, and Latinist John Rosso, Instructor of Classical Languages. Both translated into English many very difficult original manuscripts. Some were translated for the first time; the texts were written in seventeenth-century and modern Italian, Venetian dialect and early Latin. Both scholars have enthusiastically advised me, and, with much skill, helped interpret Elena's story. John Rosso greatly assisted with editing the text. Christina Braidotti, wife of Professor Braidotti and teacher of Italian and Spanish at Padua Academy (Wilmington, DE), also gave me excellent ideas and assistance with my text. In Padua, Italy, there were generous hours of consultation offered by two university professors emeriti: the late Maria Tonzig, Secretary-General of the International Cornaro Tercentenary Committee, and Fr. Francesco Ludovico Maschietto, the Benedictine authority on Elena at the Basilica of San Giustina. (In honor of her extraordinary life and dedication to the legacy of Lady Cornaro, Dr. Tonzig is to be buried in Cappella Cornaro of San Giustina.)

Two volunteer interpreters who provided their very helpful services were Dr. Tonzig's niece, Alicia Tonzig of Padua, and graduate student Sonja de Cristoforo of Milan and New York.

At Vassar College Libraries, Nancy MacKechnie, Curator of Rare Books and Manuscripts, has supported and assisted me so graciously in every way from the book's beginning. Also at Vassar, Benjamin G. Kohl, Andrew W. Mellon Professor of the Humanities, reviewed my complete work, offering insightful suggestions which have considerably enriched the story and the accompanying bibliography. I am deeply grateful to Vassar historian, Elizabeth A. Daniels, for her timely and tireless review of my work. Invaluable information and interpretation were also given by Joan Murphy, retired Reference Librarian, and the late Pamela Askew, Professor Emeritus of Art.

A major part of this book project has been, in the words of Vassar president Frances D. Fergusson, "a truly collaborative Vassar project." It seems only fitting that my Cornaro records and translations be given to the library at Vassar, where the Lady Cornaro has been honored for nearly a century. I was further inspired during a recent visit to the "Cornaro Window" at the Vassar library by a serendipitous meeting with undergraduate Mira Dittmer, Class of 1999, whose decision to attend Vassar was "prompted when I saw the beautiful window in the library and loved the sacred presence it added to a place devoted to reflection and study."

My particular thanks go to our United States Cornaro Tercentenary Committee National Chairman (1977-1978), E. Maxine Bruhns, Director of Nationality Rooms and Intercultural Exchange Programs at the University of Pittsburgh. Her great insight, knowledge, and review of the entire Cornaro story has contributed immeasurably.

I am especially indebted to Jean May Bousquet, former Supervisor of Music and Arts Services at the Berkshire Athenaeum, and presently public and parochial schools educator at the Berkshire Museum (and my cousin), who offered wonderful assistance with research, read and strengthened my manuscript; Holly Howard Stover, R.N. (and my sister), who provided important historical and medical information and reviewed pertinent chapters.

My good friends at the University of Delaware, Arnold Kerr, Professor of Civil and Environmental Engineering, and his wife, Berta, have given me very useful advice and encouragement all along; Iris Snyder, Senior Associate Librarian, Special Collections; Associate Librarian Carol Rudisell, and the entire reference and special collections staffs in the university's Hugh M. Morris Library have been a tremendous resource for me.

Grateful acknowledgment for their fine ideas and aid are due Daniel H. Traister, Curator of Research Services at Van Pelt-Dietrich Library of the University of Pennsylvania; Patricia Labalme, former Assistant to the Director at the Institute for Advanced Study in Princeton, NJ; David O'Brien, Professor of Roman Catholic Studies at Holy Cross College; William Callison, Professor of Educational Administration, California State University at Fullerton; the Venetian lecturer Maria Perale Mariutti; in Padua: Roberta Parise of the Museo Bottacin and rare books archivist Emilia Veronese at the university; and

Leonard Boyle, Prefect of Biblioteca Apostolica Vaticana in Rome. Many times, the librarians and department heads in the Italian Renaissance collections of the Newberry Library and the Pierpont Morgan Library in New York courteously advised me. Rare book staffs of the botanical library at The Arboretum School of the Barnes Foundation (Merion, PA), the New York Public Library, Bryn Mawr College, Villanova University and the Wilmington (DE) Institute Libraries furnished extensive source material.

Generously lending various works were Boston College, the University of Rochester, the University of Illinois and the University of Texas. Additional libraries used and consulted were those of Swarthmore College, Princeton University, Columbia University, Hunter College of the City University of New York, Vanderbilt University, the Rosenbach Museum and Library and Temple University (Philadelphia, PA), Newport Beach Public Library (CA), Padua Academy (Wilmington, DE), Seabury-Western Theological Seminary (Evanston, IL), Illinois Benedictine College (Glen Elyn, IL), the monastic library at Saint Vincent College (Latrobe, PA) and the library and staff of Longwood Gardens in Kennett Square, PA and the Winterthur Museum Library in Wilmington, Delaware.

Many others, especially the late Clifford Nichols, Headmaster Emeritus of Sewickley Academy (PA); C. Hax McCullough and Luisa Coraluppi, all Pittsburgh friends; the late Joanne Specker of Berwyn (PA); Carl R. Feind, M.D., Columbia-Presbyterian Medical Center; and Vassar classmates JoJeanne Millon Barton and Ann Hutchison of New York who assisted me in countless ways. I thank sincerely for the drawing of the symbolic cypress tree, artist Christine Canning, United Arab Emirates; Assistant Editor Ann McKay, M.L.S., for fine text revisions; Marsha Daigle-Williamson, Ph.D., for her very skillful review; Nancy Andrews for her fine work at the Library of Congress; Irene Decker for her timely assistance with the indexing; Kathleen Corby for the beautiful jacket design; and Peggy Lindt of Santa Barbara for the creative hand tinting of Lady Elena on the cover.

Praise is due to my splendid publisher Joseph (Trip) Sinnott of College Avenue Press, for his excellent editorial direction, his abiding, heartfelt interest, and his invaluable help in guiding me along the way with his great, good humor.

Every member of my family has been involved, most especially Jane and Charlie Birmingham, Susan and Neil Rohrer, my granddaughter Lacey Greenwalt who helped with research, my nephew Arthur Howard Domby with his legal expertise, my husband Bill for being there (from interpreting ancient, sacred music texts to educating our three daughters in the great Cornaro tradition), and my dear mother, Louise May Howard. They have made it possible for me to tell how Elena's courageous example emerged from the period when there were many heroes but few recognized heroines. Through each of these people, from this and ancient times, her great gift to all of us endures.

THE LADY CORNARO IS BURIED IN THE SACRED MONK'S MORTUARY IN PADUA'S SAN GIUSTINA BASILICA. FORMERLY KNOWN AS ST. LUKE'S CHAPEL, THE FOURTEENTH-CENTURY STRUCTURE WAS RENAMED *CAPPELLA CORNARO* IN HER HONOR. ADORNED WITH STORLATO FRESCOES, THE CHAPEL WAS RESTORED BY LOCAL CITIZENS AND BUSINESSES, AS WELL AS THE BENEDICTINES AND THE ITALIAN GOVERNMENT. IT WAS OFFICIALLY DEDICATED AS *CAPPELLA CORNARO* ON JUNE 25, 1978.

(Special Collections, Vassar College Libraries)

SOURCE NOTES

ii "Think not this is a portrait of Minerva": "Laurel-endowed" Elena, described in portrait caption from contemporary account of Rome memorial. *Le Pompe funebri.* Engraver: Jacobus Cassionus. Per il Cadorino. Padua, 1686, p. 12. Plate I. Special Collections, Vassar College Libraries.

xii "and above all": Letter to Dr. Samuel Pepys in the *Diary of John Evelyn.* Emphasis added.

PROLOGUE

5 "Try and make": Unpublished letters between John Hardman and Church Glass companies, 1904-1906.

6 "a multitude of people of all sorts and conditions, listening with astonishment and applauding her genius and ability": Church Glass to Hardman, November 2, 1904.

Chapter 1:
AN ARRANGED MARRIAGE REBUFFED

9 "I would rather elect": Deza, *Vita di Helena Lucretia Cornara Piscopia* (cited hereafter as *HLCP* or *ELCP [Helena or Elena]),* 42.

9 "The whole arsenal of beauty": *Le Pompe funebri,* 16.

10 For the sake of clarity in the text, the author has used the name "Captain Marco Contarini" for Elena's designated fiancé. No suitors' names were recorded. (Captain Contarini was listed as commanding a Venetian ship in the war against the Turks at the time.)

11 "gentledonnas": Didier, *City and Republick of Venice*, part 3, 18. (Author also called Desdier.)
12 Venetian dialect was spoken privately and in governing circles.
13 Bucentaur: Its name is thought to be derived from the figure in the bow with a man's head and bull's body.
13 "Its fittings": Cornaro, *Discorsi della vita sobria*, 213.
14 "Sea, we espouse thee": Molmenti, *Venice*, vol. 1, part 1, 214.
14 "Long live the Adriatic!": Bailey, *Daughter of the Doges*, 825.
16 "plentious food": Coryat, *Crudities*, vol. 1, 256.
19 "My daughter,": Bailey, *Daughter of the Doges*, 826.
19 "Obey, Elena,": Ibid.
21 "Ducal Chappel,": de la Houssaye, *History of the Government of Venice*, 146.
22 "Farmers of the Company": Ibid., 150.
22 "[P]roperly these Procurators": Ibid., 152.
23 "The Laws of the State": Didier, *City and Republick of Venice*, part 2, 26.
24 "as ill assorted": Rio, *Les quartres martyres*, 111.
25 "hothouse plants": Molmenti, *Venice*, vol.2, part 2, 179.

Chapter 2
BIRTH IN A GRAND CANAL PALACE

27 "Father, Sir": Deza, *Vita di HLCP*, 42.
27 "Hasten my father": Bailey, *Daughter of the Doges*, 826.
27 "Save me, father": Ibid.
28 "I don't deny that": Deza, *Vita di HLCP*, 103.
29 "in secolaro": Bacchini, *Vitae selectae*, 251.
29 "In other things": Pynsent, *Life of HLCP*, 39.
30 summer palace and winter palace: For the sake of delineation, the Cornaro Piscopia Palace in Venice is referred to as "the winter palace," Padua "the summer palace." Both, in fact, were used all year.

30 cypress: *Cupressus sempervirens.*
32 to be "the most beautiful": Ruskin, *Stones of Venice,* vol. 2, 392.
32 One source states the palace was of the "fondaco" style, erected by an unknown patron. "Tradition states that it was built by the Boccasi family of Parma and later passed to the Ziani family, although another source suggests that it was built by the Dandolo family." C.I. Gable, *Ca' Cornaro Piscopia (*1997-1998), http://www.boglewood.com/cornaro/xpiscopia.html (10 July 1998).
32 "Father, Sir": Deza, *Vita di HLCP,* 20.
33 "a glory for the family": Psychowska, *Learned Woman,* 663.

Chapter 3
BIRTH IN A GRAND CANAL PALACE

35 "Amongst the families": Rio, *Les quartres martyres,* 106.
36 "her jewels": *Encyclopaedia Britannica,* 11th ed., vol. 7, s.v. "Cornelia", 167.
36 The name Cornelii: Cornaro, *Art of Living Long,* 160.
36 Cornelia's father, the elder Africanus, a Greek scholar as well as one of Rome's greatest generals, at the end of the Second Punic War (201 B.C.) defeated Hannibal, the Carthaginian general who crossed the Alps to invade Italy. *Encyclopaedia Britannica,* 11th ed., vol. 12, s.v. "Hannibal," 920-21.
38 "parading the great models": Rio, *Les quartres martyres,* 106.
40 Procurators "becom the principall pillars": Howell, *A Survay of the Signorie of Venice,* 20.
41 "Of the throng in the Piazza": Coryat, *Crudities,* 171.
42 "great Vein": Didier, *City and Republick of Venice,* part 1, 16.
42 "hapless victim": Rio, *Les quartres martyres,* 118.
42 "studious and genial": Marzolo, *Vita Pensiero,* (486) 1.
44 "ecstatic": Deza, *Vita di HLCP,* 26.

Chapter 4
FIRST CONVENT CONSIDERED

45 "It must be reckoned": Dr. Francesco Pona (Eureta Miscocolo), Molmenti, *Venice*, Part 3, vol. 2, 111.

46 "A house of discord": Rio, *Les quartres martyres*, 125.

46 "assemblies, balls, theatricals": Molmenti, *Venice*, vol.2, part 3, 84.

46 "parlours were a field": Ibid., 80.

48 Dr. Bartolloti's first name is unrecorded.

49 G. Lanspergio's book in Italian: *Coloquio di Cristo nostro Redentore all'anima devota.* Venetia, 1669. Maschietto, *ELCP*, 82.

49 "encyclopedic culture": Maschietto, *ELCP*, 82.

49 "His Excellency": Marco Boschini, *Map of Picturesque Sailing*, "Seventh Wind", Venice: 1660, 555.

51 "made only to stay at home": Labalme, *Beyond Their Sex*, 143.

51 The mooring ring for tying them: Maschietto interview, Padua, March 1993.

51 The library had the most extensive collection: de Montfaucon, *Journey through Italy*, 93.

52 "I was leafing through": Leti, *L'Italia regnante*, part 4, 52.

53 Drawing of cypress tree by Christine Canning.

Chapter 5
EARLY FAME

55 "I have ever had two altars": Rio, *Les quartres martyres*, 111.

56 Aldus Manutius (1450–1515); also called Aldo Manuzio, Teobaldo Mannucci.

56 "This was the moment": Hunt, *Caterina Cornaro*, 172.

56 British art historian: Terence Mullaly. Hunt, Caterina Cornaro, 152.

56 Aldus' friend Erasmus claimed the anchor symbolized serious preparation preceding a work, the dolphin its swift completion. Geoffrey Ashall Glaister, *Glaister's Glossary of the Book*, Berkeley: University of California Press, 1979, 5.

58 "She is beautiful as an angel": Fusco, *ELCP*, 31.

61 "great Sages": Didier, *City and the Republick of Venice*, Part 3, 14.

61 The earliest known Cornaro was Andrea Cornaro, born in 1215. C.I. Gable, *Outline of Cornaro Family Branches*, 1997, ‹http://www.boglewood.com/cornaro/xfamily.html (18 June 1998) World Wide Web.

63 "All degrees of peeple": Howell, *A Survay of the Signorie of Venice*, 20.

64 "defined, hereditary aristocracy": Chojnacki, *Studies in the Renaissance*, 179.

66 "To my thynkyng, the trade and maner of Courtyers": Castiglione, *Book of the Courtier*, 27.

67 "noblenes of birthe": Ibid., 44.

67 "stout herted": Ibid., 50.

67 "To be well borne and of a good stocke": Ibid., 368.

67 "A Waytyng Gentylwoman" had "to be well born and of a good house": Ibid., 374.

67 "to daunse, drawe, peinet": Ibid., 376.

Chapter 6
EXTREME PENANCE

69 "What loving slaughter": Lupis, *L'eronica veneta*, 99.

72 St. Catherine also had an effect upon reconciliations in family feuds of the noble Maconi of Siena and the Tolomei, and she met with the Guelphs of Florence for Pope Gregory.

Encyclopaedia Britannica, 11 ed., vol.5, s.v. "Catherine, Saints," 524-25.

77 "There's a time for partridge": Terry Matz, *Saint Teresa of Avila,* Catholic Online Saints, http://catholic.org/saints (22 February 1999).

77 "Doctor of the Church": Oxford Dictionary of the Christian Church 3rd ed., 494.

79 "to shine": Pynsent, *Life of HLCP*, 32.

Chapter 7
ON INTERNATIONAL DISPLAY

80 Venice with its "liquid streets": Coryat, *Crudities*, vol. 1, 365.

80 "This Mayden Republic": Howell, *A Survay of the Signorie of Venice*, 190.

84 "one of the most musical centers in Europe": Burckhardt, *Civilization of the Renaissance in Italy*, vol. 2, 387.

86 Grossi dedication in seventeenth-century Italian: "Io ammiro, non senza raggione come doni prodigiosi del Cielo, le Gloriose Vocationi di V.S. Illustrissima. . . . " Tonzig, *ELCP*, 242.

88 "deep reddish gold": Hunt, *Caterina Cornaro*, 40.

90 "She walked as a puppet": McCurdy, *Essays in Fresco*, 78.

91 "Daughter of the Republic": Also "Daughter of St. Mark" in some texts.

91 "cosmopolitan Mediterranean society": Hunt, *Caterina Cornaro*, 77.

92 "melted into tears": Howell, *A Survay of the Signorie of Venice*, 85.

92 "large treasure": Hunt, *Caterina Cornaro*, 89.

96 "Merchant City": Gailhard, *Present State of the Republick of Venice*, 37.

96 "acquisition and display": Molmenti, *Venice*, vol. 2, part 1, 165.

96 "truly extravagant": Daniele, *ELCP*, 1.
98 "unimaginable wealth": Barzini, *The Italians*, 23.
98 "Besides profound corruption": Burckhardt, *Civilization of the Renaissance in Italy*, vol. 2, 406.

Chapter 8
SOCIALITE OR SCHOLAR?

100 "There are two things": Deza, *Vita di HLCP*, 21.
102 "overriding sense of civic community": book jacket of Grendler, *Schooling in Renaissance Italy*, describing Romano's *Patricians & Popolani.*
103 "Ladies of Pleasure": de la Houssaye, *History of the Government of Venice*, 71.
103 Margherita Emiliana picture, Coryat, *Crudities*, vol. 1, 260.
103 Alvina the "Curtezan": Thomas Otway, *Venice Preserv'd or A Plot Discover'd.* The Hague: Printed for T. Johnson, 1712, 29.
104 "Famoused over all Christendome": Coryat, *Crudities*, vol. 1, 401.
104 "the murrey-coloured dress": Molmenti, *Venice*, vol. 2, part 2, 247, ft.4.
104 "Stellina," Ibid.
104 "enforced bachelorhood": Norwich, *History of Venice*, 595.
105 "sedans": Gailhard, *Present State of the Republick of Venice*, 11.
107 "'Tis ridiculous to see": Spalding, *Sketches from Venetian History*, 278.
108 "nothing-things": Deza, *Vita di HLCP*, 23.

Chapter 9
RECOVERY IN PADUA

113 "If a nobleman": Marcolini, letter to Luigi Cornaro, June 1, 1544, *Art of Living Long*, 201.

113 European hornbeam: Carpinus betulus.

116 Luigi Cornaro's birth dates often vary in biographical accounts, indicated as: 1464, 1467, and 1475.

116 Also called *Trattore della Vita Sobria* and *Discorsi intorno alla vita sobria* (The Sure and Certain Method of Attaining a Long and Healthful Life).

116 "I endeavor": Cornaro, *Art of Living Long*, 98.

117 "Heady Wines" and "High Sauces": Ibid., 116.

119 "in the pleasantest Parte of Padua": Ibid., 39.

125 "classical perfection": Burckhardt, *Civilization of the Renaissance in Italy*, vol. 1, 247.

126 "Who am I more than you, dear sisters?": Pynsent, *Life of HLCP*, 23.

126 "My own Lorenza,": Ibid., 23.

126 "Ah, my little lady,": Ibid.

126 "My dear Nonnina,": Ibid.

127 "My daughter,": Ibid, 25.

127 "We are bound": Ibid, 242.

Chapter 10

IN PURSUIT OF A PH.D.

130 "What? Never! Woman is made": Fusco, *ELCP*, 36.

131 "burlesque themselves" with their "denominations of exquisite absurdity": Disraeli, *Curiosities of Literature*, vol. 2, 480.

131 "to rid the air of pedantry" and "sportive relaxations": Ibid., 490.

132 "foul imperfections": Maschietto, *ELCP*, 156.

133 "Saints should have": Pynsent, *Life of HLCP*, 33.

141 "I cannot do this": Deza, *Vita di HLCP*, 58.

143 "What? A female doctor": Fusco, *ELCP*, 35.

146 "If the women": Ibid.

147 "If the Procurator of San Marco": Fusco, *ELCP*, 36.

Chapter 11
A UNIQUE ACHIEVEMENT

149 "She was born to shine": Marzolo, *Vita Pensiero*, (486) 1.
150 Convening from the University: Ancient archives of University of Padua, vol. 365, Index Quartus Actorum Sacri Collegii Exc. DD. Philosophorum, ac Medicorum Paduae, June 25, 1678, (25-26) 1-2.
152 "multitude of people": Church Glass to Hardman, November 2, 1904.
153 "bursting a vein": Deza, *Vita di HLCP*, 67.
153 "strict cures": Ibid.
153 "raised chair": Bacchini, *Vitae selectae*, 255.
153 Title of dissertation: An. Post., 1, 2, 71 b, 19-20: *Si igitur scire est ut posuimus....* Phys., 1, 5, 188a, 26 segg.: *Quod igitur contraria quodammodum...* : Tonzig, *ELCP*, Appendice, 269.
153 "with a simple ease and dignity": Fusco, *ELCP*, 38.
155 "this 'heroine' had borne herself": Ancient archives of University of Padua, (25-260), 2.
155 "demonstrating not only her philosophical": Bacchini, *Vitae selectae*, 256.
156 "magisterial laurel": Ibid., 248.
156 "silent suffering": Rio, *Les quartres martyres*, 126.

Chapter 12
FINAL ILLNESS

157 "All literary Europe": Pynsent, *Life of HLCP*, 71.
157 "Such crazy behavior": Maschietto, *ELCP*, 125.
158 "il babuazzo": Ibid.
158 "contemporary and correspondent": Ibid., 127-8.
158 Those who wrote about her: Fabri, *La Conchiglia*, 34.

158 "The doctorate was for a man": Deza, *Vita di HLCP*, 45.

158 Her degree was officially recorded: Maschietto, *ELCP*, 120, ft. 25.

160 "*Sweeper in the Sky*": The biography of famed astronomer Maria Mitchell (1818-1889) was first published in 1949 by the Macmillan Company. That edition is now out of print. A special Commemorative Edition of the classic biography has recently been published, marking the 150th Anniversary of Maria Mitchell's discovery of a comet, as well as the opening of the Class of 1951 Observatory at Vassar College. (Helen Wright, *Sweeper in the Sky,* Clinton Corners, NY: College Avenue Press, 1997.)

162 "whatever was sensual and secular": Deza, *Vita di HLCP*, 23.

162 "the instruments of her martyrdom": Deza, Ibid., 21-2.

162 "like those of a poor townswoman": Ibid.

162 "the people with her own hands": Pynsent, *Life of HLCP*, 90.

162 "look after the tired animals": Ibid.

164 "The Lady Helen Lucretia": Visit of Cardinal Estrées, Pynsent, *Life of HLCP*, 78-85.

169 "With the joy of my studies": Daniele, *ELCP*, 1.

169 "A majestic doorway": Cornaro, *Art of Living Long*, 201.

170 "red larch": Ibid., 211.

171 "c'est pour loyauté maintenir": Hill, *A History of Cyprus*, vol.2, 319.

171 "Inform us": Tonzig, *ELCP*, Labalme speech, 165.

173 "Wait until this cypress,": Rio, *Les quartres martyres*, 138.

174 "it is not a question": Deza, *Vita di HLCP*, 100.

Chapter 13
THE HEROINE'S FUNERAL

175 "It's folly to shrink in fear": J.H. Plumb, et al., *The Horizon Book of the Renaissance*, New York: American Heritage Publishing Company, 1961, 30.

175 "ice on houses"..."floods in March": Molmenti, *Venice*, vol. 1, part 3, 95.
176 "I shall lead": Deza, *Vita di HLCP*, 68.
177 "flattering replies": This was reported in a 1925 article from a review of Italian culture by Marzolo, "Vita e Pensiero," 5.
178 "unbridled pride": Ibid., 2.
178 "This vision": Pynsent, *Life of HLCP*, 98.
178 "I see miracles": Deza, *Vita di HLCP*, 91.
178 "in humility": Lupis, *L'eronica veneta*, 93.
179 "You must sew my Habit": Pynsent, *Life of HLCP*, 91.
179 "soon rupturing": Bacchini, *Vitae selectae*, 264.
179 "such pain in silence": Pynsent, *Life of HLCP*, 102.
180 "The saint is dead": Fusco, *ELCP*, 40.
183 "first major publishing venture": Known as "the Aldine Artistotle." Hunt, Caterina Cornaro, 172.
184 "It was more like a triumph": Ibid.
184 "O passerby...": *Le Pompe funebri*, 2.
184 "She appeared to be a girl genius": Lupis, *L'eronica veneta*, 132.
185 "My daughter wanted": Fusco, *ELCP*, 40.
185 "Zanetta was silenced": Ibid., 41.
187 "It was I": In authorizing her burial site, Cardinal Barbarigo "decided that according to Canon Law the deceased enjoyed the *jus selectonis*, the right to be buried wherever she chose and, therefore, that her last wish was to be respected and executed": Fusco, *ELCP*, 41.

Chapter 14
ENDURING LEGACY

188 "Life, like a dome of many-coloured glass,": *The Complete Poetical Works of Percy Bysshe Shelley*, Thomas Hutchinson, Editor, New York: Oxford University Press, 1933, 443.
191 "extending from a side pilaster": Fusco, *ELCP*, 42.

193 "suffering from gout": Maschietto, *ELCP,* 249.
193 "The lady procuress"..."being a woman of value which is known to everyone" ... "I ask my children": Ibid.
193 "without pomp": Ibid., 245.
196 "Study is a precious gift..." John Paul II, Vatican Information Services, October 24, 1998.
196 "set a precedent": Kristeller, "Learned Women of Early Modern Italy", *Beyond Their Sex,* 99.
197 "She is a Piscopia!": Maschietto, *ELCP,* 164.
197 "adept at everything": Bacchini, *Vitae selectae,* 268.
197 "One marvels at the eclecticism": Murphy, Library Tercentenary Exhibition notes.
197 "It was her sense of belonging": Tonzig, *ELCP,* Labalme speech, 163.
197 ("Her intelligence was full of fire..."): Deza, *Vita di HLCP,* 119.
198 "as such she was part of": University of Padua brochure, *ELCP The first woman university graduate in the world,* page of English translation, 1974.
199 "Few saints": Pynsent, *Life of HLCP,* 112.
199 "the royalty of intellect": Rio, *Les quartres martyres,* 114.
200 "From her face": Deza, *Vita di HLCP,* 120.
200 "to rid herself": Labalme, "Women's Roles in Early Modern Venice," *Beyond their Sex,* 141.
202 "An exceptional woman": Ibid., 144.

Epilogue

203 "...ad perpetuam rei memoriam,": Pynsent, *Life of HLCP,* 70.
204 "The Currency of Fame": title of exhibition catalogue, New York, Frick Collection.
204 "Neidinger" used on medal rim is Germanic spelling, "Neidin" the Italian.
205 "all harmonious and original": Fusco, *ELCP,* 44.

209 "It occurred to me": M. Vassar, *Address to the Trustees,* February 26, 1861, Box 1, Folder 204, 2-3, Special Collections, Vassar College Libraries.

209 "long period of silence": Maschietto, *ELCP,* Epilogue title, 223.

211 "were quite soft": Pynsent, *Life of HLCP,* 125.

212 "companion in elegant detail": *Main to Mudd, and More: An Informal History of Vassar College Buildings,* Elizabeth A. Daniels, Revised edition, Poughkeepsie: Vassar College, 1996, 44.

212 "This promises to be a splendid work": Unpublished letters, Church Glass to Hardman, January 21, 1903.

212 Vassar student: Janice Goodson Foerde, class of 1972.

213 "a tracing of the architectural structure": Fusco, *ELCP,* 97.

213 "We have kept all the detail": Church Glass to Vassar College, November 2, 1904.

213 "There is too much purple": Church Glass to Hardman, February 9, 1905.

213 The plain cross "will not do": Ibid.

213 "The cushion on the throne..." "...it must be quite secondary": Ibid.

213 "But no man": Letter from Allen, Church Glass, to Hardman, August 23, 1905.

213 "the cherubs in the lower foreground": Ibid., July 27, 1905.

213 "[H]istorical subjects": Hardman to Church Glass, October 9, 1904.

213 "Our allowance to you": Church Glass to Hardman, March 9, 1905.

214 "Be very careful to follow...Let us have a likeness": Ibid., February 9, 1905.

214 "Mr. (Dunstan) Powell is giving it": Ibid., November 23, 1905.

214 "jewel-toned pieces": Forbush, "The triumph of the inquiring mind", *Vassar Quarterly,* Winter 1978, vol. 74, no. 2, 6.

214 "An inscription for the ribbon": Church Glass to Hardman, February 9, 1905.

216 "The Pageant of Athena": Elizabeth A. Daniels, *Bridges To The World, Henry Noble MacCracken and Vassar College.* Clinton Corners, NY: College Avenue Press, 1994. p. 159.

216 "we reproduced the original": Program for "The Pageant of Athena" by students of Vassar College, October 1915. Account of Katharine Jeffris, Library Tercentenary Exhibition, Case 3.

221 "La Prima Donna Laureata nel Mondo": Domenico Mondrone, Fusco, *ELCP*, 36.

228 "Here rests Elena Lucrezia Cornaro Piscopia": *Hic requiescit Helena Lucretia Cornelia Piscopia Nob Vene ta maximi nominis... Mœstissimo parente Jo Battã D. Marc... superstite.* Fusco, *ELCP*, 106; and Pynsent, *Life of HLCP*, 123.

264 "Aunt [Zilpha] Backus": Unpublished report, Woodwell, October 4, 1977.

265 "The dress to be white": Church Glass to Hardman, February 9, 1905.

276 "Oh I praise your continence....": "Love is not Love," dedicated to Elena Cornaro, Marie Ponsot (1921–) in *No More Masks! An Anthology of Twentieth-Century American Women Poets.* New York: Harper Perennial, 1993, 120.

BIBLIOGRAPHY

Primary Sources

Bacchini, Benedetto. *Vitae Selectae Quorundam Eruditissimo Rum Ac Illustrium Virorum, ut et Helenae Cornarae et Cassandrae Fidelis. Actorum Helenae Cornarae...florilegum.* Bratislava, Czechoslovakia: Christiani Bauchii, 1711. (Parma, 1688).

Bembo, Pietro. *Gli Asolani.* Translated by Rudolf B. Gottfried. Bloomington, Indiana: Indiana University Press, 1954. (1505).

Castiglione, Count Baldesar. *The Book of the Courtier.* 4 Parts. Translated by Sir Thomas Hoby. London: David Nutt,1561. Reprint, London: 1900. (Venice: Aldine Press, 1528).

Castlemaine, Roger. *An Account of the Present War between the Venetians & Turk with the state of Candie.* London: H. Herringham, 1666.

Cornaro, Luigi (Lewis). *Discorsi della vita sobria: Sure and Certain Methods of Attaining a Long and Healthful Life with Means of Correcting a Bad Constitution.* 3d. ed. London: Three Crowns, 1722. (1558).

———. *The Art of Living Long.* Published by William F. Butler. Milwaukee: Arno Press, 1979. (1903).

Cornelia Piscopiae Helenae Lucretia (quae and scholastica). *Opera quae quidem haberi potuerunt.* Parmae: Rosati, 1688.

Coryat, Thomas. *Coryat's Crudities.* 2 Vols. London: Printed by W. Stansby, 1611.

de Fougasses, Thomas. *The Generall Historie of the Magnificent State of Venice.* Translated by W. Shute. London: Printed by G.Eld and W. Stansby, 1612.

de la Houssaye, Amelot. *The History of the Government of Venice.* Translated by Sir Robert Honywood. London: John Starkey, 1708. (Venice, 1675).

de Montfaucon, Bernard. *Diarium italicum. A Journey through Italy in the years 1698 & 1699.* London, 1711. (Paris, 1702).

de Saint Didier, Limojon Alexandre. *The City and Republick of Venice.* London: Printed for Char. Brome at The Gun, In Three Parts. 1699.

Deza, P. Massimiliano. *Vita di Helena Lucretia Cornara Piscopia.* Venice: Bosio, 1686.

Fabri, Giovanni Battista. *La Conchiglia Celeste Del Padre Gio.* Venice: Giacomo Hertz, 1690.

Gailhard, J. Gent. *The Present State of the Republick of Venice.* London: John Starkey, 1669.

Howell, James. *A Survay of the Signorie of Venice.* London: Printed for Richard Lowndes at the White Lion, 1651.

Le Pompe Funebri Celebrate Da'Signori Di Roma Per La Morte Dell'Ilustrissima Signora Elena Lucrezia Cornara Piscopia. Padua: Cadorino, 1686.

Libro D'oro. Venice: 1714.

Lupis, Antonio. *L'eroina Veneta Ovvero La Vita di Elena Lucretia Cornara Piscopia.* Venice: Curti, 1689.

Nani, Battista. *History of the Affairs of Europe & of the Republik of Venice.* Translated by Sir Robert Honywood. London: J.M. Starkey, 1673.

Secondary Sources

Anderson, Bonnie and Judith Zinsser. *A History of Their Own: Women in Europe from Prehistory to the Present.* New York: Harper & Row, 1987.

Bainton, Roland H. *Women of the Reformation in Germany & Italy.* Minneapolis: Augsburg Publishing House, 1971.

Barzini, Luigi. *The Italians.* New York: Atheneum, 1964.

Bell, Rudolph M. *Holy Anorexia.* Chicago: University of Chicago Press, 1985.

Bouwsma, William J. *Venice and the Defense of Republican Liberty: Renaissance Values in the Age of the Counter Reformation.* Berkeley: University of California Press, 1968.

Burckhardt, Jacob. *The Civilization of the Renaissance in Italy.* 2 Vols. New York: Harper & Row, 1958. (1860).

Burke, Peter. *Venice & Amsterdam. A Study of Seventeenth-century Elites.* London: Temple Smith, 1974.

Bynum, Caroline Walker. *Holy Feast and Holy Fast: The Religious Significance of Food to Medieval Women.* Berkeley and Los Angeles: University of California Press, 1987.

Collett, Barry. *Italian Benedictine Scholars and the Reformation: The Congregation of Santa Giustina of Padua.* Oxford: Clarendon Press, 1985.

Crisis and Change in the Venetian Economy in the Sixteenth and Seventeenth Centuries. Venice – 1508-1797. Edited by Brian S. Pullan. London: Meuthen, 1968.

Davis, James C. *The Decline of the Venetian Nobility as a Ruling Class. 1508-1797.* Baltimore: Johns Hopkins Press, 1962.

Eckenstein, Lina. *Woman Under Monasticism.* London: Cambridge University Press, 1896.

Ferrante, Joan M., et al. *Beyond Their Sex: Learned Women of the European Past.* Edited by Patricia H. Labalme. New York: New York University Press, 1980.

Foligno, Caesare. *The Story of Padua.* London: J.M. Dent, 1910.

Fusco, Monsignor Nicola. *Elena Lucrezia Cornaro Piscopia. 1646-1684.* Published by United States Committee for the Elena Lucrezia Cornaro Piscopia Tercentenary. Pittsburgh: University of Pittsburgh Press, 1975.

Grendler, Paul F. *Schooling in Renaissance Italy: Literacy and Learning. 1300-1600.* Johns Hopkins University Studies in Historical and Political Science. Baltimore: Johns Hopkins University Press, 1989.

Hare, Christopher. *The Most Illustrious Ladies of the Italian Renaissance.* London: Harper & Brothers, 1907.

Harris, Ann Sutherland, Linda Nochlin. *Women Artists, 1550-1950.* Los Angeles: Los Angeles County Museum of Art. New York: distributed by Random House, 1976.

Hazlitt, William. *The Venetian Republic: Its Rise, Its Growth, and Its Fall. 421-1797.* 2 Vols. London: A. and C. Black, 1900.

Hebblethwaite, Peter. *Pope John XXIII, Shepherd of the modern world.* Garden City, New York: Doubleday, 1985.

Hill, Sir George F. *A History of Cyprus.* Vols. 2 and 3. London: Cambridge University Press, 1948.

Hunt, David and Iro Hunt, Editors. *Caterina Cornaro, Queen of Cyprus.* London: Trigraph in association with the Bank of Cyprus, 1989.

King, Margaret L. *Venetian Humanism in an Age of Patrician Dominance.* Princeton, New Jersey: Princeton University Press, 1986.

Kristeller, Paul O. *Medieval Aspects of Renaissance Learning.* Translated by Edward P. Mahoney. Durham, North Carolina: Duke University Press, 1974.

Lane, Frederic C. *Venice. A Maritime Republic.* Baltimore: Johns Hopkins University Press, 1973.

The Late Italian Renaissance 1525-1630. Edited by Eric Cochrane. London: Macmillan, 1970.

Lauritzen, Peter. *Venice – A Thousand Years of Culture and Civilization: The Baroque Facade 1600-1699.* New York: Atheneum, 1978.

Logan, Oliver. *Culture & Society in Venice, 1470-1790: The Renaissance and Its Heritage.* London: Botsford, 1972.

Maschietto, Francesco Ludovico. *Elena Lucrezia Cornaro Piscopia (1646-1684) Prima Donna Laureata nel Mondo.* Padua, Italy: Anetore, 1978.

Masson, Georgina. *Courtesans of the Italian Renaissance.* New York: St. Martin's Press, 1976.

McCurdy, Edward. *Essays in Fresco. The Lady of Asolo.* London: Chatto & Windus, 1912.

McNeill, William H. *Venice: The Hinge of Europe. 1081-1797.* Chicago: University of Chicago Press, 1974.

Molmenti, Pompeo. *Venice: Its Individual Growth from The Earliest Beginnings to the Fall of the Republic.* 3 Vols. Translated by Horatio F. Brown. Chicago: A.C. McClurg, 1906-08.

———. *La Dogaressa di Venezia.* Translation of Remington & Co. London, 1887.

Mueller, Reinhold C. *Studi Veneziani: The Procurators of San Marco in thirteenth and fourteenth centuries.* Vol. 13. Florence, Italy: Leo S. Olschki Editore, 1971.

Muir, Edward. *Civic Ritual in Renaissance Venice.* Princeton, New Jersey: Princeton University Press, 1981.

Murray, William. *The Last Italian: Portrait of A People.* New York: Prentice Hall Press, 1991.

Norwich, John Julius. *A History of Venice.* New York: Alfred A. Knopf, Distributed by Random House, 1982.

Okey, Thomas. *Medieval Towns: The Story of Venice.* London: JM Dent & Sons, 1931.

Oliphant, Mrs. Margaret. *Makers of Venice: The Doges, Conquerors, Painters and Men of Letters.* London: Macmillan, 1905.

Pope John XXIII. *Journey of a Soul.* Translated by Dorothy White. New York: McGraw-Hill, 1964.

Pynsent, Mathilde. *The Life of Helen Lucretia Cornaro Piscopia, Oblate of the Order of St. Benedict and Doctor in the University of Padua.* Rome: St. Benedict's, 1896.

Queller, Donald E. *The Venetian Patriciate: Reality versus Myth.* Urbana, Illinois: University of Illinois, 1986.

Rio, Alexis Francois. *Les Quartres Martyres. Helena Cornaro, or the Martyrdom of Humility.* 3d ed. Translated from the French. London: Burns and Lambert, 1856.

Romano, Dennis. *Patricians and Popolani: The Social Foundation of the Venetian Renaissance State.* Baltimore: Johns Hopkins University Press, 1987.

Rose, Mary Beth. *Women in the Middle Ages & the Renaissance.* Syracuse, New York: Syracuse University Press, 1986.

Rosenthal, Margaret F. *The Honest Courtesan.* Chicago: University of Chicago Press, 1992.

Rossetti, Lucia. *The University of Padua. An Outline of Its History.* Translated by Alice Hargraves. Trieste: Edizioni Lint, 1983.

Saint Benedict of Nursia. *Masterpieces of Christian Literature: The Rule of St. Benedict.* Edited by Frank N. Magill. New York: Harper & Row, 1963. (First transcribed c. 528).

Spalding, William. *Sketches from Venetian History.* Vol. 2. New York: Harper & Brothers, 1848.

Staley, Edgcumbe. *The Dogaressa of Venice.* London, 1910.

Tonzig, Maria Ildegarde. *Elena Lucrezia Cornaro Piscopia: Prima Donna Laureata Nel Mondo, Terzo Centenario Del Dottorato (1678-1978).* Published by the University of Padua and The Abbey of St. Justina. Vicenza, Italy, 1980.

Wharton, Edith. *Italian Villas and Their Gardens.* New York: The Century Company, 1904.

Yriarte, Charles. *Venice: Its History-Art-Industries And Modern Life.* Translated from the French by F.J. Sitwell. Philadelphia: Henry T. Coates, 1896.

Reference Sources

Ackerman, James S. *Palladio.* Baltimore: Penguin. Printed by G. Eld and W. Stansby, 1966.

Attwater, Donald. *A Dictionary of Saints: Based on Butler's Lives of the Saints.* Complete ed. New York: Kenedy, 1958.

Baedeker, Karl. *Northern Italy, Including Leghorn, Florence, Ravenna and Routes through France, Switzerland, and Austria: Handbook for Travellers.* 14th ed. New York: Chas. Scribner's Sons, 1913.

Baddinucci, Filippo. *The Life of Bernini.* Translated by Catherine Enggass. University Park: Pennsylvania University Press, 1966.

Balston, Michael. *The Well-Furnished Garden.* New York: Simon and Schuster, 1986.

Betham, Matilda. *A Biographical Dictionary of the Celebrated Women of Every Age & Country.* London: n.p., 1804.

Brown, Michelle P. *Understanding Illuminated Manuscripts.* Malibu, California: J. Paul Getty Museum and the British Library Board, 1994.

Butler, Alban. *Butler's Lives of the Saints.* Baltimore: Metropolitan Press Edition, 1844.

Cecil-Loeb Textbook of Medicine. Tuberculosis, Carl Muschenheim. *Anorexia.* 12th ed. Philadelphia: W.B. Saunders Company, 1967.

de'Medici, Lorenza. *The Renaissance of Italian Cooking.* New York: Fawcett Columbine, 1989.

de Waal, Esther. *Seeking God: The Way of St. Benedict.* Collegeville, Minnesota: The Liturgical Press, 1984.

Disraeli, Isaac. *Curiosities of Literature.* London: Frederick Warne and Co., 1866.

Douglas, William et al. *Garden Design. History, Principles, Arts & Practice.* New York: Simon & Schuster, 1984.

Encyclopaedia Britannica. 11th ed. 29 Vols. New York: Encyclopaedia Britannica Company, 1911.

The Catholic Encyclopedia. Vol. 4. 1908.

Enciclopedia Cattolica. Vol. 9. Firenza, Italy, 1952.

Encyclopedia Italiana. Vol. 2. 1929.

Franzoi, Umberto. *Palaces and Churches on the Grand Canal in Venice.* Venice: Edizioni Storti, 1991.

Freschot, D. Casimiro. *La Nobilità Veneta.* Venice, 1706.

Grove's Dictionary of Music & Musicians. 5th ed. Vol. 3. Edited by Eric Blom. New York: St. Martin's, 1954.

Heydenreich, Ludwig. *Pelican History of Art, Architecture in Italy, 1400-1600.* Harmondsworth, England: Penguin Books, 1974.

Lacemery, Louis. *A Treatise of All Sorts of Foods.* London: Maggs Bros., 1745.

Leti, Gregorio. *L'Italia regnante.* Parte IV. Geneva: 1676.

Lotz, Wolfgang. *Studies in Italian Renaissance Architecture.* Cambridge, Massachusetts: MIT Press, 1977.

Mabillon, Jean. *Museum italicum.* Vol. 1., 1724.

Machlis, Joseph. *The Enjoyment of Music: The Baroque.* New York: W.W. Norton, 1963.

Macmillan Encyclopedia of Architects. Vol. 1. New York: The Free Press, 1982.

The Merck Manual of Diagnosis and Therapy. Rahway, New Jersey: Merck Sharp & Dohme Research Laboratories, 1963.

Neubecker, Ottfried. *A Guide to Heraldry.* New York: McGraw-Hill Book Company, 1979.

New Catholic Encyclopedia. Washington, D.C.: The Catholic University of America, 1967.

The New Grove Dictionary of Opera. Vol. 1. Edited by Stanley Sadie. London: Macmillan Press, 1992.

The New Kobbe's Complete Opera Book. Edited and Revised by The Earl of Harewood. New York: G.P. Putnam's Sons, 1976.

The Oxford Dictionary of the Christian Church. Third edition. Edited by E. A. Livingstone. Oxford; New York: Oxford University Press, 1997.

Ruskin, John. *The Stones of Venice: The Sea Stories.* Illustrated Cabinet Edition. Vol. 2. New York: Merrill and Baker Publishers, n.d.

Sansovino, Francesco. *Description of Venice (Venetie Citta Nobilissima).* Venice and New York: Gregg International Publishers, 1968 and Martinioni, Aggiunte, 1663.

Scher, Stephen K. *The Currency of Fame: Portrait Medals of the Renaissance.* New York: Harry N. Abrams, Inc. in association with The Frick Collection, 1994.

Sill, Gertrude Grace. *A Handbook of Symbols in Christian Art.* New York: Macmillan Publishing Company, 1975.

von Pastor, Ludwig Freiherr. *The History of the Popes, from the Close of the Middle Ages.* London: J. Hodges. 1891.

Wilson, John Donald. *"The Chase": The Chase Manhattan Bank, NA, 1945-1985.* Boston: Harvard Business School Press, 1986.

Wittkower, Rudolf. *Gian Lorenzo Bernini: Sculptors of the Roman Baroque.* Ithaca, New York: Cornell University Press, 1981.

Articles and Manuscripts

Bailey, Anne Stuart. "A Daughter of the Doges." Vol. 21. *American Catholic Quarterly Review.* Philadelphia: Charles A. Hardy, October, 1896.

Chojnacki, Stanley. "Patrician Women in Early Renaissance Venice." *Studies in the Renaissance.* Vol. 21. New York: The Renaissance Society of America, 1974.

Daniele, Professor Irene. "Elena Lucrezia Cornaro Piscopia." 1970 (?) Translation, 5 pgs. University of Padua, 1896 unsigned article. n.p.

Forbush, Gabrielle Elliot. "The Lady of the Window." *Vassar Quarterly.* Poughkeepsie, New York: May 1974.

———. "The triumph of the inquiring mind." Winter 1978.

"Elena Lucrezia Cornaro Piscopia": *Journal of the American Association of University Women,* November 1974. *Kappa Gamma Pi News,* July and November 1974. *People* (National Council of Catholic Laity), June-July 1972. *Ms Magazine,* January-February 1975. *UNESCO Courier,* 1978.

Guernsey, Jane Howard. "The Case of 'The Cornaro'." *Vassar Quarterly*. Poughkeepsie, New York: Spring 1973.

———. "Two from '12 in the vanguard of the Cornaro revival." Winter 1978.

———. "In memoriam: Ruth Crawford Mitchell '12 (1890-1984)." Fall/Winter 1984.

Guida Dell' Orto Botanico. Padua, Italy: University of Padua, February 1, 1984.

Marzolo, Vittoria Scimeni. "Helen Lucretia Cornaro Piscopia." *Vita e Pensiero*. Vol. 2. Milan, Italy: V. Redlich, Rassegna Italiana di Coltura, August 1925.

Psychowska, Lucia D. "A Learned Woman." *The Catholic World*. Vol. 52. February 1891.

Ridolfis, Carlo. *Le Meraviglie dell'arte* (List of palace collections). Venice: 1648.

University of Padua diplomas:

Doctor of canon law to Octavius Colloredo von Wallsee. Chicago: The Newberry Library, March 11, 1611.

Doctor of canon and civil law to Basilius Brixia, March 18, 1659. Newberry.

Doctor of philosophy and medicine to Laurentius à Schola. New York: The Pierpont Morgan Library, May 30, 1619, Ms. M. 551.

Doctor of laws to Dominicus Ferracinus, July 4, 1620. Morgan, Ms. M. 552.

Letters, Reports and Speeches

Bruhns, E. Maxine. "The Cornaro and Her Impact in the United States and England," Tonzig, Padua, September 5, 1978.

de Santi, Angelo. "Elena Lucrezia Cornaro Piscopia (1646-1684), Nuove ricerche," *Civiltà Cattolica.* Vol. 5. Rome, 1899.

Gorini, Giovanni. "La Medaglia Di Elena Lucrezia Cornaro Piscopia." Padua: Museo Bottacin, n.d.

Labalme, Patricia H. "Nobile e donna: Elena Lucrezia Cornaro Piscopia," Tonzig, Padua, September 5, 1978.

Oliva, Giovanni Paolo."Lucrezia Cornara Piscopia," *Lettere di Gian Paolo Olive della Compagnia di Giesu.* Vol. 2. Roma: Presso il Varese, 1681.

Serena, Sebastiano. "J. Gregorio Barbarigo." *Lettere degli anni 1671, 1677-1680.* Vol.1. Padova: Antenore, 1963.

Tonzig, Maria. "Elena Lucrezia Cornaro Piscopia (1646-1684): First Woman Graduate." Primacy study taken from *Quaderni Per La Storia a Dell'Universita Di Padova.* Vol. 6. Padua, Italy: Antenore, 1974.

Unpublished letters, 1904-1906, between John Hardman Studios, Birmingham, England and the Church Glass and Decorating Company, New York, New York.

Unpublished reports of Mrs. William H. Woodwell on source of Vassar Library window, April 14 and July 16, 1975; October 4, 1977.

Exhibition

The Scholarly World of Elena Lucrezia Cornaro Piscopia 1646-1684 Commemorating the International Tercentenary of the First Doctorate Awarded a Woman, Elena Cornaro, June 25, 1678. Vassar College Libraries, March 31 – May 21, 1978.

Symbols of a heroine's lifetime are carved on Elena Cornaro's gravestone *(clockwise from the top):* Cornaro Piscopia coat of arms; emblem of San Giustina; University of Padua crest; Benedictine seal.

(Special Collections, Vassar College Libraries)

APPENDIX

Epilogue Appendix

209 In 1969 Vassar College began admitting men.

212 Correspondence between the New York and English manufacturing companies involved with the Vassar project indicates that Dunstan Powell designed Vassar's library window. Powell was the grandson of Augustus Welby Pugin, the famous architect of the interiors of the British Houses of Parliament in the early nineteenth century.

212 At the beginning of the twentieth century, Tiffany glass was widely in vogue and first-class Gothic glass was not produced in the United States. The window was ordered from Church Glass and Decorating Company of New York City; the contract for its fabrication was placed with the distinguished John Hardman Studios of Birmingham, England. Unlike in the United States, the demand for Gothic churches and stained-glass windows had continued in Great Britain.

212 Officially dedicated in 1904, the Vassar Chapel later added Tiffany, Dodge, and La Farge stained-glass windows to its elegant structure.

212 Architect Francis Richmond Allen, a senior partner of Allen and Collens in Boston, who designed the dormitories in Vassar's quadrangle, was chosen as the the library's architect. It is possible that he suggested the Cornaro window's theme to the donor, Mrs. Thompson. Allen and his wife traveled to Italy every year, and his work was very much influenced by classic Italian design. Moreover, he may have learned about Elena from Abbess Pynsent's book, published

during this time. Mary Clark Thompson, having met Abbess Pynsent in Europe, was undoubtedly familiar with the story of Lady Cornaro. It is also known that Mrs. Thompson was devoted to Mr. Allen; he and his wife visited often at the Thompson estate in upstate New York, Sonnenberg Gardens at Canandaigua. This may explain why the idea for the window was never put in writing. While the Allen-Thompson scenario seems likely, another possibility is that the idea originated with Dunstan Powell, the window's English designer and a partner in the Hardman firm.

212 During this time there were also persistent efforts by members of the Pittsburgh Vassar Club to unravel the source of the subject in Vassar's window. Whose idea was it to feature Lady Cornaro? Clues were sought everywhere.

The niece of donor Mrs. Thompson, Mrs. Walbridge Taft, suggested the originator might have been the donor's sister, "Aunt Backus," who ran a girls' boarding school in Canandaigua. There was no evidence that Aunt Zilpha ever traveled, and her school's small size and location seemed to prove otherwise. No success was reported by the archivist at Mr. Thompson's alma mater, Williams College, to whom his widow had given a chapel, designed by Francis Allen, with a series of windows furnished by Hardman Studios.

212 With President Alan Simpson's encouragement, librarians and art professors at Vassar assisted for years finding leads: Professor of Art Christine Havelock, Librarian Barbara LaMont, Reference Librarian Joan Murphy, Special Collections librarian Frances Goudy, and the current Curator of Rare Books and Manuscripts, Nancy MacKechnie.

212 Dr. James Monroe Taylor, Vassar's president during the 1906 window installation, had requested that many of his personal records be destroyed, and his nephews complied! The old window brochure sent to the college that year by Church Glass did not provide any helpful details. In the

search for the elusive story, the Historical Association in Syracuse, New York (involved in restoring the Thompsons' Sonnenberg Gardens), was contacted, as well as the New York and Birmingham public libraries, various Vassar Clubs, and museums of Birmingham and the National Gallery of Art in Washington.

212 No shard was left unturned. Vassar's Class of 1912 was enlisted, and at one of its annual reunions, attendees sat in the library studying the window. "The dress to be white, with a gold pattern over it; the inside of the dress to be of a shade like honeysuckle pink," were directions from Church Glass to Hardman Studios early in 1905. Some 1912 classmates realized that Cornaro's gown appeared to be gray with an overskirt turned back to reveal a rose lining. There they were: Vassar's original colors, rose and gray, colors of the dawn and symbols of the first woman's college heralding the dawn of higher education for women in the United States.

213 Mr. Allen was an alumnus of Amherst College, which joined the search to no avail. The Church Glass and Decorating Company had been out of business for years, and many records were burned in a serious fire at Newhall Hill in 1970 at Hardman Studios. Hardman cooperated fully with the remaining correspondence that is now in the archives of the Birmingham (England) City Library. Architect Allen's drawings and letters were dispersed when his firm dissolved after he died, according to researchers at the Boston Public Library. His architect grandson checked through his personal portfolio for possible evidence. There was none.

219 During World War II, Ruth Mitchell's work in Pittsburgh was interrupted by her decision to go to the Middle East, London and Germany with the Relief and Rehabilitation Agency of the United Nations.

222 For his service to the church, Nicola Fusco had been decorated and named Commendatore by the Italian government and was presented with an honorary doctorate of laws from St. Vincent College. In 1961 Pope John XXIII called him to Rome as a Consultor in the Commission for Discipline of the Clergy and the Christian Laity. He was appointed by Pope Paul VI in 1966 an honorary Prothonotary Apostolic with a bishop's status.

224 Visiting lecturers at the Vassar College tercentenary celebration were Natalie Davis, Professor of History, Princeton University; Patricia Labalme, then newly named Secretary of the Corporation of the Institute for Advanced Study at Princeton; Paul Oskar Kristeller, Professor Emeritus of Philosophy, Columbia University; Ann Sutherland Harris, Chairman for Academic Affairs, Metropolitan Museum of Art; E. Maxine Bruhns, Chairman, United States Cornaro Tercentenary Committee; Giorgio Fedalto, Professor of the History of Christianity, University of Padua. Vassar participants were President Virginia Smith, Dr. Havelock, Joan Murphy, Fr. Frederick Drobin, Dr. Kohl and Anne Guernsey Greenwalt, the student representative from the class of 1978.

226 Among guest speakers at the Padua celebration were Professors Paolo Sambin and Lucia Rossetti of Padua, the late Hazel Hunkins-Hallinan of the London Vassar Club, and Patricia Labalme and E. Maxine Bruhns of the United States.

227 In 1925, Dr. Tonzig had been the first person to be made a Benedictine oblate in more than a century, following the Napoleonic decree expelling the order from Italy. Her doctoral thesis was on the history of the Romanesque-Gothic Basilica of San Giustina.

Illustration Appendix

v *La Conchiglia Celeste Del Padre Gio* (Celestial Shell, or Heavenly Conch). Giovanni Battista Fabri. Chapter 5, pp. 32-38. Tailpiece. Etching: Isabella Piccini (1665-1692). Venice: Pressio Gio. Giacomo Hertz, 1690. The New York Public Library. *(Isabella Piccini was a nun. Her etching is also featured on page 233.)*

15 *La Città Di Venetia,* from works of Gioan Nicolò Diglioni. Appresso Antonio Turini, at request of Giacomo Franco. 5th Illustration. Venice, 1614. The Newberry Library.

18 *La Città Di Venetia.* 10th Illustration. The Newberry Library.

31 *The Stones of Venice. Vol. 2. "The Sea Stories."* John Ruskin. New York: Merrill and Baker Publishers. n.d. p. 392. *Elena Lucrezia Cornaro Piscopia.* Francesco Ludovico Maschietto. Padua: Editrice Antenore. 1978. p. 70.

34 *Elena Lucrezia Cornaro Piscopia.* Maria Ildegarde Tonzig. Engraving: Singolarità di Venezia II – Dep. C Palazzi di V. Coronelli, 1709. Vicenza, 1980. p. 147.

54 *Vita di Helena Lucretia Cornara Piscopia.* Massimiliano Deza. Frontispiece painted by Ant. Molinarius. Venice: Antonio Bosio. 1686. Biblioteca Civica, Padua.

57 *La Città Di Venezia.* Parta Seconda: Title page, Image only. The Newberry Library.

57 *Il libro del Cortegiano.* Baldesar Castiglione. Final leaf 195, Image only. Venice: Aldus Romanus, 1541. University of Pennsylvania.

68 Engraving: Jean Langlois (1649-1712). Cornaro Piscopia Collection. Biblioteca Civica, Padua.

89 The "Portrait of a Venetian Lady as St. Catherine of Alexandria," "sometimes identified as Caterina Cornaro," is "probably a copy of a lost original by Titian": Hunt, *Caterina Cornaro,* "Caterine 'Domina' of Asolo: Lady of the Renaissance." Terence Mullaly, 152.

95 "Cornaro Katalin." Gentile Bellini. Circa 1500. Oil on poplar panel. Szépmuvészeti Múzeum, Budapest. (Catarina Cornaro, also called Caterina.)

115 *Itinerario overo nova descrittione de viaggi principali d'Italia,* Franciscus Schottus (1548-1622). Engraving: Matteo Cadorino. Della Terza Parte, p.28. Padua, 1659. Vassar College Libraries.

121 *Elena Lucrezia Cornaro Piscopia.* Engraving by G. Valle (1784). Padua: Editrice Antenore. 1978. p. 147.

129 *L'Horto de i semplici di Padova.* Frontispiece. Appresso Girolamo Porro. Venice, 1591. University of Delaware Library.

136 *Itinerario D'Italia.* Engraving: Matteo Cadorino. Della Prima Parte. pp. 38/39. Padua, 1659. Vassar College Libraries.

142 *L'Università di Padova,* "Notizia Raccolte da Antonio Favaro." Grafiche C. Ferrari. Venice, 1922.

151 *Ragguaglio Della Vita, Virtu E Miracoli Del B. Gregorio Barbarigo.* Tomaso Ricchini. Frontispiece. Gio. Volpatto, sculptor. Padua: Giovanni Manfrè. 1761. University of Pennsylvania.

161 *Anello di sette gemme: Venezia e la sua storia.* L. Carrer. Engraving: Antonio Vivani (1797-1854). Drawing by Michele Fanoli (1807-1876). Venice, 1838, p. 697. Biblioteca Civica, Padua.

182 *Le Pompe funebri…per le morte dell'illustrissma signora Elena Lucrezia Cornara Piscopia.* p. 12. Plate III. Padua: Per il Cadorino, 1686. Vassar College Libraries.

186 *Itinerario D'Italia.* Engraving: Matteo Cadorino. Della Prima Parte. p. 38. Padua, 1659. Vassar College Libraries.

189 Photograph of Ruth Crawford Mitchell by Herbert K. Barnett. Courtesy of E. Maxine Bruhns, Nationality Rooms and Intercultural Exchange Programs, University of Pittsburgh.

201 *Itinerario D'Italia.* Engraving: Matteo Cadorino. Della Prima Parte. p.54. Padua, 1659. Vassar College Libraries.

203 Sculptor: G.F. Neidinger (Neidin) (1678-1692). Museo Bottacin, Padua. Photograph courtesy of Monsignor Nicola Fusco.

Book Cover

Front jacket Original illustration of Elena Cornaro: *Le Pompe funebri.* Engraver: Jacobus Cassionus. Per il Cadorino. Padua, 1686, p.12. Plate I. Special Collections, Vassar College Libraries. Hand tinting by Peggy Lindt, Santa Barbara, CA, 1998.

Back jacket The Lady Cornaro in the Window: In its symbolical composition, Elena Cornaro is given primacy in the central axis as enthroned and elevated figure, rendered in the most light.

Jacket flap The kingly winged lion of Venice, symbol and sentinel of valor and vigilance, is from Blaeu's magnificent atlas containing maps of Italy in Cornaro's day. The Dutch excelled in printing seventeenth-century maps. Color engraving was established with the Blaeu publication. *Theatrum Orbis Terrarum, sive atlas novus.* Guiljelmum and Joannem Blaeu. Amsterdam. 1650-55. Pars Tertia, p.30/31. Special Collections, Vassar College Libraries.

Jacket spine University of Padua commemorative medal reissued for tercentenary celebrations: 1978.

Cloth cover Laurel symbol in gold, in honor of Lady Cornaro *(also featured in the text at each chapter heading).* The laurel illustration is courtesy of Mies Hora from his Design Elements collection, Ultimate Symbol, Inc.

SYMBOL OF VALOR AND VIGILANCE, THIS KINGLY WINGED LION OF VENICE IS FROM BLAEU'S ILLUSTRATED ATLAS CONTAINING MAPS OF ITALY IN LADY CORNARO'S DAY.

(Theatrum Orbis Terrarum. Amsterdam. 1650-1655. Special Collections, Vassar College Libraries. Photograph by Charles Porter)

INDEX

Oh I praise your continence, kind life, pure form.

– Marie Ponsot, 1988
from a poem dedicated
to Elena Cornaro